A PEKING DIARY

A Personal Account of Modern China

A PEKING DIARY

A Personal Account of Modern China

by

LOIS FISHER

ST. MARTIN'S PRESS
NEW YORK

Library of Congress Cataloging in Publication Data

Fisher, Lois.
  A Peking diary.

  1. Peking—Description. 2. Fisher, Lois.
I. Title.
DS795.F57   951'.156'05   78-21424
ISBN 0-312-59997-8

To my Mother and Father, who
opened my eyes to other worlds . . .

Contents

Introduction

It was October 1972. I had just settled into life in Bonn, and was beginning to feel comfortable living there, when my husband Gerd came home one evening from the television studio, loosened his tie, sat down in his favourite leather chair, and, hiding behind his newspaper, mumbled, 'How would you like to live in Peking?'

I should have been prepared for this question, since Gerd had often talked about wanting to work in China. But the casual way he introduced the subject caught me off guard. I burst out, 'Do you really want to live behind the moon?'

Gerd and I had met in the sixties, when he was chief correspondent for German television in Washington, D.C., and I was working in the White House for one of President Johnson's assistants. At that time 'Mainland China' or 'Red China ', as Americans called it, was closed. China frightened me. It was such a remote and mysterious land. So when Gerd talked about longing to work in China, I dismissed the thought. That dream would never come true.

Then, a few years after we met, the glamour of my job had worn off and I was tired of my solitary existence behind the awesome gates of the White House. I wanted more contact with people, and since Gerd at that time was looking for a researcher who would be free to travel in the United States, I accepted the job.

Two years later Gerd was posted to Bonn, and I soon joined him as his wife instead of co-worker.

It was an abrupt change and major adjustment for me, to adapt from my life as an active, independent woman to that of a suburban 'hausfrau'. Not only did I have to learn German and settle down in a foreign country, but I was also acting as mother to Gerd's children, eleven-year-old Elizabeth and nine-year-old Boris.

The dream of China seemed to be forgotten, until the summer of 1972. Then the Chinese government invited Gerhard Schroeder, a government leader, to visit China on a historic mission that would lead to establishing relations between the two countries. German journalists were permitted to accompany Mr Schroeder, and Gerd went along with a camera team.

This one month visit revived all Gerd's passion for the idea of living and working in China. Then in October a television documentary Gerd had made about China was shown on German television, and following the broadcast we received a telephone call from the bureau chief of the Chinese government news agency, Hsinhua, who was also China's unofficial representative in Bonn. 'Eight hundred million Chinese would applaud your film,' said Mr Wang Shu.

Soon after this phone call Mr Wang Shu told Gerd that the newspaper Die Welt was to be permitted to open an office in Peking, and that if he would like to work as Die Welt's correspondent, he would be acceptable. On that day, Gerd broke the news to me.

Gerd was confronted with a decision that involved changing professions, and thus losing the benefits he had earned during twenty-five years as a prominent German radio and television correspondent. But my conflict was an emotional one.

If we decided to go to China we would have to send the children to boarding school in Germany because Peking had no proper schooling for them. I had become very close to Boris and Elizabeth and felt as though I were abandoning them. In addition, I was starting to make friends in Germany and to speak German with greater ease and confidence.

However, I knew that for Gerd the decision was as good as

made. So after pondering the decision for a few sleepless nights, I decided to give Peking a try for three years and not one day more.

In December 1972, Gerd joined *Die Welt* and for the next two hectic months we made preparations for our Peking post. Many problems had to be settled during that short period.

My American passport contained a provision forbidding travel to China, and I envisaged being told that I would have to give up my citizenship and become a German if I was to accompany Gerd. I was not willing to make this sacrifice and so went to the American Embassy in Bonn to ask what they could do to waive this regulation.

My reception was hardly what I had expected. An official informed me that the restrictions printed in my passport were no longer enforced, as a result of President Nixon's visit to the People's Republic of China at the beginning of the year. I was free to go, and the embassy people were delighted that I was to be one of the first American residents in Peking.

My next concern was Bubbles the smooth-haired fox terrier who was my inseparable four legged companion.

While Mr Wang Shu (today a leading government figure in Peking) and his lively wife were visiting us I brought up the subject of Bubbles and China. 'Can she come with us to Peking?' I asked. 'Yes, of course,' Mr Wang Shu replied. Then I gathered up the courage to ask the question that worried me. 'Do Chinese really eat dogs?'

Mr Wang Shu explained that dogs are a south China delicacy, and we would be living in the north where people do not eat dogs. I breathed a deep sigh of relief.

With the problem of Bubbles resolved, we discussed what household effects to take with us. The Wang Shus said we could bring all furniture and electrical appliances, but they warned us about the cold Peking winter. 'You must bring warm winter underwear.'

Gerd decided that he would take care of this purchase and one day returned from a shopping spree very excited about a special gift he had bought for me. When I opened the package I found to my dismay knee length angora underpants and a matching undershirt. The combination looked as though it would suit my grandmother and I could hardly imagine myself wearing such a style. 'Do you want to be warm in China or fashionable?' he said.

After that experience I decided to take over the rest of the shopping—which meant stocking up for three years. Anything we should want to import after we became residents in Peking would, we were told, be subject to duty.

A friend who worked for the German news agency in Peking advised us what kinds of goods wouldn't be available in China. Fifty pounds of dog biscuits, six cases of alcohol, two cases of canned soups, cheese, mustard, spices, coffee, washing powder, and all kinds of toiletry were a few of the things that filled our 217 cartons.

The last item the packers put into our container was a bicycle Gerd had received as a farewell gift from his office. We all thought it was an amusing joke, but later this became my most important possession in China.

Chapter 1

The Hard Beginning

FIRST IMPRESSIONS

I was finally in Peking. It was 10 p.m. local time, but my watch showed three in the afternoon German time. Twenty-eight hours ago we had left Europe, and I was glad and relieved to be at the end of this trying journey.

The pilot had landed the plane at least 1000 feet from the two-storey terminal building, that, surprisingly, was no larger than La Guardia in New York. A large illuminated picture of Chairman Mao hung over its façade to greet us. There was no bus waiting to pick us up, so we started walking the long distance to the terminal.

The cold dry February air revived us and now I started getting excited about being in China. Music was coming from loudspeakers at the edge of the airfield and I adjusted my gait to the rhythm. It could have been a John Phillip Sousa march and I was delighted to hear something familiar. Later I learned that this was the Athlete's March, a kind of Communist marching music.

When we reached the terminal a man dressed in a blue uniform led us into a room where customs authorities were standing behind counters. One official took our passports and waved us on without glancing at Bubbles, my fox terrier, or the health certificate admitting her to China.

The customs form we filled out demanded extreme detail. Instead of reading stipulations about cigarettes, perfume or liquor, we were to write down how many cameras, typewriters, radios and watches we had. How much foreign currency and what kinds of antiques and publications did we have? What jewellery were we bringing into the country?

After completing the form a customs officer read it aloud and asked in perfect English, 'May I see your watch?' He glanced at it and then gave us back our passports.

Later I heard about one journalist who had declared six watches—two for him, two for his wife, and two belonging to his daughter. The Chinese decided that this was too many watches for one family, and so they held on to two of the watches and told the journalist he could pick them up when he left China. Obviously they were worried that some of the watches would get into the hands of the Chinese.

Customs were over, without the opening of a single suitcase, and we went into the adjoining baggage area to claim our suitcases. There, we had to push through a crowd of foreigners who were waiting for incoming passengers.

Suddenly I heard our names being shouted, and saw the German Press Agency correspondent, Hans Bargmann, and his wife Jette, who had advised us about shopping for Peking. What a relief and surprise to have familiar faces greeting us. Our friends started to pick up our suitcases, all the while explaining, 'There are no porters in China.' We went to the car. Hans told us that he had come in place of the Information Department, which had planned to send someone to welcome us and take us to our hotel. I stepped into the car, feeling relaxed and satisfied that everything had been so well organised.

The harrowing ride quickly made me uneasy again. During the next thirty-five minutes I sat on the edge of my seat expecting something disastrous to happen. The two-lane paved road from the airport was lined by poplar trees and had many unlit stretches. In addition, the bicycles on the road had no lights and our car lights were mostly on dim. Assuming Hans had not noticed this, I suggested, 'Turn your lights on full, so you can see.'

'It is against the traffic regulations,' he replied. 'Lights shouldn't blind pedestrians or cyclists,' he added.

'Is it better to kill them because you can't see them,' I said, as we narrowly missed a darkly-clothed cyclist who had darted out of a side street. This was the first country I had visited where cars had to watch out for cyclists, instead of cyclists being wary of cars.

Suddenly a horse-pulled cart moving toward the centre of the road was in front of us. I don't know how we missed colliding with them, but somehow the brakes brought us to a full stop, leaving only a hand's length between us and the horses. Only then did I see the head of the driver slowly rising. He had been awakened by the screech of the brakes and was now sitting up. Unflustered, he calmly steered the horses to the side again and returned to his reclining position.

Then we turned a corner, and it was as if someone had suddenly switched the lights on. The road was wider and I could see trees on both sides and clusters of dark houses. Hans pointed out the embassy area. High iron fences and walls surrounded each building.

At each gate was a small guardhouse. Soldiers from the People's Liberation Army were standing inside or walking outside to warm up. Their thick padded khaki coats and pants looked as though they could withstand the coldest winter. Nearby, lights were shining in the eight-storey apartment buildings in which foreigners lived, also behind high fences and walls and guarded by the army. Across the street the Chinese lived in four-storey apartment buildings without fences or sentries. Everyone seemed to be asleep in the Chinese quarter and I felt we should whisper as we drove by.

One more turn and we were on Chang An, a six-lane highway, which was wider than most autobahns in Germany and better lit. But the road was almost empty. A few cyclists were returning home from the late work shift and some horses were pulling carts loaded with hay into town. Water trucks were hosing the streets, the sidewalks and the parched earth around the trees. It was only eleven thirty, but there was no sign of activity on the side streets. I wondered if Peking went to bed that early every night.

When we passed Tien An Men, a massive empty square across from the red walls of the Forbidden City, I was convinced we were really in China. I had seen both places in photographs and recognised them at once. The Forbidden City had been the home of the emperors until the first quarter of the twentieth century, and Tien An Men square was where Chairman Mao had proclaimed the founding of the People's Republic of China on October 1, 1949. Here he had also addressed one million Red Guards during the Cultural Revolution.

One block away from the Forbidden City Hans pointed out the entrance to Chairman Mao's residence, but we could see only a decorative red wooden carved gate with soldiers standing in front. In this area soldiers armed with rifles and bayonets patrolled the sidewalks in pairs.

Half a mile down the street we drove into a large empty parking lot belonging to the Min Zu Hotel, where we would be staying. Dim lights were still on in the lobby, indicating that someone was still awake. As we entered through the revolving door, two hotel employees sprang out of their seats as though an alarm had gone off.

It was clear they had been waiting for us for some time. As soon as we identified ourselves and showed our passports, one of the young men said, as if he had memorised it, 'We were expecting you and learned that your plane was delayed. You must be tired. We will show you to your room.'

I wanted to apologise for keeping them awake, and then I noticed an elevator girl who had also been waiting for our arrival. She looked very young and had rosy cheeks and waist-length braids. Rising from her folding stool, she yawned and then took us to the fifth floor. During the entire ride she kept her eyes glued on Bubbles, whose presence seemed to make her nervous.

We walked through silent red-carpeted corridors to our room. When we opened the door, a wave of stifling air hit us. Gerd went to the window to let in fresh cool air, and our two young escorts shivered and left hastily, after warning us not to get sick.

I inspected our room, which could have been in an old medium-price hotel in Europe. The beds squeaked, too much bulky furniture was crowded into too little space, the bathroom fixtures had cracks and stains, and the toilet gurgled after flushing.

But this hotel provided conveniences not even five-star hotels in Europe offered. Terrycloth robes, leather slippers, a comb, Chinese toothpaste, face cream, a thermos bottle, tea, and cigarettes were there for us to use. After pointing out these luxuries to Gerd, I crawled under the heavy green-and-gold silk-covered blanket, put my head down on a pillow that felt like a sandbag, and fell asleep at once.

Persistent honking awakened us that first morning at six-thirty. It sounded like a New York rush-hour traffic jam, and excitedly I hurried to the window to see what was happening. Instead of a car tie-up I saw hundreds of bicycles blanketing the highway in front of the hotel. The noise was coming from the few cars and buses that were trying to carve their way through the bicycle congestion.

In daylight the dullness and drabness of the surroundings startled me. The cyclists looked like grey and blue lumps, and all bicycles were a monotonous black. The walls across from us were grey. The building next door was grey. The sidewalks passing in front of the hotel were grey. Even the bare trees lining the streets and peeking out of the courtyards were grey. In the distance a grey smog had settled on part of the city and I had the feeling it was creeping in our direction.

Then twelve soldiers marched by and provided a welcomed dash of colour. They were wearing smart khaki uniforms, with tightly-belted waists, red epaulets, and a red star on each cap.

Bubbles was becoming restless and so I quickly dressed and we walked toward the elevator. An older man seated at a desk directly across from the elevator said 'Ni hao' as he observed the other people who were coming and going in the corridor. Soon several young men came out of a back room behind the desk. They smiled at me, and one of them said, ' "*Ni hao*" means hello.' This was my first Chinese word and I repeated it, while they laughed and approved of my pronunciation.

The young men looked like recent high school graduates. They were scrubbed, closely trimmed, and showed little sign of a beard. They wore clean white hotel jackets with wool sweaters underneath and wide navy-blue pants. All wore the same style of black cotton shoes, which looked soft and comfortable.

Keeping a slight distance from the dog, they started asking me questions. ' How old are you?' 'What is your nationality!' 'How many children do you have?' 'Is this your first visit to China?' 'How long will you stay?' The arrival of the elevator interrupted the one-sided conversation, which I promised to continue later. As soon as I entered the almost-full elevator, the strong smell of garlic overwhelmed me, and I held my breath for the next four floors.

A walk in the parking lot gave me a chance to get fresh air and examine our surroundings. Had Mao's picture not been hanging above the main entrance, the Min Zu could have been a government ministry in any East European country. The ten-storey concrete building was the tallest in the neighbourhood. It looked out of place; its heavy thick lines did not blend in with the curving and graceful roofs of houses nearby. Later on a hotel guest told me that the Russians had designed it in 1956, which explained its non-Chinese appearance.

A low hedge of shrubs separated the parking lot from the sidewalk. As each pedestrian passed the entrance of the hotel, he looked expectantly toward the door, hoping a foreigner would appear. If a foreigner did appear the passerby would stop and stare.

Bubbles had been playing with a stone in between the cars provided for guests, and at first we were not visible to the passers-by. Then she started barking at the stone, and one person noticed her. Within a short time hundreds of people were pointing in our direction and speaking excitedly. Even the cyclists had stopped, and people were rushing over from across the street. It was as though they had never seen a dog before.

The audience looked like a sea of blue until a father boosted his child up on his shoulder. I could not take my eyes away from the toddler, who was dressed in a bright-red silk cape with a red silk cap and white bunny ears framing the matching apple-shaped cheeks. Before long, the crowd started dispersing slowly. I noticed that a soldier with a red armband had been asking them to move on.

By the time we returned to the hotel, the sprawling lobby was alive with activity. At the money-exchange counter I heard the rapid clicking of wooden beads on the abacus, the Chinese calculator. People were queueing to buy stamps and then queueing in front of the bottle of glue that they used on the ungummed envelopes and stamps. In the corner there was a small stand selling oranges, apples, cigarettes, and candy, and across from it was a gift shop displaying Chinese-made sweaters, scarves, pens, and toiletry.

The book counter attracted my attention. I was looking for an English daily newspaper but saw only the bound works of Mao, Engels, Lenin and Stalin in various languages, some postcards, magazines published in China, and newspapers from Maoist groups around the world. I asked the young girl behind the counter when the English newspaper would arrive.

A little baffled, she looked at me and said, 'We don't have any. You should talk to the staff on your floor about subscribing to the Hsinhua bulletin.' Assuming there was a language misunderstanding, I didn't pursue the matter. Only later did I find out that no daily foreign newspapers were sold in China.

It was time for breakfast and so I returned to our room where Gerd was dressed and waiting. We left Bubbles behind and discussed whether we should eat in the Chinese or Western dining room branching off from the lobby.

We decided on a Chinese breakfast and entered the dining-room, where a radio the size of a chest of drawers, was screeching Chinese music at us. The other guests, who were mostly

Japanese and overseas Chinese, seemed at home with the noise. But I felt it would take quite a while for me to adjust to the series of shrill, prolonged notes which had a grating effect on my nerves.

The waiter gave us an à la carte menu in English and Chinese and when we asked what we should order for breakfast, he said, 'Everything tastes good.' We relied, therefore, on our neighbours' taste and ordered what they were eating.

Unfortunately they had a much larger appetite than we had in the morning. A six course breakfast arrived, including rice porridge, cakes, noodles, eggs and meat dishes, and we had room only to taste each dish. When we asked for the bill, the waiter looked at us with a disappointed expression and said, 'Didn't you like the food?' We assured him how good it was and told him we would make up for our poor performance at lunch and dinner.

We then paid the modest bill of six yuan* and left without tipping. Friends had warned us that tipping is forbidden in China, but unfortunately other foreigners had not received this message. Later on I saw guests trying to force money and gifts into the hands of very embarrassed hotel employees, who refused it.

Immediately after our arrival, Gerd wrote a letter to the Service Bureau, which was responsible for assigning staff and living accommodations to foreigners. He requested an interpreter, an apartment, a teacher, a driver, and a car, because our office car would not arrive for a while and Peking did not offer a car rental service.

I expected an immediate response, and when it did not come, I urged Gerd to call and ask when we would have an answer. But Gerd, a very patient person, told me the Service Bureau would call as soon as they had something to offer.

---

* In 1973 six yuan was roughly equivalent to $3 U.S. or £1.40. The purchasing power, however, of one yuan is considerably more in China, where the average salary is 60 yuan a month and prices are relatively stable.

In the meantime we heard from other hotel guests that all buildings for foreigners were full and we would have to wait until buildings presently under construction were completed. After learning this disappointing news we requested more spacious quarters in the hotel and on the same day moved into a suite.

The living-room looked like a waiting room in a doctor's office. It had a bulky sofa, massive chairs covered with beige cotton slip-covers and white crocheted doilies, and a beige rug that blended into the colourless surroundings. The bedroom was as cramped as our first one, but we were grateful for the extra space the suite gave us. We had no idea that this would be our home for the next four months.

Gerd's working situation was very difficult without an interpreter. He had to rely on the two Hsinhua English bulletins for current events, and that information was incomplete. The domestic daily news included only some of the articles from the two daily Chinese newspapers foreigners could receive. And the international news gave a biased and selected coverage of world events. Gerd, therefore, spent a lot of time with other journalists and their interpreters, who helped him with translations.

While Gerd was settling into his work, I was left alone much of the time. Rather than sit in our hotel suite viewing the world through a window pane, I decided to venture out on to the streets.

Since I was the only foreigner walking in the neighbourhood I always attracted considerable attention.

The Chinese being curious people, unashamedly stared, surrounded, and followed me. At first I thought they were rude and I tried to outstare them without success. Then I accepted their manners and smiled. When they smiled back, I regarded them as friends. But not everyone smiled.

Five foot ten inches tall, with a long thin nose, long narrow face and curly brown shoulder length hair, I could never blend into my surroundings and people always knew where I was. When I wandered down a dead end street or looked confused, someone would always appear from behind a closed gate and point me in the right direction. Other times people looked at me suspiciously as though they thought I was spying on them.

But I never had the feeling they were spying on me. I was more a source of entertainment, particularly for the children who had a lot of free time to accompany me. As I passed young people on the back streets they stopped their conversation and whispered to each other 'waikuojen, waikuojen' (foreigner, foreigner). Schoolboys interrupted their wrestling or angry arguments to stare. Groups of teen-age girls holding hands or boys walking arm in arm quickly separated to let me pass. Grandmothers amused their grandchildren by turning the toddler's head in my direction and pointing. Sometimes my face frightened them and they ran for cover behind a grandparent or burst out crying when they saw me.

While the Chinese were focusing on me, I studied them. Women had straight short hair chopped off at the hair line on the neck, and any stray hair was pinned back on the sides. Girls wore long braids, which I later learned were usually cut off when they married. I was surprised to see so many young people with grey or white hair mixed in with the black, while older people often had pitch-black hair that must have been dyed. The one feature that always attracted my attention was the velvet-like skin of teen-age girls.

Men's hair was always short, but the style varied. Some preferred what I called the 'porcupine' look. Short hair stuck out all over the head. The 'umbrella' look was most popular. The hair closest to the neck was very short and the hair above it was cut in layers so that the longest hair on the top of the head fanned out and covered some of the shorter hair. Occasionally a dapper young man would let the hair in front grow a little longer so he could slick it down over his forehead. Sideburns were nonexistent. Moustaches and beards did not exist except for wisps of hair on older men. It is difficult for Chinese men to grow a proper moustache, because they have so little hair on their faces.

Everyone appeared bulky, square, and shapeless in dark jackets and pants covering many layers underneath. If a woman had a shapely figure, it was well concealed.

My long walks usually took me into the neighbourhood around the Min Zu. Next to the hotel was a winding paved street that passed grey one-storey shops in need of repair. A dried patch of earth was in front of each shop door, and not a blade of grass or shrub was in sight.

Most shops had only one room, containing a counter with smudged display windows in front and dusty shelves behind, where goods were untidily stored. Usually a cylindrical black iron stove stood in the centre of the room. A clerk occasionally walked over to the stove to feed it with coal and to pour himself a tin cup full of boiling water from the kettle sitting on top of the burner. After the water cooled down he drank it slowly, without adding tea leaves. When there was no stove and kettle, a clerk sprinkled water on the floor to reduce the dryness in the air.

There were no cash registers. The money was kept in a cardboard box, and the mathematics was done on an abacus. Shops had electricity but it was seldom turned on. Only when I entered the shop would the clerk pull the string attached to the dangling light bulb over the counter. Then a dim light would appear.

In every neighbourhood there was the local 'Woolworth', which sold everything from material to chopsticks. The customers were mostly older women, bundled up in layers. Some wore the thick black padded cotton pants that hugged the ankles and a matching high-collared black cotton jacket. Many women wore a square black velvet hat with a green stone on the front, and gold earrings through pierced ears. The hair was tied back tightly in a bun resting on the nape of the neck. Later I learned this was the traditional peasant outfit, which peasants continued to wear after they had moved to the city.

The older city-born women looked very different from the peasants. They dressed in black cloth pants over layers and wore black scarves on their heads. Many had short hair pinned severely back on the sides and some hobbled on crippled feet, a result of footbinding. Although that torturous Chinese custom has been outlawed for over fifty years, women still bear the scars. The purpose of binding was to create tiny feet, which were a sign of beauty. The most beautiful foot was no longer than four inches. To achieve this, parents bound their daughter's feet very tightly with cloth at an early age until all toes except the big one curled under. The foot was then permanently deformed.

Women with crippled feet wore specially-made narrow black cotton shoes that came to a point at the big toe and then curved under, revealing how misshapen the foot was. These women had to balance themselves with every step they took.

The local restaurant catered to working men, who sat on backless stools crowded around warped wooden tables. The specialty was *jao-tze* (dumplings), a favourite northern dish. Workers dressed in long padded coats with fur caps on their heads quickly and silently devoured a bowlful. Within five minutes they had finished and given their seat to someone waiting behind them.

Near the shopping block was a brownish-grey four-storey apartment building that was dark inside. Later I learned that electricity is turned on only at certain times of the day.

Each flat had a balcony, where supplies were stored and clothes were hung. Judging from the location of the balconies and the windows, I guessed each flat had no more than one or two rooms.

Bicycles were conspicuously absent in the yard, and I noticed the balconies were enclosed and windows of flats on the ground floor had bars. Later a Chinese told me that theft was a serious problem and bicycles were frequently stolen.

Off the side street were narrow dirt roads called 'hutungs'.

These were only wide enough for one vehicle. As I walked along the side of the road high grey walls overshadowed me on both sides, and I felt as if I were viewing a fort. Only the curving roofs peeking out over the walls were visible.

Wooden doors leading to the inside were closed, and any open entrance-way in the outside wall led to another wall directly ahead. The Chinese called this wall a 'spirit wall'. Traditionally, this stone panel was there to frighten away the evil spirits which were believed to travel only in a straight line. By taking a left or right turn at this wall I could enter the courtyard, but I did not dare to trespass.

Often I would see children in the dirt courtyard trying to make kites fly. They were home-made models, out of newspaper and string.

Since the walls prevented me from seeing the life in courtyards and at home, I spent most of my first few months in Peking observing street life. I saw woman workers on the road shovelling sand through a large mesh screen. Later this would be used for cement. Shabbily dressed old wrinkled women raked through piles of refuse, pulling out pieces of paper, coal, wire, and glass they would use at home.

Often I would see a sleepy mule pulling a cart with a container whose pungent odour made me stop breathing for a second. But the old driver, who had an unlit pipe hanging out of his mouth, was not bothered by the smell. He looked content and warm in his dirty white sheepskin-lined coat and matching fur cap, which had ear flaps sticking out like wings.

He was driving the 'honey wagon', a nickname foreigners gave to the cart. The cart contained the contents of latrines in old neighbourhoods, where houses had no toilets. At the end of the day the contents of the container were processed. Later the manure was used as fertiliser on the farm land around Peking.

Each day on my walk I would notice another detail about the Chinese way of life. A few teen-age girls were chatting near a communal faucet as they filled their buckets with water.

Houses in this area had no running water. A grandmother walked by slowly pushing a low bamboo four-wheel carriage with two scrubbed children inside. While she talked to them continually, both sat like colourful stuffed animals, immobilized by the weight and thickness of their clothing. A child clad in a pink, green, and blue combination of pants and jackets was tottering along between her mother and grandmother. With every step she took, the cheeks of her rosy behind were exposed through a large open slit in her pants. I laughed at this sight just as she squatted to urinate. This is the Chinese toilet-training method, which saves dirty diapers and undressing in the cold.

THE SANDSTORM SEASON

Early in March the winds began to blow, carrying sand from the Gobi desert, hundreds of miles away, to Peking. Some days the winds were so fierce I could not leave the hotel.

Every morning the air was grey from the coal burned in stoves to heat homes. Then smog enveloped the city and limited visibility to the length of a long city block. Even the sun had a grey face and the sky, which was normally blue and cloudless, looked as though a grey screen had been pulled over it.

Just before a sandstorm, everything became still. Not even a scrap of paper or a twig moved. I had the feeling that nature was holding its breath. In the distance the grey changed to an eerie yellow brown that blocked the sun, and within a few minutes the winds began.

We felt, tasted, and ate the sand. It was blinding. It attacked raw flesh like needles. It settled on the lips and cracked them. It stuck between the teeth. It filled our noses and made us spit and cough.

Unlike us, the Chinese were used to this season and prepared for it. Pedestrians walked with their backs to the wind, and women tied gauze scarves over their children's faces. The traffic policemen put on their mirror sunglasses and the cyclists wore white mouth masks, resembling those worn in hospital operating rooms.

The cyclists riding against the wind dismounted and pushed their bicycles into the sand and wind. Those who were determined remained on their bikes, bent their heads down to the level of the handlebars, and struggled forward.

Inside our hotel room a fine layer of dust settled in the corners of our drawers, clung to the clothes in our closet and left a coating on our shoes. At night Gerd's blackened shirt collar matched the colour of the wash-cloth I used several times a day to clean my face.

The dryness made my skin peel. My hands felt like pumice stone, my heels split and bled, and the palms of my hands acquired dirt lines which did not wash out. My nails chipped and the cuticles grew black. My hair felt like straw and I developed dandruff.

Often we awakened in the middle of the night with a parched sandpaper feeling in our throats from the suffocating central heating and accompanying dryness. Soon we learned to keep a glass of water next to the bed to remedy the problem. But there was no way to ward off the continual bronchial ailments that afflicted us and left us with chronic coughs.

While the wind whistled outside, the hotel echoed from emptiness inside. Very few tourist delegations visited Peking in March and only twenty diplomats and businessmen occupied the hotel, which could accommodate over five hundred people.

THE HOTEL ROUTINE WITH UNROUTINE HAPPENINGS

Hotel living imposed a routine in our day. Every morning around eight-thirty between five and seven floor attendants filed into our living-room, usually without knocking. We never bothered to lock the living-room door because there was no need, and, besides, someone could always unlock it from the outside.

During cleaning each man had a specific task. One emptied

the soiled glasses onto the carpet. This reduced the dryness in the air, he explained. Another brought a fresh thermos with hot water. He also emptied the ashtrays into wire baskets, which unfortunately had coin-sized holes, that allowed the ashes to fall onto the floor. A third brushed the carpet with a whisk broom, and a fourth man used a feather duster on tables and chairs. The others made the beds, cleaned the bedroom, and removed our laundry, which came back the next morning freshly washed and ironed.

The room tidying-up operation was well organised but inefficient. Only the surfaces were touched and if someone were absent his work was not done. I seldom complained about the dirt under objects and in corners because I wanted to stay on good terms with the cleaning staff. They were my only informal contact with Chinese.

All were learning English and sometimes they asked me for help reading revolutionary texts translated into English. The phrases they were memorizing were useless for the kind of work they were doing, but I said nothing. Occasionally one of them was interested in learning practical expressions, but he was too shy to come alone to receive help. He would always bring a friend who would sit nearby and look at the pictures in our magazines, while he practised speaking.

On a few occasions our open-door policy led to embarrassing situations. One day while I was in the tub during cleaning hours an older man entered the bathroom and started mopping the floor. Realising at once that the Western concept of privacy was different from the Chinese, I shouted and frightened him away.

Another time I was sitting under a hair dryer when the room boys entered. They had never seen such a sight before, and they immediately put down their cleaning equipment and came over to stare at me. Soon I felt like a captive under the dryer's hood and all I could do was smile and feel foolish.

One evening a hotel employee was asked to bring drinks to

our room. After knocking quietly he walked in. Bubbles ran toward him barking. The man dropped the entire tray, breaking the bottles and glasses. The noise attracted his friends, who started laughing. I didn't think the man deserved to be laughed at, and I felt embarrassed for him. It was only later that I realized their laughter might have been from embarrassment.

The next day this man did not come to work and so we asked about him. Another roomboy said, 'He went to the hospital to have his nerves treated, and the doctor recommended a few days' rest.' I listened to this in disbelief, not knowing whether to apologise or laugh.

Three days later he reappeared and was ready to take on the dog. His friends stood around the door waiting when he entered the room, and I immediately grabbed Bubbles. He then came over to her and showed off to them as he petted her head.

After this incident the Chinese were not so frightened of Bubbles, and some threw the ball when I took her out in the corridor to play. Two roomboys even asked if they could borrow Bubbles and her ball one evening. Finding this unusual, I went along and noticed that they played in front of the elevators, so that every time an elevator girl stopped on our floor she would see them. Obviously their performance impressed the girls, who giggled and watched with wide eyes.

News of the tamed dog travelled through the hotel. Soon the staff was pleased to see Bubbles and even started calling her by name. But the old people on our floor were still sceptical about our fourteen-pound lightweight, and refused to believe that she didn't bite. A colleague of Gerd's who had lived in China during the 1950's cleared up the mystery for us.

He explained that the Chinese fear of dogs dated back to the pre-Liberation period before 1949, when half-wild, diseased, hungry dogs roamed around Peking. In the middle of the 1950's the Chinese had a campaign to exterminate all dogs because they believed they caused meningitis and encephalitis. After that time dogs were not permitted to live in the large metropolitan areas and were used mainly as watchdogs.

This rule, fortunately, was waived for foreigners. Now I knew why Bubbles was such a curiosity in the neighbourhood. Most of the children had never seen a dog before, and some pointed to her and asked, 'Is that a sheep?'

OUR FIRST CHINESE INVITATION

One morning there was a persistent knocking at our door. I knew this had to be a stranger. Otherwise the person would have simply walked into our unlocked room.

When I opened the door, a man who looked like a messenger handed me an envelope and left. The note was written in Chinese, and neither Gerd nor I could understand it. I went in search of an English-speaking hotel attendant to translate it.

The message was that a Hsinhua official had invited us to attend a banquet that evening. I was surprised that the invitation had arrived so late. Future experience taught us that Chinese invitations usually arrive on the day of the event, which often forced us to cancel other long-standing engagements. To refuse would be an affront and, besides, Gerd did not want to miss the rare opportunity to be with Chinese officials, who provided first-hand information.

The dinner was held in a private dining section of the International Club, which was open mainly to foreigners and occasionally Chinese officials. Besides a restaurant, it had a barber shop, tennis hall, olympic-size swimming pool, other recreational facilities, and reception halls.

Since this was our first banquet, I carefully noted Chinese protocol. Our host put Gerd at the place of honour, on his right side, and I sat on his left side. Three other Hsinhua officials completed the party.

I have forgotten the dishes served, but remember that my

plate was always full. I wanted to make a good impression and so I tried everything, even the green 'thousand-year-old eggs', which I didn't like. As soon as I emptied the plate my host refilled it, in spite of my earnest protests. Soon I learned to eat as slowly as the others and in that way ploughed on through the seemingly endless courses.

When our host wasn't busy filling our plates, he was making countless toasts with *mao-tai*, a schnaps that has a 65 per cent alcoholic content. It tasted like rubbing alcohol to me. Proposing many '*gambeis*' (bottoms up), he toasted to 'Friendship between West Germany and the People's Republic of China.' While Gerd kept up with the host, I sipped the palatable sweet warm rice wine.

The loud belching that accompanied the conversation forced me to take a deep breath and cover my face with the cloth napkin so I would not laugh. Later I was told that burping is a sign of a good meal to the Chinese, but I never adopted this habit. Other aspects of Chinese table manners were different from what I had been accustomed to. Spitting out fish and meat bones on the tablecloth, slurping, smacking, chewing loudly, speaking with a full mouth, picking the teeth with a fingernail, and leaning on elbows were all acceptable manners, and I would have to get used to them.

The host led the conversation, which focused on weather, food, and family. The one time he switched to politics was to recite the current political line, which attacked the two superpowers, the United States and Russia, for 'hegemony' (political dominance of others). After making his statement, our host turned to me and remarked, 'I do not mean this personally. We are not against the American people. We are criticising their government.'

The dinner, which had begun punctually at seven, was over exactly at nine, when the host suddenly rose and thanked us for coming. On the way home we realised that we had been doing all the listening and answering and never had a chance to ask a question.

THE DRIVER AND INTERPRETER ARRIVE

It was now the middle of March and we had been in China one month without an interpreter. Gerd decided it was time to contact the Service Bureau to find out what progress had been made. 'We are working on your request, Mr Ruge,' an unidentified voice responded. In subsequent calls the same sentence was repeated in response to the same question. No one apologised or gave an excuse for the delay and it was useless to try to get further information. I had heard of foreign visitors using threatening and humiliating tactics to try to get their way, but they were never successful. Gerd remained patient and calm, having experienced similar difficulties when he was a correspondent in Moscow during the late fifties. But I, a novice, fumed at the helplessness of our position.

A few days after the phone call, a smiling round-faced little man with a blue worker's cap on his head appeared. He clutched in his hand a contract written in English, which revealed that he was our driver. He would be driving us in a green Chinese-made car called a Shanghai, which resembles an old Mercedes. The rental fee for the car and driver was 25 yuan (about £5.70, or $12.50) a day, plus one yuan for every hour of overtime after the eight-hour day. Two yuan is one dollar. One yuan has 100 fen. Until then we had relied on the hotel taxi service because there were no taxis for hire on the street. The presence of a driver would make Gerd's work easier.

At the beginning, communication with our driver was difficult. We had to rely on sign language and the help of the English-speaking hotel attendants. Finally a diplomatic friend gave us a list of Chinese places and expressions written in *pinyin*, romanised Chinese pronunciation, and understanding was no longer a problem.

Two weeks after the driver arrived the Service Bureau finally called to say that we could expect our interpreter the following day. The next morning at eight-thirty sharp a bespectacled man in his mid-thirties knocked on the door. It was Mr Chen, our English-speaking interpreter.

The only information we had about Mr Chen was how much we were to pay the Service Bureau monthly for his service. Three hundred yuan certainly did not seem like a large amount, but we were sure that he would receive considerably less than this sum.

Mr Chen appeared to be very nervous when he arrived. He kept swallowing and fidgeting with his hands and feet. Trying to put him at ease, we discussed his background. He told us he had been an English teacher in high school and we complimented him on his English. 'I speak very poorly,' he said. In time we realised this was the usual modest Chinese response to a compliment.

For his first assignment Gerd asked Mr Chen to apply for an additional room in the hotel, to be used as an office. Mr Chen went to place our request with the hotel Revolutionary Committee, the managing board that was responsible for the allotment of rooms. Having become accustomed to the Chinese way of doing things, we did not expect an immediate answer.

Shortly after we had requested an additional room, Mr Chen came to us and suggested that Bubbles move out of the hotel during the forthcoming visit of the President of Mexico to Peking. Although the President would not be staying at the Min Zu, he said, other Mexican guests would be at the hotel, and the presence of a dog might make a bad impression.

I immediately protested. There was no reason, I felt, for Bubbles to move out of the hotel. But Gerd overruled me, saying he felt there might be a connection between our getting an office and the dog's temporary absence from the hotel. I thought Gerd's theory was far-fetched, but after the Mexican entourage departed and Bubbles returned, the Revolutionary Committee allotted us an additional room on the other side of the living-room. Now we had a three-room suite. The Chinese had kept an unspoken agreement, and I began to understand their subtle ways.

APRIL

It was now mid-April and the winds had died down. After so many grey weeks, I welcomed the blue sky, the sun's warming rays, and the first buds on the naked trees. With the coming of spring the winter layers of clothing started to disappear one by one and people's pants went from the stuffed to the baggy stage. The most amusing change was that the slit in toddlers' pants grew wider, exposing most of their rosy backsides.

My teacher had still not arrived and I was becoming restless. In the past I had never had enough hours in a day, but now the days were growing longer and I had to invent ways to keep myself busy. Previously I had taken short walks near the hotel, but the lovely weather encouraged me to go farther and soon I was spending four and five hours a day walking the streets of Peking. Each day I would cover a different area.

The main shopping street, Hsi Tan, in the western part of the city, was only a five-minute walk from the Min Zu and I passed it almost every day. On this street the sidewalks were crowded with pedestrians, and the sound of bicycle bells and horns filled the air.

Occasionally a shrill voice pierced the din, and I would see a woman standing on the sidewalk with a megaphone close to her lips. She was chasing away a cyclist who had parked his bike where he shouldn't have. Special areas were designated for bikes, and there the cyclist paid a two-fen (1 cent) parking fee.

Everyone was carrying a bag of some kind. The most popular was a khaki shoulder satchel, although some preferred the black plastic airline-style bags. These bags carried the most essential document a Chinese possessed, a resident's identification card, which stated where he lived. Without this card a person might have difficulty shopping. Any clerk could ask to see it, and if the customer was not a resident of Peking, he might not be permitted to buy items in limited supply, such as oil, cotton, soap, rice.

As I walked along, I could see what each family was eating that day. Shopping nets contained fresh vegetables, cooked cold noodles, steamed rolls, dried fish, eggs, fruit, and sometimes a live chicken. People on bicycles passed by, carrying large cloth sacks containing the month's ration of rice or flour.

Gradually I began to notice a difference in dress and appearance between Peking residents and visitors. The country people wore black padded pants and jackets, and sometimes the men had white towels wrapped around their head. The towels, I later learned, were used to absorb perspiration when they worked in the fields, but had become a part of their regular dress. The rural people also often wore large Mao badges, no longer in fashion in Peking. But I never saw anyone carrying the little Red Book that foreigners nicknamed the 'Mao Bible'.

While Peking families seldom appeared together on the streets, except on Sunday, the country people usually had their extended family with them, from grandmothers to grandchildren, for their once- or twice-a-year outing in the city. By the end of the day each family member was weighted down with everything from pots and pans to bags of yarn. Exhausted, they often plopped down on the sidewalk or on a store floor, with a mountain of bundles surrounding them, and took a nap before starting on the long journey home.

Chinese tourists often carried different-sized boxes tied together in a neat bundle. The decorative boxes contained candy and nut specialities from Peking. Occasionally minority groups, such as the Mongolians and Tibetans, would pass, and their non-Chinese features and different dress distracted people's attention from me. But as soon as I entered a shop, once again all eyes were directed at me.

No shop was complete without Mao's picture hanging on the wall facing the entrance. He was shown in a variety of poses. The standard portrait showed his face with round rosy cheeks, penetrating dark eyes, a receding hair line and a large mole on the chin. Another showed him standing on a beach in a long coat, which foreigners called the 'JFK pose'. He was shown sitting at a desk with a cigarette in hand and an ashtray full of butts in front of him. He appeared as a young man in an army uniform, or he wore a coal miner's helmet. Sometimes he was shown shaking the hands of workers and peasants (the Chinese term for farmer). He was also depicted wearing a flowing coat and looking saintly. I noticed all the pictures had one thing in common. The wart on his chin, which the Chinese consider good luck, was the most prominent feature on his face.

I was amazed by the variety of stores and choice of merchandise. One shop sold only sheets of glass and decorative wall and table mirrors. A department store sold not only everyday household goods and clothing, but also old foreign books, and had several restaurants. A pharmacy for Chinese medicine looked as popular as an ice cream parlour in summer, but the strong smell of wild herbs discouraged me from entering.

Another shop specialised in Chinese seals, which were used as signatures on official letters. They were made of stone or wood, shaped like a column standing about two inches high, and often were decorated with a carved animal at the top. At the bottom the stone was engraved with the name of the owner. The seal would be dipped into a red paste before stamping the letter.

Soon after we arrived Gerd was obliged to buy a seal for *Die Welt*, in Chinese. Any letter he wrote to a government organisation required this official stamp, instead of his signature.

A few Chinese practices disturbed me at first. Parents and children spat on sidewalks. In stores that had spitoons people often ignored them and used the floor. Rather than use a refuse can, people usually dropped their paper and food remains on the sidewalk or on the floor of a shop.

Nose blowing required neither a handkerchief nor a Kleenex —it was done by pressing one nostril and blowing out the other. I lowered my eyes at this action and felt slightly uncomfortable, but I learned that the Chinese regarded my method of nose blowing with the same disgust. How could I tuck a contaminated handkerchief into my pocket and then re-use it? This was considered unsanitary.

FRUSTRATION AND DESIRE TO LEAVE

At first the long walks cured my restlessness. But soon I became tired of hotel living and of being alone so much of the time. In addition, I was burdened with the feeling that I had to weigh every word I spoke in case—according to foreign hearsay—the Chinese were listening in on our conversations.

My teacher had not arrived, and after two months in China, I could speak only a few words of Chinese. I had tried to learn from tapes, but this method did not work for me. I was angry that the Service Bureau still gave us no indication when we would be able to move into a flat.

I tried to find a job, but my efforts met with failure. Embassies were fully staffed and no foreign companies had offices in Peking.

For the first time in my life I began to feel homesick. My parents detected this in my letters and started telephoning me every two weeks. Often emotion left me speechless on the telephone.

Letters took eleven days to arrive from the States and about a week from Europe, and I counted the days until I received a response from friends. In my letters I was always careful about what I wrote, assuming that any one of them could be opened and read. One letter from my mother arrived glued to the envelope, and she informed me later that one of my letters also stuck to the envelope.

Depressed and frustrated, I became even more impatient with the Chinese bureaucracy. One day, while trying to locate a fellow American who I knew was staying in our hotel, my rage exploded. I waited fifteen minutes for a clerk at the lobby information desk to search through a thick pile of American registration cards only to be told, " She does not live in this hotel'.

This was impossible, I thought, because I had seen the woman at breakfast that morning and knew she was still here. I told him this, but he calmly but firmly insisted that she did not live in the hotel anymore.

Finally I became annoyed and raised my voice. This attracted the attention of another clerk who presented me with the pack of registration cards to look through. I found her name at once and beamed triumphantly at the clerk, who refused to look up from his desk. Later I learned that I had violated Chinese rules of proper conduct. I had raised my voice and then I had forced a man to lose face, by proving him wrong in an ostentatious, offensive way. It was a lesson I was not to forget.

The person I had been trying to locate joined me and was eager to discuss her day's programme, which included a visit to a commune, a school, and a hospital. These were the places Gerd and I had wanted to see, but we had never received a response from the Information Department.

I complained to this woman about my situation and she insisted that I join her tour to a jade factory the next day. But when she told the guide she wanted to include me, he said, 'That is not convenient,' without giving any explanation. I fumed and once again felt helpless.

Then I asked to visit the hotel kitchen, assuming this would be a simple matter. I was wrong. It required a letter from Gerd to the Revolutionary Committee. After several days without an answer, Mr Chen went to inquire and came back with a troubled expression on his face. He said that I needed an organisation to sponsor me before the Revolutionary Committee would consider my request. The Information Department was responsible for journalists but not for their wives. This meant that I had no sponsor and therefore could do nothing on my own.

That day Bubbles listened to my frustrations and licked away my tears. I was fed up with this alien world and regretted that

I had ever come to Peking. I was ready to admit defeat and give up. As I started packing my bags, Gerd begged me to wait just a little longer, and I agreed.

EXCURSION OUTSIDE OF PEKING

At last Gerd was able to invite other journalists to join us on a trip to the Great Wall and Ming Tombs. During the 72-kilo-metre drive to the Great Wall, which took us about ninety minutes, we passed through the flat terrain surrounding Peking. Almost all of the land was being cultivated and only occasion-ally did we see brown clusters of rural housing, a few trees, and the slight mounds of earth that were ancestral burial places.

The fields were filled with peasants planting seeds, turning over the dry soil with simple hoes, or digging irrigation chan-nels. As we passed they often stood up and waved, looking grateful for a distraction from their hard work.

Few cars were on the road. Wagons drawn by startling combinations of a large horse and small mule or an ox and a mule were loaded with hay and vegetables and moving in the direction of Peking. Often a young colt reeled along beside its mother, then fell back to graze and, upon discovering it had been left behind, bounded down the middle of the road.

We passed trucks crowded with squashed standing passen-gers who were on their way to the Great Wall. They travelled much faster than the buses, which took three and a half hours to make the journey from Peking.

Tractors coughed up black smoke as they chugged down the road. They were driven by serious-looking young men with mirror sunglasses and dirty-white sheepskin coats lined with fur.

The bicycles on the road were carrying an odd assortment of passengers. Some had pigs, sheep, or goats, which were probably on their way to the slaughter-house, tied to the back.

Other cyclists were equipped with large straw baskets and shovels, which they would use to gather up the manure animals deposited on the road. The manure was used to fertilise small private plots of land.

Weathered, unshaven old men led lame horses along the side of the road. Wrinkled women and young grandchildren were also kept busy gathering twigs and looking after grazing goats.

A man on a well-groomed, elegant horse trotted by. This was an unusual sight, because horses were primarily work animals.

Around eleven o'clock the fields started emptying, and we knew it was lunchtime. Women with colourful bandannas covering their foreheads and tied in back talked and smiled as they moved slowly toward home. Teen-age girls with braids carried a hoe over one shoulder and held hands and giggled. The older men wore white towels tied around their head and usually had a cigarette or pipe hanging out of their mouth. Everyone wore patched, faded work clothing, which made them look poorer than the city people, but they seemed happier and more carefree.

Just before the turn off to the Ming Tombs, which we would visit on the return trip, we passed a small, sleepy, dusty adobe village. This was the feeding and resting station for horses and their drivers on the way to or from Peking. Among the horses were pigs and chickens scavenging for food.

As we approached the Great Wall, the road narrowed and started to wind and twist. We began to climb through barren hills. The countryside was rocky, parched, and mountainous and looked as though it could not support any vegetation. But the Chinese were determined to make this land arable. Workers armed with picks slowly and patiently levelled the sides of the rocky mountains. Nearby horses and carts waited to haul the rubble away and struggle with their heavy loads up the steep incline.

As we approached the Great Wall empty trucks lined the

sides of the road. Their passengers, who came from factories and communes in the area, were visiting the Great Wall.

We left our car in the parking lot and then gazed up at this 2,500-year-old man-made wonder, which is said to have taken 300,000 men over ten years to build. I had always associated the word China with the Great Wall, and now I was there, awed in its presence.

As we walked towards the Wall we stopped to watch the crowds of Chinese taking pictures or being photographed. The way women posed for a picture amused me. They looked as though they were imitating Peking opera performers. Each put one foot forward, held a hand on the hip and looked at the camera with an unsmiling, determined expression, which is the usual stance of operatic heroines.

Refreshment stands and a picnic area were at the edge of the parking lot. There, everyone ate the same lunch, a small 'vitamin bread', which tasted sweet and mealy, a carbonated orange drink, and apples and cookies. Men and women sat in separate groups with some gathered round a table and others in a squatting position. When lunch was over, men played cards and smoked, and women talked and knitted bright coloured sweaters for their children.

Finally we reached the rest of our party, who were beginning to climb up the Wall, and soon we passed those in front of us. After a fast, strenuous fifteen-minute climb we reached the sign telling us we could go no farther. Ahead of us and behind us were over three thousand miles of the unrestored wall, which had been built as a defence against the tribes from the north. Now the area on the other side of the Wall, Inner Mongolia, belonged to China. I looked out on this vast expanse of land searching for the camel caravans that our friends had occasionally seen in this area.

After catching our breath, we ran down the hill in ten minutes, passing many Chinese who were laughing at us. They were in no hurry and were enjoying the relaxation of a day off.

We had worked up an appetite and were eager to picnic at

the Ming Tombs, a 45-minute ride from the Wall. One of our group suggested going to Deh Ling, which later became our favourite tomb of the thirteen in which Ming emperors were buried.

Deh Ling was over three hundred years old and had not been restored. It had the frail beauty that age sometimes bestows on objects. A crumbling wall encircled most of the tomb. The last standing edifice was disintegrating, while trees and greenery sprouted from its sides and naked wooden roof. The yellow and green tiles which had previously covered the roof were strewn on the ground between gnarled ancient trees.

Behind the building was a large round courtyard with a man-made hill. The emperor and his treasures were buried there. A stone walkway surrounded the courtyard and when we walked around it we could see mountainous terrain and grazing sheep and goats.

Chinese visitors preferred going to the two restored show piece tombs, so we had Deh Ling to ourselves. After picnicking and enjoying the beauty and serenity of this site, we started driving back to Peking. Only then did I remember that our driver had missed his two-hour nap, a must for most Chinese.

As we entered the city at bicycle rush hour, I saw his eyes closing. I wanted to poke him in his side, but had second thoughts about awakening him in such an alarming way. Therefore, I rolled down the window and started drumming on the top of the car while singing a tune. This kept him awake for the rest of the ride.

MRS SHU ARRIVES

In May my teacher arrived and my negative attitude started to change. I liked Mrs Shu from the first time we met. When she entered our hotel room, she looked different from many Chinese I had seen. She walked with a perky gait and when she talked her eyes sparkled behind black rimmed glasses and her voice was full of life. She spoke perfect German, which impressed Gerd. I admired her confident and relaxed manner and I decided it had been worth waiting three months for this teacher.

I started learning Chinese from an elementary conversation book, which I soon discovered didn't contain the vocabulary I needed in town, where no one spoke English. And so I asked Mrs Shu if we could put aside the book, and proposed that I write my daily lessons. This meant that I went around with a notebook the entire day, jotting down the words and phrases I needed, but did not know, when I spoke with Chinese. Mrs Shu agreed to my system, which focused on conversation rather than reading and writing.

The May weather had suddenly become sticky and warm. Old men sat outside with their pants and the layers underneath rolled up to their knees, while I pushed my shirt sleeves up above my elbows.

The ship carrying our personal belongings and all of my summer clothing had not arrived yet and so I was stuck with winter clothes. I tried to buy ready-made blouses in stores, but they were intended for short waisted, flat chested women, which excluded me.

But Hong-Kong, which was famous for its twenty-four-hour tailor service, was enticingly near. In addition, I needed a change of scenery. The first months of adjustment had been very difficult, and I yearned for a juicy sirloin steak, stylish shops, a modern, immaculate hotel room, and free conversation.

I decided to go to Hong Kong but before leaving Peking, I had to have a travel permit, and this meant that Gerd had to go through the Chinese bureaucratic channels. He wrote a letter to the Information Department requesting a travel permit for me. When the permit was granted I then had to go to the Public Security Bureau, where my travel permit was stamped with the latest date I would be permitted to return to China. Only then could I make a reservation with CAAC (the Chinese national airlines) and buy a ticket to Canton.

THE SHOCK OF HONG KONG

I had the choice of spending two nights in a train on the 36-hour journey to Hong Kong or taking a plane first to Canton, and I decided to fly. The 1600-mile flight to Canton gave me plenty of time to rest and work up an appetite. It took six and a half hours with stops and no food was served along the way. (A year later I made the trip in two and three-quarter hours in a Boeing plane that China had purchased from America.)

The young stewardesses looked like recent middle school graduates. All of them were very pretty. They wore uniforms consisting of blue pants, white blouses, and blue jackets, and the tailoring gave them more shape than the baggy Peking style.

Each had waist-length braids, a velvet complexion, and a warm smile, and when they served me they spoke a few words of English. 'Would you like an orange drink or tea?' 'Please take more candy, cigarettes and gum,' they said. But these did not fill the hole in my stomach or appease those foreigners whose request for alcoholic beverages met with the response, ' We don't have any.'

In addition to foreigners, there were well-dressed Chinese on board who looked like experienced travellers. They must have been on business trips because private travel in planes, I understood, was not allowed. Judging from the way they were dressed, in well-cut suits with high collars, I thought they must be leading government officials.

I was puzzled by the fact that a few passengers did not remove their caps, even though perspiration was rolling down their cheeks. I had noticed that caps never left men's heads in winter, but now that the weather was warm, there was no longer any need to protect the head. Only later did I learn that for the Chinese, who lived according to the moon calendar, it was still spring, which meant that caps should be worn.

'It is unhealthy to dress for summer before it officially arrives,' a Chinese friend explained.

Since no air service operated between Canton and Hong Kong I had to continue the journey by train, after an overnight stop in Canton. The train for the border station, Shumchun, left in the early morning.

I found Canton and Peking as unlike as New Orleans and Boston. While Peking is quiet and unexciting and the people are reserved and staid, Canton, by contrast, was lively and noisy and the people appeared to be relaxed and gregarious. The Cantonese dressed in brighter colours and looked sloppier than the northerners, and spent their days and evenings on the streets and sidewalks where it was cooler. At night, at about the same time that Peking residents went to sleep, the restaurants and streets in Canton were still full of people.

The next morning other foreigners and I made the two-hour ride to the border in a special air-conditioned train that had adjustable reclining seats fitted with white covers and lace doilies. The windowsills were freshly dusted and the young train hostess frequently mopped the spotless red linoleum aisles. She also served tea, the only refreshment available, while other Chinese functionaries sitting in our car changed Chinese currency into foreign currency. It was illegal for Chinese money to leave the country.

The inside of the train seemed unusually bare. The only decoration on the walls was a picture of Kweilin, a city in southwest China that was famous for its rock formations.

I pushed back the white lace curtains to see the lush green southern landscape. Peasants wearing wide straw hats were knee deep in rice paddies, planting seedlings. Water buffalo were ploughing the fields or resting contentedly in water covering all their bulk except for the two big nostrils. Occasionally old men with sticks walked along beside grazing buffalo that were carrying young passengers on their back.

When we reached the border, customs clearance was routine and I did not have to open a bag. Then, for the first time in my life, I walked across a border. To leave China and enter Hong Kong, everyone had to walk across a wooden railroad bridge.

When I turned around to catch a last glimpse of the People's Republic of China I saw a familiar sign, 'Long Live the Unity of the Peoples of the World,' and 'Long Live the People's Republic of China.' Army guards in khaki uniforms and caps with red stars stood at attention on the bridge. I looked ahead of me and was startled. The Hong Kong customs authorities, who were Chinese, were dressed in white Bermuda shorts, white caps, white shirts and white knee-length socks. This contrast in dress and the sudden noisy confusion were jolting.

After clearing customs on the Hong Kong side we boarded the train foreigners nickamed the 'gin and tonic express.' Imported liquor was not sold in the People's Republic, and this train got its nickname from the favourite drink served on board, gin and tonic.

The windows of the hot train were opened to let in a breeze, but at the same time coal dust and cinders flew in. The stench from the bathroom made me wait the ninety minutes until the trip was over. The seats were torn and mine would not go back. When the person in front of me put his seat back my knees pressed against it. Paper and bits of food were scattered in the aisles, which needed a good cleaning. The inside of the train was plastered with advertisements selling *mao-tai*, the schnaps from Kweilin, Laryngitis pills, Viceroy filter cigarettes, etc.

Wrinkled and shrivelled old women, dressed in black, walked up and down the aisle shouting out their wares in pidgin English. 'Pretty black umbrellas, must have,' 'Sweeties, sweeties, why you no want?' The call for 'gin, whisky please' required no coaxing.

As I looked out of the window my eyes feasted on the sparkling blue ocean and the soaring mountains in the background, and then I saw the garbage heaps and scattered debris. I noticed unwashed children in rags, shacks with cellophane windows and hovels with tar-paper roofs. These signs of poverty erased the beautiful backdrop. As we approached the end of the line, high-rise apartment buildings with broken windows, balconies full of laundry on bamboo poles, and Chinese women in curlers came into view. I began to feel very disoriented.

Twenty-four hours after leaving Peking—almost as long as the flight from Paris to Peking—I arrived at Kowloon, a city on the Hong Kong mainland side. Outside the railroad station a scrawny bent old man put out his veiny trembling hand for money. This disturbed me, because I had forgotten that beggars existed. In the People's Republic begging was forbidden.

As I walked toward the hotel I passed Chinese girls in low-cut snug-fitting shirts and short skirts. Their painted faces were like masks and their long finger-nails were carefully manicured with red polish. Their black hair either flowed down their backs or was set in tight curls, sometimes with dyed red or blonde streaks. They looked like prostitutes compared with the women in Peking, who wore shapeless clothes, severe hair styles, and no make-up.

Old rickshaw drivers sprinted past on muscular legs, their strength surprising because their faces revealed their advanced age. Their passengers—Western tourists—laughed and enjoyed this exotic means of transportation. This, too, was a new sight. There were no rickshaws in Peking. They had been outlawed because the Chinese believed that this kind of work was for animals and not for people.

I was surprised to see young couples in the streets locked together in embraces; some were even kissing. In Peking couples hardly dared to touch hands publicly. All these sights shocked me, and for the first time I was aware that Peking had made a great impact on me.

When I registered in the Hong Kong Hotel a small note on the registration card caught my eye 'Guests should put all valuables and money in a safety deposit box for security reasons.' In Peking my jewellery and money were in our un-locked room, and safety deposit boxes did not exist.

When the porter brought my suitcase to the room, I thanked him, but he still didn't leave. Suddenly I remembered I had not tipped him. After he left I saw a sign on the inside of the door, instructing guests to lock the double lock from inside whenever in the room.

Assuming I would soon get over the culture shock, I went out to shop for summer clothes. But the fast pace of the life in Hong Kong baffled me. Chauffeur-driven Mercedes dropped their expensively-dressed Chinese passengers in front of exclus-ive jewellery stores that had locked doors and guards standing outside. Street hawkers approached me and tried to sell bar-gains that looked like stolen merchandise. Pushy saleswomen told me that everything I tried on looked beautiful. Blaring Western hits competed with Chinese music.

These scenes were strange to me only because Chinese were playing the main role. I was used to the conduct, appearance, and pace of the Chinese in the People's Republic and felt un-comfortable here. Confused and disappointed, I decided to shorten my stay. Instead of remaining a week, I finished my shopping in three days and returned to my secure Peking cocoon.

Chapter 2

Summary

MOVING INTO THE APARTMENT

While I was in Hong Kong Gerd received word that the ship carrying our household containers would soon be unloading in Hsinkang, a port three hours from Peking. It was the middle of June and the humid and rainy summer season was beginning. Foreigners warned us that the port had no sheds for protecting the cargo. Concerned about the rain drenching our belongings, we contacted the Service Bureau and requested that it provide a shelter for our things.

We still did not have an apartment, but within a few days the Service Bureau called and asked us to visit an apartment in a new block. We drove through the gates of a fenced-in compound reserved for foreigners. A man from the Service Bureau was waiting to receive us at the first entrance to an eight-storey brick building. After entering a poorly-lit corridor, we passed a lift lady who was sitting and reading a newspaper in a lighted cubicle across from the elevator.

The apartment the man showed us was one of two on the ground floor, and had been vacant since the building's completion six months ago. We opened the door and went into the entrance hall, which led to a spacious living-room, adjoining dining-room, and kitchen. We walked through the living-room and entered the other side of the flat, which had a bedroom with a built-in wardrobe closet and another bedroom with an enclosed balcony. The size of the bathroom and its king-size bath impressed me, and Bubbles showed her appreciation for the bidet by jumping into it and sitting down to cool off.

The large kitchen was my greatest joy. It was fully equipped with built-in wall cabinets, a three-burner gas stove, storage room, sinks, and an outdoor balcony with a garbage chute.

We then walked through another corridor branching off the entrance hall and found a small bathroom with toilet and shower and another bedroom, which was destined to become the office.

The rent for the flat was 400 yuan, or about $200, a month and we accepted it immediately, noting the regulation that we could not make holes in the walls or remove the ceiling light fixtures. These terms set down by the Service Bureau led people to believe 'bugging' devices were overhead, but no one ever had evidence to prove this.

Our front windows looked out on a garden with forsythia bushes and pink blossoming almond trees. Behind the young trees was a fence, and about twenty feet farther was Chang An, the main highway through Peking.

From our kitchen we had a perfect view of the entrance to our compound. Two People's Liberation Army guards with pistols on their belts stood outside the gate. They let foreigners through, but screened the Chinese, who had to show a pass before being permitted inside. When I asked why these guards were necessary, I was told 'to protect the foreigners living within.' I wanted to ask what this meant, but knew it was not the time and a Service Bureau employee was not the right person to confront with such a provocative question.

The six-month accumulation of sand and dirt gave us reason to hire a cleaning woman full time, who would cost us 120 yuan a month. I was used to having help a few hours a week in Bonn but realised that the Peking climate would require a lot more housework than I was able to do.

The Service Bureau sent us a timid Chinese woman who looked frail and very frightened. Mrs Yin came directly from a factory and had no experience doing housework for a foreign family. We were probably the first foreigners she ever spoke to, and she was nervous. In addition, the size of our flat must have overwhelmed her. Her family of four, like most Chinese families, probably lived in one or two rooms that were about one quarter the size of our flat.

For ten days Mrs Yin and I worked together to scrape off the layers of dust from the walls, which were once white, and to clean and polish the parquet and tile floors. Noticing how pale and tired she looked, I dismissed her early one day, saying I was too exhausted to continue working. After she heard from the observant elevator lady that I had continued to clean, she refused to go home in the future until I stopped working.

Our containers came by truck to Peking, and when the packers opened them, they found the plastic covering inside already sagging from the weight of accumulated water. One more day of rain and everything would have been wet.

Gerd, the interpreter, the cleaning woman, and I joined in to help the packers unload. The heat was so oppressive that Gerd took off his shirt as he carried the cartons. To our surprise the unpacking, which was supposed to take two days, was completed in one day. Mr Chen later explained, 'Mr Ruge's assistance inspired everyone to work harder,' except for the driver, who sat like a Buddha behind the wheel of the car until the bikes were unpacked. Only then did duty call. He stepped out of the car and volunteered to fill the tyres with air.

Within a week familiar furnishing, scattered nick-nacks, pictures hanging on the walls, and green plants on the window-sills made us feel at home. The office Mercedes had arrived and so had our new driver, Mr Liu. For Mr Liu's service we paid 150 yuan a month, which was less than one fifth what the hired Shanghai with a driver had cost us.

Mr Liu was an attractive and lively young man. He was proud of driving a Mercedes, the most prestigious car on Chinese roads, and he dusted, washed, and pampered it daily.

Our staff worked a five-and-a-half day week and it took time for me to get used to having people around me from nine to five every day. Gerd needed the interpreter and driver for the full working day, but I often sent Mrs Yin home much earlier.

I was pleased that the three worked so well together and

often helped not only me, but each other. On one occasion Mr Liu and Mrs Yin included me in a joint activity.

Mrs Yin needed household cleaning supplies, and Mr Liu said he would drive her to a local store. After stepping into the front seat carefully, she immediately reached for the dashboard and, when we started moving, gripped it so hard that I could see the pale, taut knuckles on the back of her hand. She, like many other Chinese, had never been in a car.

When the three of us entered the shop, the other customers, upon seeing me, stood aside and a clerk stopped waiting on a woman and came over to me. Mr Liu and Mrs Yin explained what they wanted as the clerk slowly handed them each item, which they inspected thoroughly while discussing it. If they were not satisfied, the clerk went to the back room and returned with new merchandise that was not on display. I noticed that no other customer in the store was receiving such treatment, and felt guilty about the fuss made over me. But Mr Liu and Mrs Yin were clearly enjoying it.

Ninety long minutes later, we left laden with a heavy floor mop, made of long coloured strips of cotton remnants, a duster, made of chicken feathers attached to a bamboo handle, a short straw whisk broom for sweeping the floor and carpet, a wooden washboard for washing clothes, fly swatters, an aluminium pail, soap, and detergent. I was tired from the time-consuming shopping trip, but Mr Liu and Mrs Yin beamed and looked very satisfied with their purchases.

Although we had ample household cleaning equipment at home, I felt it was better for Mrs Yin to do things her way. The first job every morning was to go through the flat and kill the flies, and during the day the swatter was always within arm's reach. Killing flies was an important part of the Chinese hygiene programme, I noticed, and even air hostesses were armed with fly swatters. On one flight the stewardess serving me tea paused for a moment, took a fly swatter out of her pocket, killed a fly, and then gave me my cup of tea.

After our house was fly-free, Mrs Yin did the washing. This

entailed scrubbing and slapping our clothes forcefully against the washboard. Soon I began to worry that our material would be worn thin after such abuse.

There was a washing machine in the kitchen, but it had not been used yet. I thought it was time to start using it. First I had to explain how it worked. Mr Chen, Mr Liu, and Mrs Yin lined up for a demonstration. The first time I turned it on the three stood silently with wide eyes and open mouths. They looked as if they were watching a suspense programme on television.

One week later Mrs Yin invited me to come into the kitchen. I knew that Mr Chen had been teaching her the technique, and she was very proud to show me that she could now operate the machine alone. But she still did not give up using her wash-board for very dirty clothes.

The vacuum cleaner did not impress her at all. I showed her how it worked and explained that it made cleaning easier, but for some reason I never understood, she did not use it, and went back to sweeping the carpet.

Now that I was settled, some of our neighbours in the building stopped by. Gerd's colleagues asked us for dinner and embassies sent us invitations to receptions. This wave of popularity resulted when our names, phone number, and address were added to the journalist's telephone booklet, published by the Foreign Ministry and distributed to foreigners. In addition, we received a separate telephone manual listing diplomats according to embassy and rank. But there was no Peking telephone book available for our use.

At first I was happy to be invited to participate in activities in the small foreign community of about three thousand people. There were bridge and mah-jong groups, yoga and *icabana* (Japanese flower arranging) classes, foreign language conversation circles, a choir, and English for foreigners. But I turned down all these invitations, and instead joined an exercise class that met three times a week in an embassy basement. I also enjoyed playing tennis on embassy courts or at the International Club, and occasionally accepted invitations to women's tea parties and luncheons because I was anxious to meet other women and hear how they were spending their time in Peking.

We met in an embassy residence or someone's flat. There I was able to devour such luxuries as imported foreign chocolates, cookies, cheeses, and wines. The only thing that bothered me was the conversation. Everyone had a gripe to air. The Chinese food was too greasy. Meat was tough. The tailors had ruined a piece of silk. A clerk in the Friendship Shop was impudent. The Chinese were lazy.

My greatest frustration had nothing to do with these complaints. I wanted to be closer to the Chinese, to understand them, their way of life, and even to make friends, if this was possible. And so I withdrew from these foreigners and escaped on Gerd's bicycle into the Chinese world.

PREOCCUPATION WITH THE WEATHER

The Chinese are always preoccupied with the weather. It was part of everyone's conversation and soon part of mine as well. In summer the Chinese sounded like qualified meteorologists, basing their knowledge on the Chinese moon calendar, which divided July and August into four hot periods.

On scorching days when the temperature reached 37 degrees C. (100 degrees F.) and the humidity was 95 per cent, a Chinese friend would offer comfort by telling me when the hot cycle would be over and on what day the temperature would fall. When the prediction came true, I started to believe in the wisdom of her calendar.

The Chinese never complained about the heat, but I did constantly that first summer. When it was warm they fanned themselves with a fan that was always within reach, and I panted. They moved slowly on hot days and drank a lot of warm tea. I hurried as usual, with perspiration running down my face. After lunch they slept for two hours, and I found things to do. Only when I slowly succumbed to their ways during the following summer did I find the heat more bearable.

The nights were the worst times for me. Unlike the Chinese, we had air conditioners—when they worked. Frequently two air conditioners running at the same time blew a fuse, and then we would have to wait until the next morning for the electricians to arrive.

After four breakdowns in a hot, sleepless week, I asked if we could have the key to the fuse box and flick the switch ourselves. 'That is our duty,' the electrician said, and I knew from experience there was no way to change his mind.

My teacher, Mrs Shu, arrived punctually at eight-thirty every morning, and after one glance at the shadows under my eyes she knew whether the heat had kept me awake. 'Why don't you try the Chinese method of sleeping in summer?' she asked. 'Buy a straw mat and put it on top of your bed. Then buy a terry-cloth blanket as a cover. I sleep well almost every night.'

I did not get around to following her suggestion the first summer. But when I finally tried her method, I regretted my former stubborn and sceptical attitude, because for the first time I slept through the whole night without the heat interrupting me.

The summer weather was so variable that no bicyclist, except for me, would leave home in the morning unprepared for a downpour. The Chinese folded up blue or grey plastic raincoats into a fist-size package and put them into the indispensable shoulder or hand bags they always had with them.

Usually I was on my bicycle several miles from home when the sky suddenly became overcast. While the Chinese quickly donned their raincoats, I would start racing toward home. But I seldom beat the rain, which came down in torrents and drenched me within seconds. Other cyclists, who remained dry under their raincoats and umbrellas, laughed when they saw me looking as wet as a fish. I wondered how they survived the heat of the plastic cover.

On hot days rain was a gift to children, who had very few

places to swim. They sloshed through streams of water and splashed in the mud until they looked as though they had been dipped in chocolate.

For about six weeks in summer we had downpours every day, but they lasted no longer than an hour. Then the sky cleared, and the burning sun appeared. Pavements steamed, raincoats were packed away, pedestrians fanned themselves, and I dried off.

But the rain provided only temporary relief. Within an hour the soil was dry, the puddles were gone, and the water trucks were once again on the roads spraying the trees, sidewalks, and delighted children.

MORNING ACTIVITY IN THE PARK

I rose regularly with the summer daylight at about five-thirty or six and saw joggers passing our windows and workers returning from the night shift. Since this was the coolest time of the day, it was ideal for bicycling, and sometimes I would join the 7 a.m. traffic. At this hour few cars were on the road, but bicycles were everywhere.

Some people stopped to buy breakfast on their way to work. Three-wheel bicycles were parked on the side of the road and a clerk from a local restaurant sold cigarettes and 'you bing', which are flat, almost circular pieces of fried dough that the Chinese liked for breakfast. I enjoyed the taste of *yo ping* but could eat no more than one, which was delicious warm, but difficult to digest when eaten cold.

Usually I headed toward the 'Altar of the Sun' park, where Chinese in our neighbourhood gathered in the morning. Judging from the number of bicycles standing outside the gates of the park, I was always one of the last people to arrive.

A brown cloud of dust hit me in the face soon after entering the park. The women cleaners had already begun sweeping the sidewalks. When they looked up and saw a foreigner emerge from behind the `dust, instead of a Chinese, they seemed surprised and giggled from embarrassment. In town, sweepers always stopped their work until I passed.

A circular garden planted with neat rows of red geraniums was a short distance ahead. I went by without stopping, while Chinese stood around the garden, pointing out and admiring individual flowers. They loved flowers, which, in Peking, were a luxury grown only in parks.

A wide dirt passageway framed by rows of carefully nurtured flowers led to the centre of the park. On the way I met another group of cleaners who were wearing white chef's caps, surgical masks, faded blue denim pants, and jackets. They were brushing this walkway at a tempo resembling slow motion. They paused as I went by and then continued collecting the papers and fruit peels people had discarded on the ground. Empty rubbish containers were nearby, and I wondered why no one bothered to use them.

On both sides of the walkway were photographs of China's new factories and mechanised agricultural implements, displayed in glass-framed panels. Interspersed between these photos were pictures of Chairman Mao greeting foreign dignitaries, and government leaders visiting workers and peasants.

People stood in front of each picture, reading aloud the accompanying text and staring for long periods at each scene. Similar exhibits were also set up on main streets and side streets, where they were a leading attraction. These were like sidewalk museums.

I had passed these pictures often and so went directly to the end of the entrance-way, where four retired men in their sixties shared a green park bench. We greeted each other like old friends. Whenever I visited the park, they were sitting in the same place and wearing the same clothes.

One of the four had already tucked his grey patched pants up to his knees and was in the midst of rolling his white long-sleeved shirt up to the elbows.

Another, who looked like a monk with his shaved head, was waving his bamboo cane in the air and speaking in an animated tone. When he saw me, he stopped to smile, revealing many missing teeth.

The third wore knee-length shorts, which had probably been long pants at one time, a white torn T-shirt over his pants, and black cotton shoes. He listened to the conversation while grunting and tapping a green plastic umbrella on the ground.

The fourth man had long wisps of white hair growing from his chin, which was a sign of old age. I guessed he was between sixty-five and seventy-five. His main interest seemed to be filling his pipe from a leather tobacco pouch hanging on the wooden pipe handle. The absence of glasses for his squinting eyes struck me immediately. Later I found out that glasses and false teeth were expensive, and many people could not afford them.

Songs from Peking revolutionary opera seemed to burst out of different clusters of bushes, but I couldn't see anyone. The singers had hidden themselves behind trees and obviously did not want to be seen. As I continued walking, two teen-age boys, who looked as though they were out for a lark on the way to school, mimicked the invisible singers.

The music came from all directions. Beside baritone and soprano voices, musicians started to play instruments. An accordionist sat on top of a small man-made hill while friends sat around him singing. A trombone player was not disturbed by a trumpeter practising musical scales nearby. Before long the park sounded like an orchestra tuning up.

The almond and forsythia trees provided more than shade and beauty. One stocky woman in her fifties lifted her leg slowly and stretched it against a low branch of a tree. Another solidly-built older woman held on to a young trunk as she did knee bends. Suddenly the tree collapsed, but she was unhurt. She started laughing and the others joined in.

In the background a man was punching a tree with his fist. He had hung his bird cage, covered with a white cloth, on a branch of a nearby tree. On the same branch were the man's blue jacket, matching cap, and a canvas shoulder bag.

Older men and women in groups under trees were shadow boxing, a traditional Chinese sport. They looked as though they were dancing a ballet in slow motion. Only later, when I took part in a two-months shadow boxing course at the International Club, did I realise how difficult this exercise is. It consisted of 173 consecutive movements, which demonstrate positions of attack and defence against imaginary opponents.

The first unforgettable words of our teacher were 'Don't glare. Tuck in your bones. Slope your shoulders. Salivate, relax.' This combination was in itself difficult to do, but at the same time I had to remember a sequence of movements, maintain a continuing rhythm, and control the position of each part of my body. Had I known, during those first walks through the park, how much practice and discipline shadow boxing required, I would have paused longer to admire this art and the people who had mastered it.

Shadow boxing was a sport that was passed down from the older generation. A few older people in the park were leading classes of middle-aged men and women, but I rarely saw young people participating.

Ahead of me, crowds were gathered around one performer whom I could not see. I arrived to find a young man, under five feet tall, balancing himself on one hand that was resting on a small slab of stone. He looked like a piece of rubber as he twisted and contorted his body. A few people tried to imitate his seemingly effortless movements, but they gave up quickly.

Next to him was a sword-dancing class. Each person had a crude home-carved sword for the drill. This sport looked as though it required the same discipline as shadow boxing. The instructor thrust the sword forward and withdrew it in smooth, controlled movements, while displaying an elegant body harmony and co-ordination. Walking on, I almost collided with a teenage runner, whose teacher was timing him in a fifty-yard dash.

Music coming from a green-and-blue wooden pavilion attracted me. A blind musician was playing an *erh-hu*, a traditional Chinese two-string violin. Young and old people sat around him on low wooden folding stools brought from home.

Then a grey-haired woman with a leathery, hard face rose from the audience. After taking one last puff on her cigarette, she let the butt dangle in her yellow stained fingers and started to sing. Expecting a rough and throaty voice, I was surprised to hear a beautiful and tender tone coming from her as she sang classical Peking opera.

When she finished, a worker wearing a grey cap and holding a grey plastic satchel sang the next song. Then he went off to work and the unrehearsed entertainment continued.

The audience was very mixed. People with sensitive and intelligent faces listened attentively and nodded and smiled at familiar tunes they had not heard for a long time. Old workers sat in a corner rolling cigarettes and talking. Grandmothers played with grandchildren, fed them fruit and cookies, and coaxed them to sit still a few minutes and listen to the music.

Leaving the music behind, I walked toward a large circular marble altar after which the park is named. I had read in a guide book that the emperor had come to this place over 450 years ago to make offerings and pray to the sun. Now it was the stage for two six-year-old children, who were practising sword dancing under the critical eye of an instructor. Dressed in blue athletic pants, matching T-shirts, and black cinch belts, showing off waists that looked the size of my neck, they went through the drill. The precision, confidence, and grace they exhibited astounded me and I joined the large approving audience surrounding them and applauded.

The marble arch, about the size of a skating rink, was the stage for other activities. Two boys played badminton. Teachers, dressed in white smocks like nurses led a freshly scrubbed kindergarten class in morning callisthenics. Another teacher shouted marching orders to teen-age school children who were filing through the centre of the circle in pairs.

By eight A.M. the park was left to the retired, who sat quietly on park benches reading books and newspapers, chatting and knitting, while their grandchildren played. As I left an orchestra of cicadas screamed their farewell.

THE COOK ARRIVES

I returned home to hear the good news that our cook would arrive that day. I was interested in Chinese cooking, but there were no courses for foreigners. Gerd, therefore, decided that we should have a cook to prepare lunch for us, and from him I could learn the art of the Chinese cuisine. He would be our 140-yuan, monthly luxury.

The Service Bureau had warned us that we would have to wait a long time for a cook specialising in Chinese food. But they could offer us almost immediately someone who made Western food. This was my specialty and so we decided to wait.

When Mr Yu walked in I was surprised at his youthful face and tiny stature. He was twenty-seven years old and I towered over him. I had always seen cooks who looked like their own best customers, but Mr Yu did not follow this pattern. He was no more than five feet tall and weighed about one hundred pounds. At once I liked his warm smile, large dark eyes, and his short hair, which stood up like bristles.

His shyness made him speak almost in a whisper and I strained to hear what he was saying. He told us it was his first job with a foreign family and he was anxious to please us. 'What do you eat?' Mr Yu asked. I was willing to try everything except for slimy sea slugs, an expensive favourite Chinese delicacy, and jellyfish, which I had once mistaken for crunchy noodles and sampled. Mr Yu promised to prepare a menu for us with simple dishes.

'What kind of menu should I prepare for the dog?' he asked, with a very earnest expression in his face. I assured him she could eat leftovers. Later I saw the raw tidbits he was putting aside for her. Bubbles was eating choice meat daily! Not wanting to offend him, I suggested that Bubbles eat in the evening. As soon as he left the house after lunch, I made Bubbles' meal into our dinner stew or goulash, and she got the remains.

Two weeks later Mr Yu presented me with the hand-written menu he had promised, but it was written in Chinese and I couldn't read a character. Mr Chen then provided an English translation next to the Chinese characters. The completed menu reminded me of a bill of fare from a Chinese restaurant in New York. It had fifty selections, numbered and arranged according to category: fish, fowl, meat, and vegetable dishes. Although the menu looked familiar, Mr Yu's food was much better than any Chinese food I had eaten in the States.

After lunch each day, Mr Yu asked me to make a choice for the next day. When I chose two dishes, he insisted on three. 'Two dishes are enough for one person, not for two,' he explained.

At the beginning I noticed that Mr Yu discarded leftovers from lunch. Being frugal, I promptly told him not to throw away anything that was still eatable. But he persisted in throwing away the cold leftovers. I knew that Chinese wasted nothing themselves, and so I wanted to find out why he did this. At first I mistakenly thought that he did this because he considered us rich, and therefore, assumed he did not have to save food.

I discovered the real answer by speaking to other Chinese friends, who told me that they never rewarmed cooked food in summer because the food might have spoiled. Chinese do not have refrigerators and in summer buy fresh food for each meal and prepare only the amount that will be eaten at one sitting. Not understanding the advantage of refrigeration, Mr Yu was sceptical about it, and followed the Chinese custom in summer.

Careful not to insult or offend Mr Yu, I slowly started to show him how I used the refrigerator. After lunch I cleared the table and put the leftovers in the refrigerator. The next morning I greeted Mr Yu by thanking him for the delicious dinner he had prepared ahead of time for us. I told him I had warmed up his lunch leftovers and that they had tasted marvellous.

My quiet persuasion lasted a few weeks, until he started using the refrigerator regularly and no longer threw away food. His confidence in the refrigerator led him to try out the freezer. On the day he prepared a large lunch for guests, he proudly showed me that he had made some dishes ahead of time and had frozen them.

STREET LIFE

The summer heat had a mellowing effect on Peking and its residents. People who had been reserved and withdrawn in winter started talking to me on the street. ' *Tienchi hen hao*,' (It's hot today) someone would remark and I would agree. '*Ni hao*' (hello) another would shout as he passed me on a bicycle.

A few times, when it was cooler, young men challenged me to bicycles races. When I rode past them, they suddenly sped up, overtook me, and then turned around and smiled. Then they slowed down, waiting for me to catch up with them. When I did, the race continued, until I wilted and reluctantly gave up the chase.

The doors leading to courtyards and housing were open and the grey walls lost their chilling winter appearance. I looked inside and for the first time saw what was behind the formidable walls.

In the courtyards were vineyards, laden with green grapes that had not reached maturity. Ten-foot-high golden sunflowers were stabilised by sticks.

In the shade of graceful willow trees, old barebreasted women sat on low stools washing clothes on washboards. A grandfather sat and dozed while his grandson played with stones on the dry earth. They both had shaved heads, which made them look alike. Girls under five also had a practical summer hair cut. Their heads were shaved up to the ear line. Very short hair sprouted above the ear.

A mother walked by with her blouse open, breast feeding a child at least two years old. And a man rode by slowly on a three-wheel bicycle, carrying a rapidly melting hunk of ice destined for the neighbourhood market.

The monotonous winter and spring façade of all blue disappeared. The removal of the jacket and its replacement by a colour other than blue made people look less stiff and the atmosphere more congenial. That first summer most men and women wore dark cotton pants and a white shapeless shirt hanging outside the pants and covering the hips. Black rubber sandals were very practical footwear during downpours.

Occasionally my teacher appeared in a black, full skirt that covered her knees. When I commented about the style she had an instant explanation. 'Today it will be very hot.' When I asked why she had not worn it on former hot days, she commented, 'I would never wear a skirt before the first of July,' the start of summer that year by the moon calendar. Unlike their mothers, girls wore bright-coloured skirts with elastic waists.

In the following summers colours and styles changed. Men wore blue shirts and women wore ready-made blouses, produced in prints and bright pinks, greens, and blues. Then dresses appeared in stores.

A popular clothing store that sold only ready-made items displayed different styles of dresses and two-piece matching skirts and blouses. When we visited this exhibit behind glass the store employee brought to our attention the dress collar, which imitated the collar worn during the Tang, 618-906, period. I found not only the V shaped neck attractive, but also liked the flat pleated skirts and belted waists.

We had heard that similar dresses had been shown in Shanghai shop windows, with a sign next to them saying that Chiang Ching, the wife of Mao, had participated in the dress design. Once I had seen her appear publicly in a mid-calf-length shirtwaist dress.

The purpose of the Peking exhibit was to find out which styles people liked best. One Chinese who had seen the exhibit commented to me, 'The dresses are too modern, expensive, and require many coupons.' Cotton, like grain products and oil, was rationed and each person received six yards a year. This woman's reaction seemed to represent the general sentiment in Peking, where I saw only one woman wearing a dress in the street.

By the summer of 1975 army uniforms for women changed from pants to an A-line khaki knee-length skirt, jacket, overblouse, short white socks, and sandals. When army women walked down the streets everyone's eyes were fixed on this new Chinese style. Obviously it met with their approval, because soon ordinary women started wearing slightly fuller polyester skirts.

By 1976, instead of women wearing ready-made skirts, they were creating their own fashions. Flat pleats appeared and skirts revealed waists, which overblouses had formerly concealed. Lengths wavered around the knee and sometimes even above it. Some women put on ten-year-old straight skirts which they had last worn before the Cultural Revolution.

Nylon and polyester blouses became fashionable and in every store there were long queues in front of blouse counters. When my teacher appeared in a new nylon blouse one day, I asked her how she could wear such hot material in summer. She admitted that it was warmer than cotton, but then raved about its advantages: 'It washes easily, dries quickly, and requires no ironing.' I agreed that this was a very practical material, knowing that Chinese had little free time and no help at home.

The new fashions revealed for the first time during our stay the figure of the Chinese woman. Until then I had no idea how they were built because they were always wrapped in layers. Women's legs were often short and shapeless and their hips looked broad. Waists were small and chests were almost flat. Later I heard from a Chinese friend that Chinese girls with

large breasts suffered. She had heard old women comment
about one girl, 'Her breasts look as though she is six months
pregnant, but her stomach is flat.'

After coming from a society where people tended to overeat
and show the results, I was surprised to see so many trim, firm
bodies. An overweight Chinese was the exception.

In the heat of summer, stores were stuffy and hot, but I never
smelled the odour of perspiration. This fact puzzled me until I
met an American doctor visiting Peking. He said that Chinese do
not have the glands which create the perspiration odour.

In the back of my mind I remembered a visit we had made
to a clinic in Shanghai. The doctor had told us that minor
operations were performed there, such as removing the smell
glands from the few Chinese born with them. Assuming the
interpreter had made an error in translation, we ignored this
detail. But now I understood what he meant.

Later on a Chinese girl told me that she had a friend in
middle school who had a body odour, and none of her school-
mates would go near her. 'They made fun of her and left her
alone, so I became her friend,' she said.

At times, I noticed that my smell also disturbed members
of our household. When I put on perfume before going to a
lunch one day, and then got into our air-conditioned car, Mr
Liu immediately opened the window to get fresh air. Another
time my teacher asked me what the strange smell was in the
living-room. That morning I had put on perfume.

After lunch everyone in our household and most of Peking
rested. It was the hottest part of the day and no one ventured
out on the streets unless it was unavoidable. Between two-
thirty and three the city started to awaken and streets and
sidewalks became alive with activity and colour. This was
the time I usually started bicycling.

The Chinese were not used to having a foreigner among
them and sometimes my presence created an unexpected
series of events. Once a three-wheel motor cart loaded with
cucumbers passed me on my bike, and when the driver saw

me he stared so long that he bumped into the truck in front of him and his cucumbers tumbled onto the street.

In the late afternoon horse-drawn carts, allowed only on side streets, and trucks were the main traffic on the roads. They were loaded down with eggplants, cucumbers, string beans, onions, and other vegetables grown on nearby communes. Coming from the outskirts of Peking, they were bringing in the afternoon delivery of fresh produce.

People had started queuing in front of the empty counters of outdoor markets long before the delivery. But when it came, others rushed toward the stand, pushing and shoving their way into line.

The unloading process always fascinated me and I often paused to watch. Fruit and perishable vegetables were usually packed in baskets that could be unloaded quickly. The clerks then covered them with straw matting to protect them from the sun. The firm vegetables like cabbage, potatoes, lettuce, turnips, and radishes were dumped or shovelled onto the sidewalk in separate heaps, which were protected under the straw roofing of the stand.

Melons, especially, required a lot of unloading time. A few people stood waist deep in the melon mountain on the truck or cart and tossed each piece down to catchers on the sidewalk, who passed them on in an assembly line fashion.

Melon was the favourite fruit in summer and on every main and side street melons of different sizes, shapes, types, and shades were stacked. Customers could buy a whole melon or eat a piece at the stand. A basket for seeds and another for the rind were nearby, and unlike other times, everyone seemed to be using them. The rind would be food for the pigs and the seeds would be dried and salted, and later I saw them sold as a favourite winter snack.

Selecting a watermelon was an art, and many customers were professionals, who felt and tapped thirty or forty before buying one. Knowing nothing about this specialty, I relied on the judgement of the sellers.

One day I wanted a ripe melon to serve that evening. I bicycled to a stand only five minutes from our door. There, a long wall of watermelons faced me. To me they all looked alike. The clerk saw at once that I was a beginner, and he offered to assist me. The only thing I told him was that the melon must be ripe, and later on I found out that this was a mistake.

After lifting, shaking, patting, and listening to many melons he called another clerk over for consultation. The other clerk and he were not in agreement and soon four others joined the search, while customers waited silently for me to be served. As I looked at the busy clerks, dressed in white caps and white aprons, I thought of doctors examining patients.

Forty-five minutes later they agreed on the perfect melon. But when we cut it that evening, I was disappointed. The melon was mushy. Only later did I realise that 'ripe' by Chinese standards means soft, and I never asked for a ripe melon again.

Ice cream vendors were as popular as the watermelon sellers, but they had a different status. The government gives licences to needy, old people to sell ice cream and their salary is ten per cent of the amount they sell. Unlike workers, they do not receive a fixed monthly salary. In addition, the ice cream sellers own their white wooden carts, which are like their shop, while all other businesses are government owned.

Most of the sellers looked as though they had had hard lives. Their hands were calloused, their faces deeply lined, and their clothes worn. In another country these old men and women might be beggars, but in China they worked for a living.

After picking up the daily ice cream supply each seller pushed his cart to the same corner every day. Then the vendor put on a white cap and apron, required by hygiene regulations, and called out in a raspy, trembling voice 'pinguar' (ice cream on a stick). The carts had no refrigeration, but padded white cloth blankets kept the ice cream from melting.

I was one of their regular customers. After trying the four flavours—vanilla, pineapple, soy bean, and chocolate—I decided chocolate tasted the best. But chocolate was not sold every day. Usually only one flavour was sold each day in Peking, and I would often have to settle for that flavour.

Noticing that the prices differed between three fen and five fen for a stick, I asked a friend for an explanation. He said that the cheapest kind was made of water, flavouring and saccharin, and the other had sugar in it. The most expensive ice cream was creamy vanilla, costing ten fen, but this was available only in government-owned stores and not from the street vendors.

During our first summer in Peking people relied on watermelon and ice cream to cool them off, but the following summer the drink automat was introduced. I saw only two in the city and they were set up as stands in the busiest areas of town, where crowds descended on them.

Before the customer went to the automat, he had to fetch a porcelain tea cup from an attendant. Then he placed it under the outlet of one of the seven faucets of the machine, and at the same time put four fen into a slot. Soon a lukewarm sweet orange drink came trickling out. When he was finished he had to return the cup to the attendant who washed it in a basin of water and passed it on to the next customer. Those who were not using the machine were content to stand by as spectators, and watch this new form of entertainment.

When people returned home from work in the late afternoon their flats were hot. After preparing dinner on a coal or gas stove, the temperature indoors was so unbearable that they had to go outdoors to eat. The air was much cooler there and so some remained outside until midnight.

Every evening Chang An, the main highway that passed in front of our building, was crowded with people who turned the street into a promenade, and often I joined them on my bicycle. Mothers and fathers who had not seen their children all day would play with them on the streets, and often I was surprised to see young children awake past midnight. Young couples walked together talking and sometimes their shoulders touched. Some people sat on the curb knitting and rolling yarn into balls. Others would be carrying watermelons bought from a night stand, which was open until the late summer hour of ten P.M.

Old people would often be seen lying on the sidewalk with straw mats under them and a terry cloth towel on top. This was the method Mrs Shu had recommended for me to keep cool.

A community of senior citizens gathered every evening on the same busy corner. Each brought along a folding stool, a cane, and a long thin wooden pipe. Sitting and rarely speaking, they looked as though they were enjoying being together and watching the activity around them.

The most popular night-time recreation was card playing. Although the cards looked like ours, not being a card player, I did not recognise the games, that often went on past midnight.

Children were as avid players as their parents and grandparents. Many were squatting around a page of newspaper they used as a playing board.

One evening I saw four middle-aged men, dressed in undershirts and pants sitting under a street light. They had brought folding stools and a table from home and it looked as though the card game would last a long time.

Many spectators stood silently watching this group play. I never saw money exchanging hands during card games because gambling is illegal. But I heard from Chinese that sometimes the loser treated the winner to a meal.

The street lights attracted not only card players but people reading books. Under one lamp two primary school students had set up a small class-room. After putting their desks and stools on the street, they did their homework, seeming oblivious to the noise around them.

Teen-age boys had set up a badminton net between two electric lights. One young girl had a street light to herself as she sat alone blowing bubbles and watching them rise until they burst. Another girl was combing her freshly washed waist-length hair that glistened in the light. Other children were jumping over a long half inch elastic band, which they had stretched out and attached to two fixed objects. The only people who avoided the light were the shadow boxers, whose slow moving silhouettes were visible in dark areas.

COURTING

Before summer arrived I saw very few young people in pairs. But on summer evenings, the parks and streets were filled with couples walking hand in hand, sitting on benches close together, and whispering under the shadows of trees.

Most young couples looked shy and unsophisticated. While giggling and making small talk, the girl and boy carefully avoided looking at each other. I never saw any couple more involved physically than the boy resting his head in his girl friend's lap or the girl putting her head on the boy's shoulder. Kissing is not a Chinese custom, but a friend remarked, 'Lovers kiss,' and then laughed.

Other foreigners said they had seen young people in secluded scenic spots doing much more than holding hands. There were also many stories about the sexual freedom high school graduates from the city enjoyed while working in the countryside.

The area behind the Military Museum in Peking had a reputation for being a meeting place for young people. Its hilly landscape provided privacy, and when I took walks there I saw that many people were taking advantage of the seclusion it offered. Next to each hill there were two parked bicycles, but their owners were seldom in sight.

Although I never saw 'promiscuous' couples, I didn't doubt that they existed. But I was certain that only a small group of young people belonged to this set. In China premarital relations are taboo, and rape receives the death sentence.

When we were visiting a hospital in Shanghai, Gerd asked

if abortions were performed on unwed mothers. After a long embarrassed silence, a doctor said quietly, staring at the floor, 'Exceptionally few girls who are not married ask for abortions.' A middle-aged woman then spoke up in a loud, excited voice, 'Those who are unmarried and ask for abortions must be educated by the work organisation.' I had heard about girls sent to the countryside to do physical labour because they had too many boy friends, and I assumed this was the type of education she meant.

Any girl who is seen with different men is a 'bad girl,' I was told. I never recognised this type of girl, but the Chinese saw them at once. Girls who smoke, wear their hair loosely braided with wisps of hair falling on their faces, or in summer wear sunglasses, are immediately labelled as 'bad girls.'

The uniform dress and hair style made most young women look plain. Once, when I saw a girl with loose hair that was drying, I commented to our interpreter, 'What a pity girls are not permitted to look this pretty all the time.'

'Everyone would laugh at them if they always wore their hair in that fashion,' Mr Gu replied.

Another friend was more specific. 'No girl should stand out. It is better to look like everyone else, and then you won't be criticised,' she said.

Sometimes I saw beautiful young girls walking down the street, and found it unusual that I was the only one staring at them. The men passing by did not even seem to notice them, although a friend later said, 'Those girls who are pretty know it, and the young men do not miss them.'

This led me to ask a Chinese what his ideas were about a beautiful woman. 'She should have long eyelashes, skin like a peach, big almond-shaped eyes, the nose should not be too flat and the mouth too big, and she should have a double layer of skin above the eyes,' he said, pointing to mine. When I inquired about her figure, he said, 'She should not be too fat.'

Boys and girls do little mixing before their early twenties, and when a girl appears in public with a young man it means they will marry one day. Before they became engaged, both sets of parents meet the future son- or daughter-in-law. When gifts are exchanged, this is a sign of approval on both sides.

According to Chinese custom, when a gift is given, a gift of approximately the same value should be returned. I know of one couple whose families were constantly exchanging gifts. The future mother-in-law made a blouse for the future daughter-in-law and then the future parents-in-law gave the future son-in-law a polyester shirt. Later, tropical fish in an aquarium, an ornamental stone mountain, shell lamps, and other items exchanged hands.

Often an engagement would last a few years while the future daughter-in-law got to know her future mother-in-law, in whose house she would be living. During this period both the boy and girl saved money for the furnishings and household items they would need when they married.

Few Chinese men or women over thirty were unmarried, and no couple who could have children was without them. But there was a recommended marriage age—girls should marry after twenty-five and boys after twenty-seven.

Pamphlets were published discouraging early marriage and early pregnancy. A booklet entitled *Adolescent Hygiene* said that early marriage led to too much sexual activity, and it implied that this could have adverse effects on the body's development. The booklet indicated that over-indulgence led to impotence, and advised that young people abstain from sexual activity until their mid-twenties.

The pamphlet warned that masturbation led to impotence in men, irregular and painful menstruation for women, and brain damage and shortsightedness for both. In order to overcome the inclination to masturbate, it was recommended that adolescents study Marx, Lenin, and Mao diligently. 'Only when the proletarian world outlook is developed can the right ideological foundation be laid for giving up the habit,' it stated.

Young people who could not sleep were advised to do physical exercises. They were also told to get up early, not to sleep face down, not to cover themselves with too many blankets, and not to wear tight underwear. Those who still had problems sleeping were encouraged to take up shadow boxing or even undergo acupuncture treatment.

Adolescent Hygiene warned that a pregnancy before the age of twenty-five could cause anaemia and bone softening in women. It cited a study showing that out of 781 grossly deformed infants, 24 per cent were born to young mothers. It neglected to mention, however, the dangers of late pregnancy.

The booklet informed its readers that contraceptive devices and the pill are distributed free in factory clinics and on communes. This was the extent of the 'sex education' a young person received formally.

After learning that 'the pill' was sold in pharmacies, I asked if unmarried girls could buy it. 'Why should they? They don't need it,' a Chinese friend answered curtly.

Knowing that a family of four to six people sometimes shared two rooms, I wondered how a couple could have privacy. 'It's easy,' a friend told me. 'We send the children out to do errands.' But other Chinese admitted that the close living conditions provided a built-in birth control system.

PEITAIHO, THE SUMMER RETREAT FOR FOREIGNERS

The foreign community had separate 'cooling off' facilities from the Chinese. The Olympic-size swimming pool of the International Club was the main attraction for the people remaining in Peking during the summer. Those who wanted to leave behind the heat and humidity of the capital could go to Peitaiho, a seaside resort located on the Gulf of Po Hai, a branch of the Yellow Sea.

Having heard many glowing reports about this spot, Gerd and I decided to go there for a long weekend. As usual, we had to apply to the Foreign Ministry for permission to leave Peking, and, in this case, we received it immediately. Then we boarded a train for the six-and-a-half-hour journey which took us north-east of the capital.

Unlike the majority of Chinese who sat in the 'hard class', on crowded, wooden benches, we were given no option but to travel first class. First class meant comfortable, clean compartments, seating six or fewer people.

Since we had the compartment to ourselves, we stretched out on the two long upholstered seats that faced each other and that could be converted into beds. There were also two bunks above where we had put our suitcases. As soon as we settled down, a young train attendant brought a thermos with boiling water and bags of tea.

A small wall fan worked hard to cool the area, but it was not up to the task. And so we left the sliding door open, hoping for a breeze. Instead we received many long surprised stares from Chinese walking through the train.

In the next compartment were older army officers, who wore no sign of rank. They must have been important people; otherwise they would not have been permitted to travel first class. While first class was mandatory for us, it was a privilege granted only to leading Chinese, who were supposedly travelling on business.

A few hours before mealtime, the train attendant brought us a menu that catered to both Chinese and Western tastes. At breakfast fried eggs, white bread, and jam were available. For lunch there were typical Chinese shrimp, fish, and meat dishes, and cucumber and tomato salad. After we each ordered what we wanted the attendant left. He fetched us for lunch when the Chinese had finished eating.

When we entered the dining car I was impressed with the decor. Each table had a white tablecloth, a potted plant, and a variety of wine, beer, and schnaps bottles. As soon as Gerd and I tried to sit together, we were directed to separate tables. When I asked why we couldn't eat together the waiter said, 'Because you have different nationalities.' 'But we are married,' I replied. He seemed amazed and then agreed that we could sit

together. It never occurred to him, or others, that two people
of different nationalities could be married. Some months later
we had a similar experience on the Hong Kong border. Gerd
was assigned to eat with the Germans and I with the
Americans.

Nationality played an important role in our life in the
People's Republic. Whenever we had a request, the first question was, 'What is your nationality?' Even when I went shopping, salespeople would note this on the receipt.

Around the time the United States opened a Liaison Office
in Peking in May, 1973, Westerners found it difficult to get
taxis at night, and people said that Americans were being given
priority. After a friend was unsuccessful in getting a taxi, she
urged me to call the taxi bureau for her. The man asked the
usual question, 'What is your nationality?' When I replied,
'American,' he said, 'The taxi will come immediately.' A few
minutes later the taxi was tooting its horn outside the gate.

When the train stopped at stations the spectators did not
think about nationality. It was our foreign faces that interested
them most. People swarmed around the train window and I
could read their lips saying *waikuojen* (foreigner). Based on
their expressions, I knew that many Chinese were seeing a
waikuojen for the first time.

Occasionally we stepped out of the train for fresh air, and
immediately felt like animals in a zoo. Luckily we had train
escorts who held back the inquisitive bystanders.

The train attendant usually sat in a room next to the
Western-style lavatory. When she saw a foreigner coming, she
unlocked the bathroom door. Otherwise it remained locked.
When Chinese passengers approached this toilet they were
sent to the toilet at the other end of the car. That one was a
typical Chinese toilet with two holes in the floor.

When the train arrived in the Peitaiho area, chartered buses
met us. On the thirty-minute drive to the resort we passed
large beautifully kept estates with high walls and two-storey
houses. Before Liberation in 1949, Peitaiho was the favourite

summer spot for foreign missionaries, diplomats, and business-men, who had built the villas and bungalows we were passing. Now the Chinese government had taken them over and was using them as rest houses for the Chinese leadership. During one of Mao's visits to Peitaiho he wrote a poem and dedicated it to this place.

The outskirts of the town reminded me more of a typical Chinese countryside. Peasants were in the fields weeding, watering, and tending the wheat crops.

As we drove through Peitaiho I was charmed by this lovely, sleepy resort town, which used to be a fishing and farming village. Chickens scavenged for food and women washed their clothes by a stream. The housing needed repair and fresh paint.

Then we came to the main street, which looked different from the other part of town. The shops were showpieces, with newly-painted façades, clean windows, and immaculate sur-roundings. Unlike Peking, I saw many more signs in English in front of stores. There was a food store, a handicrafts store, a bakery, restaurant, and even a shop for stencilling slogans on T-shirts.

The bus then brought us to the hotel, which was around the corner from the main street. The sign in front said, 'Rest House for Diplomatic Guests.' Army guards, as in Peking, were stationed at posts, screening the Chinese who entered this area.

The moment I stepped out of the bus I could smell the sea air and pine trees. My eyes scanned the sandy beach, the blue Gulf of Po Hai, and the blossoming orchards. Birds were sing-ing, and suddenly I realised how long it had been since I had heard this sound, which was absent in Peking.

Our hotel room was spartanly furnished with two creaking beds that had mattresses listing to one side, a desk, and a chair. But the simple accommodations did not bother us, because we had come here to spend our time outdoors.

Early the next day I awakened to the sound of a bugle blow-ing reveille in an army compound nearby. Dressing quickly, we decided to take an early morning walk on the beach.

From the beach we had a better view of the splendid housing, which made Peitaiho look like an exclusive Long Island summer resort. One- and two-storey freshly-painted pink, yellow, and white houses were spread out over large estates. The trimmed grass and clipped hedges had a gardener's touch. Occasionally we saw someone walking in a yard, but the person was always too far away for us to guess who he was or what he did that entitled him to this luxury.

Then we passed a stretch of beach with parasols and empty chairs. A house was hidden behind high hedges and a wall, and we wondered who lived there. We were not left in suspense long. Two older army men emerged from that area and started walking on the beach. This must have been a guest-house for senior army officers.

After walking about twenty minutes, we reached a sign written in English, Chinese, and Russian: 'Out of bounds to foreign visitors'. We regretfully turned around and started in the other direction.

We passed our white-washed hotel, which looked splendid in its parklike surroundings. It was located on a hill that overlooked a piece of beach belonging to the foreign compound. Other guest-houses, which foreign families could rent in summer, were built on the lower parts of the hill.

A rocky area extending into the sea was to the right of our compound. Many Chinese were fishing, crabbing, and walking there. They looked like people on holiday, and I saw they were coming from a large, plain-looking building. Later I learned that this was a sanatorium where factory workers in the province were sent to rest and be treated for ailments.

Farther ahead we met the local people. Fishermen dragged nets near shore and when they brought the catch to the beach, villagers surrounded them and bought the fish.

After we had walked for about forty minutes, once again a sign appeared telling us we could go no further, and so we turned around and started walking back, feeling discriminated against.

By the time I reached our patch of beach, I no longer noticed the beauty of my surroundings. I only thought about the confinement the Chinese were imposing on us. No Chinese could stop on our beach, and the swimming area in front of the hotel was exclusively for foreigners.

I didn't come to Peitaiho to be stuck with foreigners the entire time, and so I decided to go into town, which was a five-minute walk away.

On the corner of the road leading to our hotel there was a former Austrian bakery, now run by Chinese. Not noticing that the bakery had two entrances, I went into the first one, which was crowded with Chinese customers. Immediately, a clerk told me to go to the next entrance, which was for foreigners. The sight of German *stollen*, rich creamy cakes, salt sticks, macaroons, French bread, and doughnuts calmed me down. Soon I was sinking my teeth into pastry I had not seen for months.

After leaving the bakery I visited a few shops where most of the clerks spoke English and most of the customers were foreigners. This dampened my enthusiasm for shopping and I headed back toward the hotel. Next to the bakery I passed a restaurant that was set back from the road. Its specialities were fresh flounder and crab, my favourite dishes.

That evening we ate on the restaurant's patio, next to other foreigners. The silverware, engraved with the name 'Kiesling and Bader', reminded us that the former owners were Austrians. After dinner we drank coffee in the moonlight and I overheard a woman next to me saying, 'This is the best evening I have had since coming to China.'

By the end of the weekend I was fed up with the isolation and special treatment the Chinese had imposed on us and could hardly wait to get back to Peking. When our train arrived in the evening I rushed home and jumped on my bicycle. I had missed Peking and needed to feel, see, and smell it again.

Chapter 3

Autumn

THE CABBAGE SEASON

In October and November the Peking plain no longer looked flat. Hills of long-leafed green cabbage, known abroad as 'Chinese cabbage', were everywhere. Bicycle parking lots, sidewalks, street corners, curbs, and the unpaved area in front of shop doors were piled with cabbage.

Suddenly the fields around Peking were full of people picking, stacking, and loading cabbage. The work force was mainly students, army men and women, teachers, and doctors and administrators who were doing *laotung* (physical labour), an essential part of everyone's work and study programme.

Trucks and horse-drawn carts filed into the city daily to deliver a fresh supply of cabbage. The new batch was unloaded in front of customers who had been awaiting its delivery. The leftover wilted cabbage from the day before was stacked beside it and sold at reduced rates.

Cabbage buying was a family affair. The grandmother carefully selected and examined each head while the grandchildren amused themselves playing on the large metal or wooden scale. After the cabbage was weighed, everyone joined in carrying it home.

Usually there were not enough hands to carry the load and so other means of transportation were used. Bamboo prams, bicycles, three-wheel vehicles and squeaky homemade carts were piled with cabbage.

The tons of cabbage that poured into the city often left a trail of leaves behind, and during the unloading process the loss was great. But these leaves seldom went to waste. Withered women in tattered clothing collected the loose leaves in plastic nets and took them home to cook.

Some families bought more than one hundred pounds of cabbage. They then stored it in a place where the sun and air would keep it dry for the next few months. There was usually no rain from mid-September until June, and so the cabbage was stacked in courtyards and on roofs and balconies.

During the season cabbage cost less than three fen a kilo, but a few months later the price would be at least six times more expensive. In winter the choice of vegetables grown in the greenhouses around Peking was limited, and if a person wanted variety, such as green peppers or carrots, he had to pay a hefty price. Cabbage, therefore, was the main winter vegetable, and was eaten at almost every meal. It was fried, pickled, boiled in soup, used as filling for *jao-tze* and combined with other dishes.

Another sign of autumn was the appearance of coal briquettes drying outside. I only saw these in old neighbourhoods, where coal-fed stoves heated the houses from November until March. Old men squatted in front of the walls on the unpaved back streets and mixed water and coal dust. They made coal patties from this mixture and then lined them up in rows on the ground or stuck them against walls to dry. Homemade coal briquettes were cheaper than factory made and burned more slowly, a Chinese friend told me.

Many people, however, did not have time to make their own coal briquettes, and so they ordered them from the neighbourhood factory. The coal was then delivered in bushel baskets on three-wheel bicycles.

Those people who had moved out of the old housing into four-storey apartment buildings no longer had to worry about a winter coal supply. They had central heating from mid-November until mid-March. But it was only turned on two hours in the morning and two hours in the evening, when most people were at home.

The autumn weather in October was ideal for bicycling. The temperature was in the upper sixties and low seventies, the sky was a bright blue and the sun was shining.

On the way I would pass large billboards containing Mao, Lenin and Marx quotes, written in white characters on a shiny red background. Winter clothing was being aired on clothes lines hung between trees and poles and an older person would sit nearby, keeping watch over them. Black cotton shoes dried on window sills or tree branches. Young children, sitting in a squatting position, helped their grandmothers wash and separate cabbage leaves.

While both parents worked the older children had considerable responsibility. They had to take care of the younger family members and often do household chores. The affection that brothers and sisters showed for each other was always very touching. Tall and short pairs walked together arm in arm, talking and laughing.

The dirt roads were obstacle courses. I had to steer around the potholes, hills of sand, and piles of cabbage. I had to be careful not to run into children who dashed out of doors without looking either way. On one occasion I narrowly missed being hit by a bucket of water that a woman threw out of her door.

Around 11.30 the streets always started to empty. At the same time the smell of fish, pickled vegetables and seasonings filled the air. Once a school boy passed and shouted 'Chu la ma?' (Have you eaten?) a typical greeting around lunchtime.

I was always on the lookout for my favourite autumn snack, tiny candied hawthorn apples on a stick. Very few markets sold them, but as soon as I saw people walking with them, I would ask where they had bought them.

Soon I would be riding down the street eating my treat, and people would smile and laugh. Until then, very few smiling faces had greeted me.

Seeing me pass, the children sometimes disappeared into courtyards, shouting *waikuojen* (foreigner). I was never sure whether this reaction was merely curious, or hostile. Later on I heard from a Chinese friend that Chinese did not understand why foreigners would want to ride around back streets, when they could travel in cars on main streets. She told me about one student in her classroom who mentioned seeing a foreigner on a bike in a back street, and the teacher had said to the whole class, 'You must beware of spies.'

The two-storey houses in the old parts of the city displayed beautiful and intricate wood carving, desperately in need of repair. Their balconies and window sills were full of plants that thrived on an egg shell diet.

The Chinese love plants and often I stopped in at the only local plant shop I had found in Peking. Sometimes it was so full of customers I could not enter. But when I did, I saw there were as many people looking as buying.

The buyers brought along friends to help and advise in the selection. Each petal and leaf had to be examined, discussed and then compared to its neighbour. Purchasing a plant was not a hasty transaction and often required at least an hour.

I often passed sewing workshops where mostly older women were employed. Their sedentary jobs did not give them much opportunity to move, and so sometimes they would take exercise breaks, and I would ride by when they were lined up in front of the shop doing light calisthenics.

On one of my bicycle rides I saw a young boy, perhaps ten years old, in front of me. He was practising riding his parents' bike which was too big for him. While I was chuckling at this sight, his bike hit a bump and suddenly he was on the ground in front of me, crying. Other cyclists paid no attention to him and passed by, but I rushed over to see if he was injured.

As soon as the other cyclists saw this, they parked their bikes on the main street and came over too. Thanking me, they said everything was fine and I could leave. I immediately understood that my presence was causing an awkward situation and so I left.

It was not the first time I had witnessed this apparently indifferent behaviour. When the wind scattered sheets of card-board that an old man was carrying on his three wheel bike, no one helped him gather them. A man, having difficulty balancing a heavy sack of rice on the back of his bike, received no help when rice started trickling out of a hole in the sack. Two runaway horses galloped down Chang An one day during rush hour with one old man running behind them. But no one joined in the chase.

This conduct perplexed me, because I had heard so much about the legendary Lei Feng held up as the model for all children to follow. He helped old women carry heavy loads. He took off his warm coat on a cold day and lent it to a poor peasant who did not have adequate clothing. He gave his lunch to a fellow worker who had forgotten his food. He stood up on a train to give his seat to an old woman.

I wanted to know why people were not responding to his example, and a Chinese friend provided me with a possible insight. When she was young, she said, she saw a bicycle fall over in a parking lot and wanted to go over to stand it up again. But her mother held her back. 'If the owner comes back he will think you are trying to steal his bike. It is best to mind your own business and not get involved, because you never know what the consequences will be.'

WASTE NOT

Often I passed three-wheel bicycles parked on street corners. They were loaded with scrap, and next to each one was a woman wearing a white cap, blue denim overalls, and an apron. People gave her pieces of glass, bottle tops, tin cans, rags, tangerine peels, feathers, hair, dry meat bones, paper, shoes, cloth, and aluminium. After weighing the items indi-vidually, she paid the customer.

I knew that rags were made into newspapers and mops, and braids into wigs for export. But only later did I learn that tangerine peels were made into medicine and bones into tooth-brushes, buttons, and cigarette holders.

A Chinese girl showed me a beautiful new white sweater she was wearing and said, 'My relative made it for me from five pairs of work gloves she had unravelled.'

Most people bought wool sweaters instead of cashmere, which were cheaper and warmer. I didn't understand the advantage of wool and asked Mrs Shu. 'The yarn in wool sweaters can be unravelled and used again. You cannot do this with cashmere,' she said.

The recovery, reuse, and recycling of used articles to avoid waste was not only a family concern, but a national policy. A furniture factory we visited had a separate division for making rulers out of wood shavings.

In a Hsinhua bulletin I read that scrap copper is used for high-voltage transmission lines. Forty per cent of China's cement is made of slag from iron and steel works. Winery waste residue becomes sugar-fermented pig feed. Soaked and treated cigarette butts produce insecticide. Chemical fertiliser, animal feed, lubricants, chemical products, and building materials are derived from factory waste and residue.

Hsinhua also reported that a Shanghai chemical plant, which specialised in using refuse, sent people out daily to collect the oil and fats that lodged in the sewerage system. As a result of their work, during a three-year period more than six hundred tons of materials were rescued and three million bars of soap were made from the oil extracted.

The no-waste policy also applied to us. During our stay in the hotel, a clean and pressed pair of torn pyjamas, which I had discarded in the waste-basket, came back in the laundry the next day.

At home I did not dare to throw anything away before asking if we could use it for another purpose. Worn-out shirts and underwear became dust rags, shoe cleaners, and towels for drying dishes. The buttons from old shirts went into the sewing box. Mr Yu used old telex paper for shopping lists and menus. Glass jars were ideal for storing food and seasoning, and at the same time they provided a safeguard against ants and cockroaches invading our food.

Mr Liu used a marmalade jar for tea. Plastic bags and aluminium foil were used many times before throwing them out. Johnny Walker scotch bottles contained boiled water, oil, and sauces.

When a wooden handle of a carving knife split, the driver and interpreter went to several shops to inquire if they would make a new handle for the knife, but no one was willing to do this work. One weekend Mr Liu asked to borrow the knife. The following Monday he brought it back with a beautifully carved handle of fine workmanship. When I asked him who had made it, he looked down and said quietly, 'I did it badly.'

When we were in hotels and trains it was difficult not to discard unnecessary things. On a journalists' trip one woman in the group threw away a pair of ripped stockings. After we got off the train, an attendant came running toward us holding up a pair of stockings and asking who had forgotten them.

In Canton, the lobby of the Dung Feng Hotel, where foreigners stayed, had a display cabinet containing lost and found items such as combs, Chinese stationery, an almost empty box of candy, playing cards, ballpoint pens, etc. Based on the contents in the cabinet, it was clear that no one could discard or give away anything in China.

THE BICYCLE HAS THE RIGHT OF WAY

While the bicycle was a means to bring me closer to the world outside the foreign ghetto, the Chinese used it for transportation. Unlike cars or other motorised vehicles, the bicycle was privately owned.

All bicycles were made in China and looked alike to me, but not to the Chinese. They could see at once the difference between the 'Ford' and 'Rolls-Royce' of bicycles, varying in price between 140 and 180 yuan.

Bicycles were not only a luxury item requiring several months' savings, but they were in short supply. In order to buy a bicycle a person had to present a letter of recommendation from his work organisation and the necessary number of industrial coupons, earned after working several years. Few women's bikes were made, and so women usually rode men's bikes.

Two of the bikes belonging to our staff were over ten years old, and still in very good riding condition. Mr Yu's bike, which was three years old, looked new. Every day he dusted, cleaned, and polished it.

The bike was the most precious possession a person owned and no one left his bike unlocked. At bicycle parking lots the attendants made certain that the owner returned the slip of paper or stick with the same number as the one stuck on the bike.

I had lost the key to my bike, and when I took it to parking lots the attendants always reminded me to lock it. When I told them that I had no key, they often stood guard next to it until my return.

Stealing bicycles was a common crime among the Chinese, but I never worried about this because my bike was foreign and too conspicuous to steal. Very few foreign articles were sold in Chinese stores and no one would risk being caught with something foreign unless he had permission to have it. But I did hear of a few cases where foreigner's Chinese watches, Chinese clothing, and money disappeared, and then sometimes reappeared again after the crime was reported.

Our staff was always worried about my 'open door' policy of an unlocked door. They were amazed to learn that I had left my purse on the front steps the whole night and the next day it was where I had left it, untouched.

I had heard many stories about theft in the Chinese community and began to believe them when I saw the number of things people locked. Windows, chests, trunks, drawers, even purses often had locks. Ground-floor flats had bars on their windows and balconies had fences or walls around them. One Chinese said, 'Everything that can be stolen is stolen. Bike bells, knobs of doors, even laundry disappears.'

When a Chinese friend was in the hospital and his wife stayed with him overnight, the nurse asked her how she could leave her house empty for a night. 'Everything will be gone when you return,' she warned. Fortunately, this was not the case.

Whenever I left my bike in town, it attracted attention. Unlike Chinese bikes, which were usually black, mine was a bright orange and looked like a dwarf next to the neighbouring black giants. It could be taken apart and its tyres were half the size of the Chinese tyres. The Chinese examined these different features, but their main interest was the wire basket attached to the front of the bike.

Chinese bicycles have no baskets in front and people must carry everything on the back part of the bike. I saw tall swaying trees, bulky furniture, sewing machines, sheets of glass, and one hundred pound sacks of flour or rice secured to the area behind the cyclist's seat. One day I mistook a bound pig sitting upright on a bicycle for a backseat passenger.

Once I bought a bamboo chair about half the size of my bike. When I told the clerks I would have someone pick it up later, they said this was unnecessary and went to work tying it down on my bike. Within minutes I was on the road, hardly aware of the load, until I looked back and got frightened.

Cyclists maintain the attitude that they have the right of way and sometimes nearly lose their lives proving this point. At intersections they cut in front of moving cars, which infuriated Mr Liu. Coming to a screeching halt, he rolled down the window and shouted at the fleeing person, 'Do you want to kill yourself?' but this was usually to no avail. By then the cyclist was out of hearing distance.

On one occasion we were driving down Chang An when a cyclist started riding in our direction. Assuming she would cross over Mr Liu did not slow down. At the last minute when a collision seemed inevitable, she jumped off her bike and stood in front of our oncoming car. Fortunately Mr Liu had faster reactions than I would have in the same situation. He braked, just in time, and came to a stop inches from her. When I opened my eyes, I saw a woman standing and giggling in front of our car. Then she rode off, almost nonchalantly, while I sat stunned, and Mr Liu caught his breath and for the first time was left speechless.

Traffic policemen seemed to have little more success in imposing order on the bicycle chaos. If a policeman stopped a cyclist, this drew a large audience who sided with the cyclist. Knowing that a traffic policeman has no power to arrest, the crowds often called him names and shouted at him.

The policeman's main defence was to give the violator a lecture and sometimes the lecture would last a long time. Under unusual circumstances I had heard he would grab the key out of the bike's lock so the cyclist could not escape, but I never saw this happen.

THE HAZARDS OF DRIVING

To drive in China I had to have a Chinese driving permit. This was easy for me to obtain because I already had a driving licence and was in good health.

A physical examination was required, which included measuring my blood pressure, checking my eyesight and hearing. I passed these tests, but friends who were colour blind and had a high blood pressure, failed. The next time they took the test, however, they passed, after taking pills or memorising the numbers in the colour blind test.

Those who did not have a foreign driving licence and driving experience could take a driver's training course, costing 240 yuan. A Yugoslav friend participated in the six month course and told me about her experience. The final driving exam was worse than her university finals, she said, and it took longer.

There were four sections to pass, and a failure in one would mean that the other parts were postponed until she passed that section. The first week she passed the written rules of the road test. She completed this at home with the help of her husband, who explained questions and filled in the correct answers. The second week she passed the motor repair test while her husband was standing nearby, giving her instructions in Serbian. The third week she passed the parking test.

During the fourth week she took the road driving part and failed it. Disappointed, she pointed out to her instructor that she had done everything he had taught her and did not understand what mistake she had made. He did not respond directly to her remark, but praised her for passing the other three parts of the test. 'No one has passed the entire test the first time. You have done better than any other foreign student.' She then had the feeling that her failure on the last part was necessary, in order not to set a new precedent. A week later she passed that part and received her driving licence.

When I went to the Traffic Bureau to pick up my licence the clerk said I would have to exchange my foreign driving permit for the Chinese one. I had only one American driver's licence and needed it for identification and driving abroad. But the clerk would not accept this excuse and told me what the regulations were. I had had regulations read to me before, and knew that he was in no position to make an exception.

After the clerk assured me he would return my permit at any time, I handed in my American licence in exchange for the Chinese one. I then received a little red plastic pocket folder containing a document written in Chinese with my picture pasted on it.

When I first sat behind the wheel of our car, I assumed that the Chinese rules of the road were similar to those in the United States. The Traffic Bureau had given me no instructions or manual and so there was no way for me to know that I was wrong. It was through a trial-and-error method that I learned the traffic regulations in Peking, the only city in China where foreigners may drive.

At night on unlit streets or on dark stretches of main roads I put my lights on the full beam in order to see. But as soon as a car or truck came in my direction, the driver would flash for me to turn down my lights to dim, which I used for fog in America. If a policeman saw my full beam, he would shout at me and on occasion stop me and reprimand me for blinding the other drivers and cyclists.

During the day a policeman waved me to the side of the road because I had three people in the front seat, instead of the maximum number of two. Then he waited until the third person moved into the overcrowded back seat before permitting me to drive on.

A friend was stopped for driving while chewing gum and another for having an unlit pipe in his mouth. Drivers may not eat, smoke, or talk while driving, according to the Chinese rules of the road. Policemen were strict about enforcing the first two regulations, but I noticed that the third was difficult to implement and our driver certainly took advantage of that. While driving, Mr Liu would often ask me to translate a Chinese word into English. Then he would race to the next red light to write down the sound of the word in Chinese and repeat it for my correction.

Since our arrival almost a year ago the traffic had increased. Horses no longer walked down Chang An during the day, and the old East European cars were now taxis for the Chinese, instead of for us. A fleet of three hundred shiny Toyotas had replaced them and were the new, more expensive taxis for foreigners. In addition, trucks, jeeps, buses, three-wheel inexpensive transport only for Chinese, foreign cars, and Chinese-made *Hongchis* (Red Flag) and Shanghais occupied the roads.

The *Hongchi* is a long black limousine that is reserved for government ministers, leaders, the visiting heads of state, and chairmen of important delegations coming from abroad. It has heavier lines than the older chauffeur-driven Cadillacs in New York City and comes in different sizes and models, which reflect the rank of the passenger. The Shanghai is modelled after the old Mercedes 180 and is reserved for middle-level Chinese and foreign visitors.

Before leaving China, foreigners often sold their cars to the Chinese government, and the Mercedes was the favourite. Sometimes the government paid the owner the original price of the car.

Although there were many foreign cars on the road driven by Chinese, it was easy to see which cars belonged to foreigners. The licence plate was one clue. Diplomatic licence plates had a Chinese character, meaning diplomatic corps, written in red, followed by numbers in white on a black background, while the Chinese plates were white on blue. In addition, the Chinese cover their back and side windows with a white, beige, or grey curtain that looked like stocking material. This concealed the identity of the passenger sitting in the back seat.

Sometimes I had the feeling the streets were racetracks, but no policeman was interested in the speed of a car until an accident occurred. From a starting position foreign drivers had an advantage over Chinese drivers, whose main interest was saving gas. They did this by starting in second gear and then moving quickly into third and fourth gears before gathering speed. Once they were underway no risk was too great to take. They passed on the left, right, and even in between cars, and an oncoming car did not discourage them from overtaking. In a close call they expected the car approaching them to pull over to the side.

When a foreigner got behind the wheel, he drove with the constant fear of colliding with a cyclist. During our stay three diplomats had accidents in which cyclists were killed. Following a police investigation, each was pronounced guilty and asked to leave the country. No other punishment could be imposed on them because they enjoyed diplomatic immunity.

In each case the authorities set the sum of liability, which the foreign insurance company paid. One liability sum was $10,000.

In one of the three fatal accidents, the driver believed the cyclist was at fault. The cyclist had darted out of a side street, ignoring a red light. After listening to the driver's story, the police measured the brake marks, talked with the eyewitnesses, and later concluded that the driver was more at fault than the cyclist bcause he had been driving too fast.

Mr Liu had an accident, and this gave us our first insight into how Chinese bureaucracy functions. He collided with a tractor, resulting in damage to both vehicles, but no injuries. A police investigation then followed the accident to determine the cause.

Four months later, while we were still awaiting the results, Mr Liu came to Gerd and told him that he would no longer drive for us, and that a new driver would come at noon. He said that the Service Bureau had made this decision.

Gerd called the Service Bureau immediately and informed them he would accept no other driver and would rather drive himself. In addition, he wrote an angry letter, complaining that this decision was made without explanation, and he asked for a meeting to discuss the matter.

The next day Mr Liu did not come to work and Gerd drove himself to his appointment in the Service Bureau. The head of personnel received him in a conference room. After offering Gerd tea and cigarettes, the official began the conversation: 'We are old friends. You a friend of the People's Republic of China. We want to promote friendship between West Germany and my country. We respect each other. . . .' While he was talking, a secretary sat nearby taking notes, and our interpreter translated these familiar phrases.

The personnel chief then said, 'The change in drivers has nothing to do with you, Mr Ruge. After the accident Mr Liu did not want to drive for you anymore. Once you have been bitten by a snake, you do not wish to work in that field again.'

Gerd said that this was a faulty, almost a Confucian political attitude, and that the personnel chief should do ideological work with Mr Liu so Mr Liu would return to driving. The meeting ended with the official saying, 'It might take a long time to convince him.' Gerd reassured him he could drive himself and was willing to wait and see if the ideological work was successful.

Gerd heard nothing for a long time and then asked for a second meeting at the Service Bureau. The atmosphere was the same and the personnel chief said that Mr Liu was still not willing to drive.

In the meantime, we heard a different version of the story from other Chinese drivers. Following the accident, the police had taken away Mr Liu's driver's licence and issued him a temporary licence. During that time he was supposed to take and pass a driver's test to obtain a permanent licence. But he refused, saying there was no need for him to do this because he was not responsible for the accident.

The temporary licence expired and Mr Liu continued to drive without a licence until the Service Bureau stopped him from driving. That was on the day he came to us to announce that he was being replaced.

His friends told us he was now on holiday. After a visit to his family on an island off the coast of Shantung, a province known for its hard-headed people, he had brought his wife back to Peking to show her the city. He was receiving his monthly salary and still refusing to take the driver's test.

At a cocktail party, Gerd spoke with the head of the Service Bureau, who was familiar with the case. On that occasion, he reassured us we would have our driver back within a few weeks. Once again Gerd heard nothing for several weeks, but a Chinese told us that Mr Liu had gotten his licence back without taking the test, and was now insisting that he drive only for us.

The personnel chief thought it was bad enough for Mr Liu to defy regulations and be given a licence, but he would not permit him to drive for us. With his characteristic stubbornness, Mr Liu was making serious trouble for himself, and a Chinese friend advised us to help him out of this difficult situation by writing a letter to the Service Bureau and accepting the veteran driver they had originally offered us.

During that period we finally received the results of the investigation. Both the tractor driver and Mr Liu shared the blame for the accident, but Mr Liu was more at fault because he had been speeding. We then paid 180 yuan for tractor repairs, several hundred dollars for new car parts, and an exorbitant customs duty to import the parts from Hong Kong.

GETTING CLOSER TO OUR STAFF

Our new driver was also called Mr Liu, but he was very different from the first Mr Liu, who had been young, handsome, colourful, stubborn, and confident. The new Mr Liu had deep lines in his gaunt cheeks that made him look much older than his forty-two years. He spoke very little, seemed shy, and was always calm. After adjusting to his retiring personality, I began to like him very much.

With the new driver, a new cleaning woman arrived to replace Mrs Yin, who had stomach problems. Mrs Lee was a short, firmly-built woman in her mid-thirties. She had worked for another foreign family and required no explanation about household chores. Mrs Lee was a tireless, quiet, and steady worker, and it was a pleasure to have her around me. She spoke very little, but her warmth and tenderness required no words.

And then a new intepreter arrived. He was Mr Gu, a German-speaking interpreter, and he replaced Mr Chen without explanation. There was no way to know if these changes were coincidental or planned, but Gerd was so angry at the abrupt change of staff that he told the Service Bureau that if they also took away Mr Yu, our cook, he would leave China. Mr Yu remained with us.

Our new interpreter, Mr Gu, had a large moon-shaped face,

which made him look very boyish, although he was thirty-two years old. Black-rimmed glasses and a porcupine hair style suited his broad, filled-out frame, which showed his love for food.

At first I found him stiff, uncommunicative, and too serious, and the others also reacted strangely to his presence. There was not as much chatting, joking, and sitting together in the office as before. I also detected a tension in relationships I had not felt when Mr Chen was with us. Gerd, however, considered Mr Gu an excellent interpreter, which he needed more than a sparkling personality.

It took several months before the harmony returned to our household. Mr Gu became more relaxed and self-assured, and I started to like him as he loosened up. I even felt guilty that I had judged him so severely at the beginning. What I had thought was aloofness was acute shyness, and no doubt he had sensed my negative attitude when he had started working for us.

I noticed good relations developing among our staff when they started doing things together and for each other. Mrs Lee sewed on Mr Yu's buttons when they fell off, and she washed his aprons. Mr Liu, Mrs Lee, and Mr Gu loved to tinker, and when a vacuum cleaner part broke, they worked together to repair it. Once when Mrs Lee was sick and I did the wash, Mr Liu the driver hung it up. Another time, when Mr Yu was away, Mr Liu put on his white cotton driving gloves and brought me tea on a tray. Mrs Shu, my teacher, and Mr Yu were good friends, and she would often give him recipes and suggest that he make those dishes for us.

When we had many guests for lunch, everyone would help in the preparations. Mr Gu chopped and Mr Liu stirred. When lunch was being served, Mrs Lee remained in the kitchen to wash the dishes, while Mr Yu was busy at the stove.

Some days Mrs Lee brought lunch for Mr Liu or Mr Yu made lunch for them. Mr Yu would heat up his favourite dish of noodles and vegetables, which he had brought with him, or

Mrs Lee would offer all of them *jao-tze* she had brought to work in her rectangular aluminium lunch box.

Whenever I offered them food, they refused, saying they had enough to eat. Later I learned that Chinese working for foreigners were not allowed to eat food belonging to foreigners, or to take it home. The official explanation was this would put them at an advantage over other people, who could not afford meat and similar delicacies. On the other hand, I learned that every Chinese working for a foreigner received a ten-yuan 'hardship' allowance.

As we got to know each other better, our staff talked more about their families. Mr Liu's wife had a heart condition and could not work. He never mentioned his children, but through a coincidence I discovered he had a teen-age daughter in middle school. While we were driving down a street one day he waved to a schoolgirl. Mr Gu laughed and I asked who the girl was. 'Mr Liu's daughter,' he said. It seemed strange to me that Mr Liu was too shy to tell me himself.

When we had an extra ticket to a sports event, I found out that Mr Liu had a son. After I asked if anyone in our household wanted the ticket, Mr Gu said, 'Mr Liu's son loves sports and you should give it to him.'

It suddenly occurred to me that they were not only working colleagues, but had become friends, who saw each other outside of work. When Mrs Lee forgot something in our flat, Mr Liu volunteered to drop it off on his way home.

Everyone called Mr Yu 'hsiao' (small) Yu because he was the youngest (twenty-seven) in our household. He was married, but lived in a Service Bureau dormitory for bachelors, while his wife, mother, and two children lived on a commune that was a three-hour ride from Peking. During the slack farming season his wife came to be with him in Peking, and he visited her on the commune twice a year for a few weeks. They lived apart because there was no employment for Mrs Liu in Peking.

Changing a residence in China was a very complicated procedure, requiring government approval and a job. People who wanted to move posted slips of paper on telephone poles, stating what their job was and where they wanted to live. Then they waited, hoping that someone from that area would be willing to exchange positions with them.

Mrs Lee had three children, two girls and a boy, between five and thirteen years old. When I asked to see a picture of them, she brought a picture in the next day and showed it to me secretly. She never mentioned her husband, but later I found out that he was working abroad in an embassy. She had been raising the family alone for the last two years.

One Monday morning Mrs Lee walked in with red, swollen eyes, and I asked her what had happened. Tears started rolling down her cheeks as she told me that she had just brought her five-year-old daughter to overnight kindergarten for the first day. When they separated, she said, they both cried. Then, wiping away her tears, she said she would pick her up on Saturday morning for the weekend and that was only five days away.

Mr Gu returned home every day during his lunch break to prepare the meal for his seven-year-old son. His wife had a very serious asthma condition, he told me, and was often bed-ridden or in the hospital. Therefore he did the housework, shopping, and cooking, but he never complained to us about his burden.

The Chinese had a firm policy of keeping the family in the background and I never met any member of our staff's families. In addition, when Chinese invited us to dinner, it was always in a restaurant, and although I was included, the wife or husband of our Chinese company was not.

THE HEALTH 'TIC'

When our staff arrived in the morning I always asked them out of politeness how they were feeling. Discussing health and taking care of it were favourite Chinese hobbies, and the people around me could not understand why I did not share this interest.

After returning to the flat, the first thing I usually did was to take off my shoes and go barefoot. This disturbed Mrs Lee very much. At first, she put my shoes in conspicuous places. After I ignored her hint several times, she gently rebuked me by saying, 'You will either get sick or catch a foot disease.' I tried to please her by mending my ways, but it was not easy to give up a lifetime habit.

Chinese had fixed notions about water. They said tap water was polluted and therefore they always drank boiled water. On the other hand, I loved drinking cold tap water, which the Peking Health Ministry said was free of germs. Everyone in my household complained, but I never got sick.

Mr Yu, Mr Liu, and Mrs Lee could spend hours discussing their physical problems. On one occasion Mr Yu came to work with a suffering look on his face. When I asked him the usual question about his health, he seemed relieved to discuss his ailment.

He had great pain in his elbow and upper arm because he had slept in a draught. He then described his sleeping position, the direction of the draught, and exactly where he had the most pain.

Noticing that his face was drawn and that he moved with difficulty, I suggested that he rest his arm for the day. But he refused to do this because we were having guests for lunch. After making an excellent lunch he went home and rested there for the next two days.

Mrs Lee had a recurring pain in her shoulder and Mr Liu had problems with his elbow. On days when they complained of these difficulties, a long discussion was useful, and sometimes the discomfort diminished after the therapeutic talk.

When anyone in our household had a cough, sniffle, or looked tired, I immediately recommended *hsiu hsi* (rest). *Hsiu hsi* was one of the most common words in the Chinese language, and was used for every occasion.

After lunch, *hsiu hsi* was obligatory for the health, and few people stirred between twelve and two. Small shops closed. No one was available in government ministries. The larger stores were almost empty and the salespeople rested with their heads on the counters. Drivers pulled to the side of the road to sleep and there was little traffic.

After a factory tour, our guide said '*hsiu hsi*,' meaning we should sit down, drink tea, and rest. When I told Mrs Lee to go home, I would say '*hsiu hsi*.' At the end of my Chinese lesson Mrs Shu would say '*hsiu hsi*.'

Doctors were generous in authorising rest. When Mrs Lee had a cold, it was an automatic three-day *hsiu hsi*, and when she had a fever it was a seven-day *hsiu hsi*.

I had heard that some people took advantage of the easy-to-obtain *hsui hsi* leave and the rule that a person could be out of work up to six months without losing his job or pay. Some stayed out of work on sick leave just short of six months, returned to work for one day, and then resumed the *hsiu hsi*.

Doctors were sympathetic when anyone had a health complaint and I was told that many people used tricks to feign poor health. Doctors considered high blood pressure a serious problem. This could be achieved by running before the physical examination or by pushing the heels against the floor while the doctor was measuring the blood pressure. Keeping hot water in the mouth before having a temperature taken resulted in an instant fever.

One man put a drop of blood in his urine specimen, and the doctor gave him several weeks *hsiu hsi* to recover from the supposed bladder infection. However, the trick was discovered during the next examination. He did not lose his job or wages, but he was criticised at his place of work.

In the event of a real or pretended sickness it was necessary to go to the hospital, where doctors examined patients and granted *hsiu hsi* leaves. I once passed through the Chinese section of the hospital and was appalled by the conditions. Hundreds of people were crowded into a hall. Some waited several hours before being examined. The noise, dirt, cramped space, and seeming confusion contrasted with our section of the hospital, the Clinic for Foreign Patients.

Foreigners usually went to the Capital Hospital, formerly the Peking Union Medical College. Funded by the Rockefeller Foundation during the 1920's, it was later called, during the Cultural Revolution, the Anti-Imperialist Hospital, located on Anti-Imperialist Street. The Capital Hospital was a beautiful large Chinese-style building with a curving green roof and glazed mythical animals standing guard at the roof's corners.

Once we went to the hospital because Gerd had injured his back. As we arrived outside the high steel entrance gate, a very sick old woman was being brought to the hospital on a three-wheel bicycle (the local ambulance). After passing through the gates we climbed a staircase leading to a stone courtyard, where patients clad in hospital robes and pyjamas were sitting on benches or walking around.

Straight ahead was the Chinese section, which had four fading red columns in front of its door. We turned right and walked up another flight of stairs to the foreign section. Its columns had just been painted and were a shiny, gaudy red.

We entered the quiet hall and registered at a desk. There we paid a two-yuan admission fee and gave Gerd's name, nationality, and medical file number, which everyone was assigned on the first visit to the hospital. The two small waiting rooms with ornately carved wooden chairs were occupied, and so we sat on benches in the clean, serene yellow hall. It was not long before the nurse called our name and nationality and Gerd was seen by one of the older doctors, who spoke English with an American accent. When I remarked about his accent, he told us he had been educated in the United States during the thirties.

The doctor recommended *hsiu hsi* for one week, but Gerd said that was impossible because of his work. Understanding the problem, the doctor sent for two other specialists and a therapist, who were working in the Chinese section of the hospital. They arrived a short time later, and then the four of them discussed the case in front of us. After fifteen minutes of a lively exchange, they once again suggested *hsiu hsi*, and hearing Gerd's refusal, decided on heat treatments, which began immediately and provided relief.

I had occasion to visit the hospital again when I developed a tennis elbow and could no longer shake hands. The doctors gave me a choice of cortisone injections, an operation, or acupuncture. Curious about acupuncture, I decided to try it.

The treatment lasted three weeks with ten half-hour sessions. First the doctor put two needles painlessly into the back of my hand and wrist and a third into my lower arm. Then she held candles next to the needles to heat them. Another time she attached electric prods to them so they would vibrate, and this created a strange, but painless, sensation. Only once did I experience pain, when the needle was injected in the wrong spot. During the treatment the elbow improved, but when it was over one handshake made me wince again.

At the same time I was having acupuncture I had to wear a piece of adhesive on my ear lobe. Under the adhesive were tiny pellets of Chinese medicine. The nurse instructed me to rub the adhesive often, saying it would be good for my elbow, and as I did this, I wondered what my ear had to do with my elbow.

On the streets I passed many Chinese wearing adhesive on their ears and assumed it had to do with acupuncture. But after a visit to another hospital I discovered that this was also part of the treatment for heart patients. For some reason wearing adhesive on the ears with hard green peas underneath was supposed to alleviate heart problems.

During and after my elbow problem, Mr Liu insisted on helping me. He followed me through stores and carried whatever I bought. Then he explained to the clerk at each counter about my elbow. When they finished talking, the clerk would ask me sympathetically if I had pain. I was embarrassed at the fuss that was being made over such a simple injury and always responded that I was fine.

Then I sprained my ankle very badly and, after a visit to the hospital, came home on crutches. This created great excitement among our staff. During the first days, while I was immobile, they enjoyed smothering me with attention and care. Seldom had I given them this opportunity.

Mrs Lee adjusted my pillows regularly and stood by to support me if I had to move from one place to another. Mr Yu kept on refilling my tea cup and made me my favourite Chinese dishes. Mr Liu and Mr Gu asked me often how I was feeling and if they could do anything for me. Soon the elevator operator, the other staff in our building, and the maintenance team in our compound were inquiring about my health.

When I felt better, I naturally became more active, and this distressed everyone. The doctors had told me to *hsiu hsi* a few weeks, but after a few days I was already moving around with the help of crutches. 'If this had happened to one of us, we would rest several weeks,' Mr Gu remarked, and everyone in our household agreed.

Unlike them, I regarded *hsiu hsi* as a punishment and was a bad patient. Eager to get back on my feet again, I followed the advice of a friend who had had a similar injury. She told me that after the swelling went down massages would remove the tenderness. Although the doctors in the hospital had not mentioned this treatment, I decided it was worth trying.

The one masseur who treated foreigners was located in a bathhouse about one mile from us. I had heard about blind masseurs, but they only handled Chinese.

I arrived early for my first appointment, and sat on a bench at the end of the hall. I watched girls in their late teens and early twenties come out of the bathing room and stand in front of a full-length mirror combing glistening waist-length hair. They had paid 30 fen for a shower that often lasted three hours.

People did not have baths or showers at home. Most went

to a bathhouse only once a year, around Chinese New Year. Those who bathed 'often' went once every three months, I was told. When I lifted my eyebrows in astonishment, my friend told me that the Chinese were very clean, something I had noticed myself. Every day they washed themselves with water from a basin and spent a lot of time cleaning their feet. Most changed their underwear daily, but this was not necessary with the other layers, she said.

Before the massage began, a strongly built, sprightly man greeted me with a broad smile. Later, when he told me he was sixty-five and ready for retirement, I had difficulty believing him. After taking me into a small cubicle with only a hard bed, he said, 'unless you have pain the treatment will not be effective.' This warning startled me, but soon I realised he was telling the truth.

For five days I submitted to vigorous massages that were so painful around my ankle I thought I would faint. It was his continual conversation about his family and questions about mine that enabled me to endure the treatment. At the end of five days when he asked, 'Do you still have pain?' I answered 'no,' and he dismissed me, telling me to come back only if I had pain again.

The Chinese have a remedy for everything, and sometimes it works. Acupuncture is commonly used not only to remove pain, but to alleviate headaches and mental stress.

In addition, the diet is believed to play an important part in a person's recovery. A Chinese friend told me about old food cures her mother had passed on to her. 'Eat one bud of garlic daily to cure tuberculosis.' 'After a difficult birth, the mother should drink turtle soup daily for one month to get back her strength.' 'A mother should remain in bed resting at least one month after a birth.' (Paid maternity leave is between fifty-six and seventy days.) 'Take white vinegar against high blood pressure.' 'Put a slice of fresh ginger and brown sugar in boiling water against a cold.' 'Eat raw chili to warm up the body against the cold. But pregnant women should not eat

chili because it creates high blood circulation in the baby.'
'When a baby is born with red cheeks, the mother ate too
many spicy foods during pregnancy.' 'A certain kind of squash
makes hair fall out.' 'Peanuts eaten in their skin are good for
the kidneys.' 'Drink black tea on an empty stomach, and when
you come in from the cold.' 'Drink green tea for digestion and
in summer.' 'Salty duck eggs are good for old people.'

'People suffering from face paralysis should put the head of
an eel in the mouth; then let the eel's mouth hook onto the
inside of the cheeek and bite it. The paralysis will disappear.'
I heard about this remedy at the time Chairman Mao appeared
in pictures looking as though he had recovered from a facial
paralysis.

In addition to eating the proper foods when sick, Chinese
medicine was prescribed. The window of one pharmacy had
an exhibition that was a conversation-piece for foreigners passing it. It displayed a calf's foetus in a bottle, the antlers of a
deer, and various kinds of roots, which were sources for
medication.

The antlers created the greatest interest among some Westerners who believed that the powder from deer's antlers
increases potency. Curious about its use here, I asked a Chinese,
who responded to my question in a very matter-of-fact manner.
'Old people who are sick and weak take it to increase their
strength. Then they can live longer.'

I had tried different forms of traditional medicine that had
no noticeable effect on me. One kind was round pills, so small
that ten could cover a finger-nail. A friend had to take fifty to
one hundred pills a day, and half jokingly I told him that part
of the cure was remembering the amount to take and the
time to take them.

After my ankle injury, the doctor suggested that I chew
and swallow soft medicine the size and shape of a ping pong
ball. Its herbal taste was too unpleasant for me to swallow
more than once.

A friend who was suffering from high blood pressure and

dizziness cooked special roots and herbs in a clay pot the Chinese called a 'medicine pot'. Then he drank the liquid. I tasted the pungent muddy brew and thought to myself, the sickness would be more bearable than having to drink a cup of this vile concoction daily. But he believed in it and told me that he felt better every day because he drank this mixture.

One tourist I met was anxious to buy a particular Chinese medicine he thought was made from marijuana. We found it in the form of tiny brown pellets with an herbal aroma. I never heard if his theory was true, but a Chinese friend took these pills for nervous tension and said they had a relaxing and soporific effect.

Pharmacies for Western medicine were never as full as those for traditional medicine. When I asked a doctor why Chinese medicine was so popular, he said, 'The Chinese tradition and habit is taking pills. Traditional medicine is not as powerful as Western drugs and can't do any harm.' Previously I had thought the majority of Chinese people were hypochondriacs, but now I realised that the obsession with health stemmed from a cultural difference.

Doctors were particularly careful in diagnosing complaints of foreigners. After considering all the possibilities, they invariably gave the most pessimistic opinion and recommended the strongest dose of medicine. When a person had a bad cold, he was treated for pneumonia and given heavy doses of antibiotics, sometimes resulting in unpleasant aftereffects.

Hepatitis patients had the worst plight. They were put in a hospital for infectious diseases and had to lay for six weeks in complete isolation. Two of my friends had this disease, and before visiting them I had to receive clearance from hospital authorities.

When I entered the white halls of the antiseptic-smelling hospital, a nurse led me to the waiting room and gave me a white surgical gown. Then a doctor entered the room and spoke to me. 'Your friend does not know the gravity of his condition. Do not talk about anything that will excite him, and do not stay long because you will tire him out.'

I walked into the spacious single room with an adjoining bathroom and shower. A very agitated friend greeted me. It was the second time in twenty years he had had hepatitis and he was familiar with the treatment, requiring rest and a fat-free, bland diet without roughage.

The kitchen had been giving him fatty fried food and cabbage regularly, and he was uncomfortable. He had complained and requested other food, but he was still receiving food swimming in oil. Now he was going on strike and would eat nothing more, he said, unless it complied with the recommended Western diet for hepatitis.

While doctors were quick to prescribe strong medicine, they were reluctant to perform surgery unless it was absolutely necessary. One foreigner had a high fever and severe pains on his right side while he was in Tsingtao, a naval port several hours from Peking. The patient thought the source of his problem was his appendix, but the doctors could not agree on the cause of the ailment. While they stood around his bed discussing the matter, his appendix burst, and this provided the evidence they needed. The patient was hospitalised for several weeks and was lucky to recover.

Whenever the doctors were baffled by an ailment they would say, 'The reason you are not feeling well is because you eat too much meat and too many dairy products. You do not have enough vegetables in your diet.'

In certain areas the Chinese were extremely competent. A friend was rushed to the hospital with third-degree burns on the upper third of his body. The Chinese specialise in burn treatment and after two months of hospitalisation and constant nursing care, the patient recovered without complications.

Every year a few foreigners contracted encephalitis and the Chinese prompt diagnosis and treatment saved their lives each time. A few days after the July, 1976, earthquake a girl went into a coma and was rushed to the hospital. The doctors said she had both meningitis and encephalitis and gave her little chance of recovery.

Due to the earthquake and constant post-quake tremors, the conditions in the hospital were perilous, but nurses sat by her bedside around the clock, and doctors were in constant attendance. In addition, other medical specialists were flown into Peking from Shanghai to examine her. After being in a coma for five days she recovered consciousness. Later she had no visible after effects. Her mother said, 'The devotion and care of the hospital staff saved her life.'

The Chinese are famous for their success in sewing on severed limbs. In one hospital we visited, the doctors showed us an album with gory pictures of people immediately after losing a limb and then pictures one or two years later, showing them back at work, once again using the limb.

A Yugoslav seaman severed his foot on board a vessel in a Chinese port. A helicopter rushed him to Peking and within seven hours of the accident he was in the operating room. The seaman was treated one year in a Peking hospital, and during that time the Chinese assigned him a full-time Serbian speaking interpreter. In addition, leading government officials visited him.

Following the lengthy treatment, he walked out of the hospital on two feet. A year later he wrote a letter to the hospital staff who had cared for him. He was playing soccer again, he wrote, and this would not have been possible without their treatment and 'moral support'.

Chapter 4

Winter

THE BEGINNING OF THE COLD AND DRYNESS

Because I am a New Englander, I am used to snow covering the naked winter landscape. This does not happen in Peking, and the winter weather was a great disappointment for me. Snow was rare, and when it fell the flakes usually melted before touching the ground or turned into brown slush within a few hours.

Only during our second winter did snow settle on the ground long enough to create a temporary hazard for the three million cyclists. The problem, however, was resolved within a few hours. Hundreds of middle school students were mobilised to assist the street cleaners. Using straw brooms, they swept the streets, made snowballs, laughed, and had as much fun as young people anywhere in the world after the first winter snow.

Around the middle of November smoke from the coal stoves made the air grey. In addition the branches were bare, clothing was once again drab, and the outdoor vegetable stands, which had added colour to the surroundings, were gone. Although the sky was cloudless and the sun visible, I was only conscious of the gloomy cold weather and the harsh dryness.

By the time we had endured our third winter even our furniture protested. Wooden chairs fell apart and tables cracked.

As the temperatures fell, the Chinese put on more layers. The central heating and coal-fed stoves did not provide enough warmth at home, and so they slept in their layers of clothing. On the coldest days of winter, when it was minus 25 degrees C., my teacher said she could fit five layers under her blue pants and jacket.

By the end of December the lakes around Peking were frozen solid and people went skating and sledding. The homemade sleds consisted of a board with squat wooden legs to which runners were attached. The parent either pulled the sled over the ice or the child pushed himself along with thin metal rods.

Four weeks after the skating season began it came to an end. A layer of dust and sand had settled on the ice, making skating impossible.

As soon as the ice reached a certain thickness, large ice-cutting machines were set up next to lakes. They cut ice into blocks, and horses and trucks brought it to underground caverns, where it was stored until summer and used to cool perishable food.

The holiday preparations distracted me from the dreary outdoors, and I started planning our Christmas meal. The local stores provided everything I needed. Potatoes, turnips, canned vegetables, and even live turkey were available. I did not want Mr Yu to slaughter a turkey in my kitchen, however, and so I asked the clerk in the market if he could prepare the largest turkey for me and I would pick it up the following day.

'Tomorrow I'll have a bigger selection of live turkeys here, and you can choose yours. Then I'll prepare it for you while you wait,' the butcher said.

'Can't you select the largest turkey for me, kill it, and clean it before I come?' I asked.

'I would not know which one you wanted. It would be better if you choose your own turkey,' he replied.

Explaining my squeamishness to him would have made me seem foolish, and it probably would not have changed his mind. This was my decision, and he did not want to be held responsible.

I went home and discussed the problem with Mr Gu and Mr Liu. To my relief they volunteered to make the choice.

On Christmas Eve a midnight mass was held in the old South Church, which was the last functioning Catholic church and open only to foreigners. But on this occasion thirty or forty

Chinese attended the service. Dressed in their finest black pants and jackets, they sat in the back rows with hands folded in a praying position. They knew the Latin service and hymns by heart, and did not even glance at the prayer book.

Officially the Chinese constitution permits freedom of religion, but after Liberation, the churches, which had been open to Chinese and foreigners, were closed. Now they are surrounded by barbed wire fences or are factories, living quarters, or government facilities.

During our stay I never saw anyone practising religion, but I assumed there were still many old people, like the ones selected to attend the Christmas mass, who practised religion privately.

THE CHINESE PREPARE FOR THEIR NEW YEAR

A few weeks after we celebrated our Christmas and New Year, I heard the first sounds of the approaching Spring Festival, the name which the Chinese give to their New Year. This three-day holiday fell between the end of January and mid-February each year and marked the beginning of the Chinese lunar year.

Schoolboys tried out the firecrackers they had just bought. The loudest met with the greatest approval. I understood why. In the old days, people believed firecrackers would frighten away the evil spirits.

Before New Year the market was flooded with new goods and the shops were packed with people. Some were so crowded that a monitor stood at the entrance and stopped more people from entering.

New Year was the time when families took money out of their bank account to purchase expensive items. Mr Yu had been saving over a year to buy his watch, which cost 120 yuan. Other luxuries were sewing machines, 140 yuan, bicycles, at least 140 yuan, and transistor radios, 60 yuan. A few years after my first Chinese New Year, the most lavish New Year gift was a black-and-white television set, which cost between 300 and 450 yuan, and was in limited supply.

Many people went to second-hand shops to purchase foreign cameras, radios, watches, and other electrical equipment. These articles had belonged to Chinese or foreigners who had sold them to the government for what, I was told, was only one tenth of the amount written on the price tag.

New Year is the time of year to give gifts. I asked our staff what they had bought for their families. Mr Yu showed me his daughter's gift—a red plastic purse with a picture of a panda bear on its side. Mrs Lee had knitted sweaters for her children and had bought a plastic inflatable doll for her youngest daughter. Mr Gu had a toy rifle for his son.

I had noticed that Chinese were usually non-drinkers, but most families wanted to celebrate the holiday with wine or schnaps, and Mrs Shu had bought a bottle of wine for her husband. When I asked her what she would give her parents, she said, 'They are living far away and need nothing. But as a token of respect, I will send them a little money.'

This custom is an old tradition that overseas Chinese, living abroad and separated from their families, also observe. One of my friends had left his family in Shanghai twenty-five years ago and now lived in Hong Kong. Since he had left China, he told me, he sent money annually to his relatives.

In spite of the strict rules forbidding giving gifts to staff, I wanted to give our people something small. I asked foreign friends for suggestions. One person told me that employees must turn in their gifts to the Service Bureau. Another warned me not to give anything bought abroad. He had done this last year and later found all of the gifts hidden in the back of a closet.

Finally I decided that food was the answer, and so I made banana bread for each family and stressed that it was good for their health. They accepted it and later told me it was delicious.

During the following years I bought items which I called

'work tools' instead of gifts. Mr Yu was delighted with a Hong Kong cookbook containing recipes of Western dishes written in English and Chinese. German dictionaries helped Mr Gu and Mrs Shu.

In addition, I gave Mr Gu a Chinese ballpoint pen which, I thought, was more practical for taking notes during a discussion than the fountain pen he always used. Unexpectedly, this work tool later created problems.

When we went to CAAC to purchase an airlines ticket, Mr Gu used the ballpoint to fill in the amount of money in Chinese characters on Gerd's signed check. At first the clerk refused to accept it, but, following a long discussion that I didn't understand, she reluctantly took it.

After leaving the building, I asked Mr Gu about his conversation. The clerk had reprimanded him for copying the foreign habit of using a ballpoint pen, instead of following the Chinese custom of using a fountain pen. Years ago the ink from Chinese ballpoint pens had faded after a few months, he said, but he had told the clerk that the quality of the Chinese ballpoint had improved and she should consider it as good as a foreign product.

NEW YEAR: A TIME TO EAT WELL

Food was on everyone's mind as the New Year approached, and I had the feeling that this was more important than the three days off from work. Trucks stacked with frozen pig halves started pouring into the city at least a week before the holiday began. Each truck stopped at different stores, and the bundled-up men who sat on top of the pig pile heaved the halves onto the sidewalks.

On one corner people had lined up in front of a shop waiting for this delivery. When it arrived, a large automatic saw, placed on the sidewalk, was used to cut the frozen halves into pieces. They were sold immediately to customers.

Wicker baskets full of apples cluttered sidewalks and long

queues wound around them. Some markets sold mandarin oranges from south-west China and Vietnam, and bananas bore labels saying 'Panama'. Live Peking ducks in cages were loaded onto tractors and deposited at markets and restaurants. A truck full of fresh fish passed, and I wondered if it came from the Summer Palace, where we had seen a team of men and women making holes in the ice and netting carp.

In contrast to the previous four months, every market had a large selection and supply of vegetables and meat for the New Year. My favourite indoor market was Hsi Tan, located in the western section of the city. It was a fifteen-minute car ride from the foreign community living in the eastern and north-eastern part of the city, and the distance discouraged most foreigners from shopping there.

Hsi Tan's doors opened at 7:30 A.M. to waiting throngs and closed at 6:30 P.M. From the inside it looked like a large barn. The ceiling was about three storeys high and towered over the ground floor, where each year more than nine hundred different kinds of food were sold. Counters adjoining each other ran along the sides of the hall, often with window displays in front and shelves filled with supplies behind.

Upon entering the chilly hall, the first thing I saw opposite the entrance was the dramatic sixty-foot-long display of fresh vegetables, which looked, from a distance, like a wall tapestry of geometric designs. After weaving my way around long queues of warmly dressed customers, I came to the eight-foot-high exhibit. It was in an elevated wooden frame, which was behind a counter and out of the customer's reach.

From close up I could see that the triangles were made of carrots, cucumbers, and turnips. Circles were created with onions, potatoes, and green peppers. Stars were made of yellow and red tomatoes. In the middle of the exhibit was a large basket full of carved vegetables resembling a bouquet. Its banner read, 'Serve the People'.

A few months earlier I had seen a special summer squash in this display, and now I felt very lucky to have found it again.

When I decided to buy the squash, the clerk hesitated and then spoke to her colleagues. After the discussion she took the squash out of the design and gave it to me. Only later did I find out that the displays were not for sale and that the clerk had done a special favour for a foreigner.

The New Year vegetables in Hsi Tan were grown in the hot-houses of the Nan Yuan Commune in a southern suburb of Peking. We had visited the production brigade on the commune responsible for supplying Hsi Tan with vegetables, and had spoken with the brigade leader there.

He told us that the national goal is for communes to feed the city they surround. Peking's population of more than seven million people was fed by thirty-three communes, which planted over 30,000 acres of vegetable land and had over 10,000 hot-houses.

Each commune was assigned to supply different food markets with fresh provisions and Nan Yuan's production brigades provided Hsi Tan with vegetables daily, about 110 different kinds over the course of a year.

The Nan Yuan brigade informed the market regularly about what it had available, and Hsi Tan told them if there was too little of one kind of vegetable or too much of another. In addition customer's opinions were solicited. Based on their suggestions, Nan Yuan altered its crop plan to include more sweet radish, less white turnips, and more vegetables for *jao-tze*, the favourite northern dish.

The main task of the production brigade, the leader explained, was to produce fresh and tender vegetables, guarantee a winter supply and even distribution throughout the year, and provide a rich choice for the festival days. All of this was done at a low cost to the customer, who paid an average of less than four fen a pound for vegetables.

I could see that Nan Yuan had kept its promise at New Year. I counted about thirty different vegetables that were being sold. Next to the vegetable section was the meat department, with a white tile counter in front and a row of pig halves hanging on hooks behind. Usually this counter had short lines because meat is expensive and most people cannot afford it regularly. Every family, however, was willing to splurge for the holiday and spend an average of forty-five cents a pound for pork. Some were asking for half a pound of ground pork to use as filling for *jao-tze*, the dish prepared on New Year's Eve.

A separate department sold beef and lamb, but only *Hui*, a Moslem (non pork-eating) minority, could buy this kind of meat. It was scarce, and before a customer was waited on he had to present an identification card showing that he belonged to the *Hui* minority. Everyone, however, could go to eat in *Hui* restaurants, where mostly mutton dishes are available, and no one had to show identification at the special store counters selling cakes and cookies made with peanut oil instead of lard.

Customers with empty bottles were lined up at the oil counter, where the clerk weighed each bottle before filling it. The weight was important because every family was rationed a few pounds a month.

I wondered how the Chinese could get along with their small ration, especially since northern cooking consists mainly of fried dishes, which require a lot of oil. A Chinese friend provided the answer. 'Sometimes we buy lard and melt it down.'

Although we could have had our bottles filled with as much oil as we wanted at the Friendship Store, Mr Yu was very sparing. After cooking he drained the oil and put it back in the bottle to be used again.

Eggs were also rationed, and when customers bought eggs they gave the clerk a booklet in which she entered their weight. Every family could buy two pounds a month. During summer, when chickens laid more eggs, they were no longer rationed.

Usually only dried and frozen fish were available, but now the fish counter was full of shrimps, squid, and the cherished fresh fish. The fowl counter had wooden cages full of chickens, ducks, and turkeys, which children were teasing. At the same time their grandparents were carefully examining different birds before making a selection. Fowl was very scrawny and most of the chickens we ate did not have enough meat to feed two people.

Chickens were relatively expensive, averaging one yuan a pound, but there was no waste. Everything was eaten on the bird except the feathers, which were sold to the government to be used for feather dusters. The bones, neck, and feet went into the soup and then the soup was served with these parts in it. Even the blood was used in a Szechuan hot and sour soup.

Some customers put the live chicken into a net, already filled with vegetables, and others carried it by bound legs, so that it swung back and forth with every step the owner took.

Those who did not want to do the slaughtering at home left it to the butcher, who bled, cleaned, and feathered the bird on the low counter in front of the customer. I was the only one disturbed by this sight and I rushed away. As I left I noticed that dead hare and frozen sparrows were also offered as a New Year's speciality.

In other parts of the market more food staples were being sold. One counter had dried, smoked, and pickled soy bean products, the main source of protein in the Chinese diet. Seasonings such as pepper, paprika, sesame, and curry were sold by weight and wrapped in a piece of paper. Pickled vegetables and smoked and cured meats were also available.

The variety of canned goods was astonishing and most had labels in English or German, indicating they were being exported. I had tasted the delicious baby carrots, string beans, and mushrooms. Gerd regularly ate a pork luncheon meat that tasted like Spam. Among the canned fruits I saw not only the usual tins such as pineapple, pears, peaches and apricots, but there were also seedless grapes, bananas in syrup, mandarins, lychee, dragon eye, loquats, and strawberries. The fruits were too sweet for me, but nothing seemed too sweet for the Chinese.

During the holiday period Hsi Tan had an average of 100,000 customers a day, and in order to facilitate shopping outdoor stands were set up to sell frozen fish and fowl, and three-wheel bicycles loaded with vegetables, were sent directly to the residential areas.

The Chinese had four official holidays a year—May 1st, Oct. 1st, Jan. 1st, and New Year—and no other vacation time. Around New Year, however, couples who were separated and people who wanted to visit close relatives received several days' leave from work.

Travelling by train provided the only means for private long distance travel and the area around the railroad station was chaotic days before the holiday began. The sidewalks in front of the station looked like a refugee camp; only the tents were missing. Hundreds of people leaned against the bundles they were guarding; others slept or smoked before being allowed into the station to catch their train. Travellers walked toward the railroad station, balancing their load on bamboo poles. Others were staggering under the weight of almost bursting plastic and khaki bags tied together by a belt and slung over the shoulder. One father pushed a bicycle carrying his wife, two children and their luggage which hung from the handlebar.

In addition, many people stood in long queues in front of outdoor ticket counters, hoping to get a place on a train at the last minute. Mr Yu did not want to take any chance and he bought his ticket seven days before going to visit his family. Mrs Shu already had a ticket for her ten-year-old son, who would travel about twenty hours to visit his grandparents.

This was a very long journey for such a young child, and when I expressed concern, she told me a railroad attendant would look after him. She gave him enough fruit, cookies, boiled eggs, and chocolate to last the entire journey.

When I asked our staff how they would spend the three days, they said that they would eat *jao-tze* to end the old year, and in the new year they would have shrimp, pork, and chicken dishes. In addition, they would take walks, visit friends, and relax. I assumed part of relaxation meant playing cards, which I noticed was the first item to be sold out in stores.

The last shopping day of the lunar year was as hectic as the day before Christmas in America, and so I stayed at home. In the evening the streets suddenly emptied. The red Chinese flag with its five gold stars appeared in every neighbourhood, and round red lanterns with yellow tassels hung from the entrances to government buildings and stores.

For the first time I saw restaurants only half full. Students and army people, who had not gone home, were celebrating the year's end in small groups. At midnight the skies burst into colour with hundreds of firecrackers, and the noise from the explosions went on until morning.

New Year's Day was a family day and parks were full of families strolling together. Young children attracted the most attention with their new toys and dazzling coloured new jackets. Their mouths were full of peanuts, candy, watermelon seeds and even popsicles, and their tiny hands clutched treasured balloons or pulled quacking wooden ducks.

Young boys played war games with their new toy rifles, and some of the older boys had saved a few firecrackers to set off. Primary and middle school girls walked arm in arm, in their new identical plaid and checkered jackets and long waist-length braids tied with ribbons. The older people wore spotless, freshly-pressed black pants and jackets, and I could see that the material was finer than what they wore on normal days.

Tien An Men was crowded with families who were trying out their new cameras and taking pictures of each other. One young man pulled up the sleeve of his jacket so his new watch would be in the picture. Those who did not have a camera joined the long queues in front of the government photographers who had set up their tripods on the square.

The nearby Peking Hotel was another attraction. People

gathered on the sidewalk in front to watch foreigners coming and going. A year later a new air-conditioned seventeen-storey addition to the hotel drew hundreds of people, who appeared more interested in the electronic doors at the entrance than in the foreigners.

At night, parents walked through the quiet streets with their young children who carried paper lanterns lit with candles. A friend told me that this was an old custom, practised only by the natives of Peking.

Most families were at home celebrating reunions. Children had returned from working in the countryside, after a two-year absence. Unmarried army sons were enjoying their first home leave in several years. Overseas Chinese were visiting relatives they had not seen for twenty-five years. Wives and husbands were reunited briefly after the long separation their jobs had created. Each year people looked forward to the New Year, with the hope that the family would be reunited.

THE CHINESE AND I BEGIN TO SHARE A COMMON OBSESSION:
FOOD

The bleak, depressing months of February and March followed the Chinese New Year. We had arrived at this time a year ago and I knew how disagreeable the dryness and sandstorms were. They forced me to lead a confining indoor life, and so I looked for an amusing distraction. Food became the answer.

During my Chinese lessons I focused on learning a food vocabulary. I wanted to be able to cook with Mr Yu and order in local restaurants where people seldom spoke English.

One Peking-born friend estimated there were at least 500 eating places in the capital. Some of those that I had already eaten in catered only to foreigners. Others served mainly Chinese customers, and these were the places I wanted to visit.

Once we were the guests of a German industrial delegation in the Big Peking Duck restaurant, where our twelve-course meal included the most noble dishes in the Chinese cuisine.

There were at least seven duck dishes with duck tongue and feet as special treats, swallow's nest soup, sea slugs, silver ear (a fungus growing on trees), and shark fin.

On another occasion we were invited to a vegetarian restaurant, where we had a room to ourselves. There all the dishes were made of soy bean products and were named after their flavour, such as 'duck's liver', 'fish', and 'beef'. When a foreign friend invited us to a meal that would feature exotic dishes such as bear's paw, bull's penis, salamander, snake, cat, and dog, I politely turned down the invitation.

Most dinners began no later than 6:30 because the kitchen wanted to close at 8:30 or 9. Restaurants often specialised in the food of a particular province, and Chengtu (the name of the capital of Szechuan) was a favourite among foreigners. This restaurant was known as much for its atmosphere and history as for its spicy food.

It was rumoured that Yuan Shih-kai, the first President of the Republic, who had tried to become emperor, had used this small palace for entertainment. When a foreign guest asked a waiter if this was true, he said, 'Yes, I heard it from another foreigner.' Reputedly Teng Hsiao-ping, the vice-premier, ate many meals here before the Cultural Revolution.

Located behind walls on one of the back streets, Chengtu was difficult to find the first time. Fortunately, an attendant in a white jacket was standing on the narrow street. He directed us to pass through the front gate and park in a courtyard behind. There, traditional Chinese architecture surrounded us and took us into a different world than the one outside, where the buildings had straight, heavy lines. Inside, there were curving roofs, belonging to different wings of the former palace. Narrow passageways led from one courtyard to the next, and, while walking past each separate section, we admired the ornate wood carving on the walls.

Our dinner, hosted by a German, was being held in a room that looked like someone's former living-room, but the arrangement of furniture made it stark and formal. A stiffly furnished section, where friends were sitting and drinking tea, was at one end, and a dining area at the other end.

We sat down in bulky beige chairs and the attendant immediately offered us tea and cigarettes. An unopened package of Chunghua cigarettes, the brand usually offered foreigners and infrequently sold in local shops, was sitting on the table next to a *cloisonné* ashtray and a matching matchholder. A radiator provided a little heat, but not enough for me to take off my coat.

Before going to the table I went to the bathroom, and was surprised to see that it had a bathtub, sink, and flushing toilet. This contrasted with the usual restaurant toilet, which was just a hole in the floor.

The arrival of the cold platter was the sign that dinner could begin. On the white tablecloth each setting had a cloth napkin arranged in the shape of a fan, a small plate, a row of different-size glasses, a fork, knife, and spoon, and ivory chopsticks. The hard wooden straight-backed chairs did not permit slouching; this was not the kind of meal meant for relaxation.

We had a choice of beer, wine, schnapps, orange soda, and even chilled water, which Chinese would never drink themselves because they considered it unhealthy. A hand-written menu in Chinese and English prepared me for the number of courses our host had ordered. Some of the names, such as 'ants climb the tree' and 'lions' head' were more mysterious than informative. I was a little sceptical about the poetic names when I recalled that one restaurant menu had included 'fragrant meat', which guests later discovered was dog meat. When the 'ants' dish arrived I was relieved to see that it was ground beef with glass noodles. The 'lion's head' was spicy pork meatballs.

After ploughing through seven courses, soup arrived, signifying the end of the meal. At the same time the attendant asked us in English if we wanted a bowl of steamed rice. According to old Chinese tradition, if the guest accepted the rice it meant he was still hungry, and so he should be served more food.

During the ninety-minute feast, the attendant stood in the background refilling our glasses when they were three quarters full and changing our plates after each course. At the completion of the meal he gave us damp perfumed towels to clean our hands and faces. As usual, I had messed up the tablecloth but I didn't have to apologise here. The Chinese had the proverb, the table-cloth should look like a battlefield after a good meal.

The attendant led us to the sitting area where we had first drunk tea. We were offered oranges, apples, pears, and more tea which, the Chinese believed, was good for digestion. After the meal our host paid a bill amounting to twenty yuan a head. Then some staff lined up outside the door, and we shook their hands and thanked them before leaving.

I rarely enjoyed this kind of evening because the atmosphere was so stiff, formal, and uncomfortable. Instead, I preferred eating in the lively, noisy, simple surroundings of the 'masses' restaurants', the foreigners' nickname for the restaurants where the Chinese ate.

But it was not always easy to receive the same treatment as the Chinese. On one occasion I had a difficult time convincing the waitress that we wanted to eat where the Chinese were sitting. She thought we should eat alone in an empty adjoining room and refused to understand me. Even if my Chinese was not clear, my gestures were. Finally I saw a free table in the crowded section and we went over to it and sat down. The staff did not look pleased, but there was nothing they could do but serve us.

Some foreigners had complained that a few restaurants would not serve them because they had no separate dining area. This was never my experience, and I assumed that the policy of 'special treatment' by segregating foreigners was the decision of the restaurant staff.

We always tried to go to restaurants with only one dining-room to make certain that we would eat with the Chinese. There, the prices and service were different from the Chengtu. One of the masses' restaurants, which became our favourite was located in a brick two-storey building on a busy main street. It featured Szechuan food and was clean, spacious, and well lit with neon lights.

The first floor sold only noodle dishes and so we walked up the wide tile staircase to the second floor. There a menu on the blackboard had dishes ranging in price from thirty fen to 2.10 yuan.

When one of the waitresses saw us, she disappeared into the kitchen. A concerned-looking man wearing a chef's cap appeared and walked over to us. He was worried because the restaurant was full and there was no table for us. I said we would wait.

Chinese traditional politeness demanded, however, that foreigners be served first, and so the cook went over to one table and asked the people to double up at another. I protested but this didn't help. I was embarrassed that we had taken someone else's place.

It took me many months to realise that our conspicuous standing around embarrassed the cook, who felt he had to seat us. Later he would greet us with a bright smile and shake our hands every time we arrived. We finally avoided the problem of unseating Chinese by stopping by the restaurant during the meal hours (6–9 A.M., 10:30 A.M.–1:30 P.M., and 4:30–7:30 P.M.) and asking when it would be convenient for us to return and eat.

The wooden backless stools we were sitting on seemed more comfortable than the stiff-backed chairs in the Chengdu. But maybe it was the atmosphere that made me feel relaxed.

The white plastic tablecloth still showed the signs of the last dinner guests, and so the chef wiped the remaining food onto the floor and put wooden chopsticks and small plates in the middle of the table. I liked this kind of informality and simplicity.

During that first meal I ordered very spicy meat, cabbage and fish dishes, which later became our standard meal. Only after many months did the chef feel he knew us well enough to recommend a delicious bean curd dish. After this we started asking him regularly if he had any suggestions.

While waiting for our food we looked around and saw that everyone's table was set like ours and people were eating the same kinds of things we had ordered. Then two men in their twenties, who were sitting a few feet away and had heard me speaking Chinese, asked in Chinese, 'What is your nationality?'

I was pleased to have someone speak to me and answered immediately. When he heard that I was American, he replied 'very good' and then said, 'How long have you been in China? You speak very good Chinese.' I told him, 'My Chinese is very bad, I wish I could speak better.'

Noticing that our conversation had started to interest other people, I asked both young men what they were eating and then commented about the weather. I was careful to avoid asking a question which could create problems for them later.

An experience I had on a bicycle parking lot a few months ago still haunted me. A young student had approached me and started speaking English. It was clear that he wanted to practice his English, but this attracted attention and people stopped and watched us. I was concerned that he would have trouble later and tried to end the conversation, but he continued. Finally, after getting away, I turned around to see him surrounded by people. I assumed he had to explain to someone in the group why he was speaking to a foreigner and what had been said.

Two steaming plates arrived and interrupted our conversation with the two men. I had learned to eat like the Chinese and dipped my chopsticks into the communal dish and then put them in my mouth. Others around me were placing the spicy food on top of rice, in order to cut the sharpness. Then they brought the bowl up to their mouths and moved the chopsticks so quickly from the bowls to their mouths and back again that it looked like a continuous movement.

There was not enough space in our tiny saucers to put fish bones and so we followed the Chinese custom and spit them on the tablecloth. I had brought along Kleenex, which came in handy as napkins when we started to perspire from the Szechuan specialities, which featured chili.

At the same time our food had warmed us up so we could take off our coats and still feel comfortable in the unheated room. But the people around us, who were mostly men, remained bundled up, with their caps pulled down close to their ears.

Warm beer, served in a pitcher, quenched Gerd's thirst, but I wanted water. When I asked for it, the chef said, 'We don't have any.' Then I pointed to a faucet and he replied, 'You can't drink that.' And so I became accustomed to drinking 'white tea'—clear boiling water—unless I remembered to bring along a few tea bags.

One time when I brought tea bags to another 'masses' restaurant, where foreigners seldom ate, I had to wait one hour before the tea arrived. Only when the waitress presented me with the empty cloth bags, I realised why I had waited so long. The people in the kitchen had obviously not known what to do with the tea bags and they were too embarrassed to ask. Finally they had decided to cut them open and empty their contents into a tea pot.

While we ate slowly and talked during the meal, the Chinese around us were silent. Later a Chinese friend said, 'Unlike you, when we eat we concentrate on our food and do not talk until we are finished.'

People usually ate all the food in front of them, but if there were leftovers, they would bring them home in their aluminium lunch tin or plastic bag. We paid 1.50 yuan a head for our four courses while the average customer paid less than one yuan for more vegetable dishes. In addition, the Chinese gave the waitress coupons for the rice they ate because rice

Street Scenes

Above: Traffic on Chien Men Wai, one of my favourite streets in the southern part of the city

Below: **Yoping**, a fried piece of dough, is a popular breakfast for those on their way to work

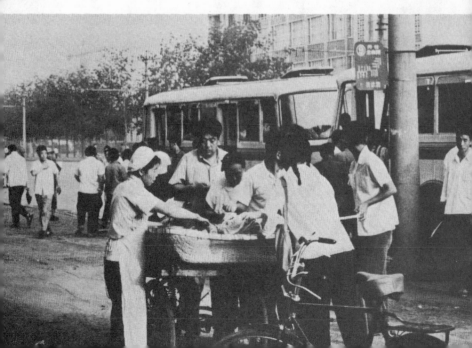

Above: This is a shopping side street, branching off Chien Men Wai

Below: Many back streets are so narrow that a car has a tight squeeze passing

Above: These people are patiently waiting for the bus

Below: But as soon as the bus approaches, the scene changes. If you don't push and shove you'll be left on the street

Below: Sometimes a policeman and cyclist do not agree and crowds form to take sides

The Bicycle

Top left: The bicycle is the most important possession many people own

Centre left: It carries large loads . . . even a sewing machine

Bottom left: Bicycles are not supposed to be parked at random. There are bicycle parking lots

Above and right: It transports the family

Below: Some bikes have a homemade side compartment to carry the child

Market
In summer, outdoor fruit and
vegetable stands sell fresh
produce

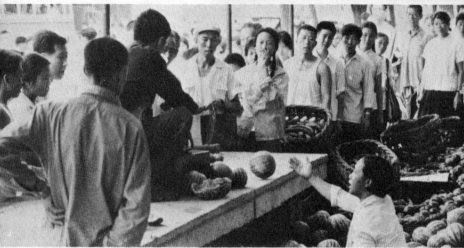

Above: Live fish netted in a lake near Peking are being delivered to a local market

Below: Chopping ice – during winter ice is cut out of lakes, and stored underground until summer arrives. Then the chunks of ice are used in markets to refrigerate perishable food

In the indoor market, the items for sale are stacked on counters. Above: Fish, Centre: Frozen ducks, and below: Vegetables

abbage. During three weeks in autumn the streets are heaped with cabbage, which most amilies buy in enormous quantities

elow: Every kind of transport, including the baby carriage is used to carry the cabbage ome

Fashion

Above and below: Everyone bundles up many layers to keep warm in winter

Left: Two old women, huddling togeth under one raincoat, are seeking shelter from the summer rain

Top right: The baby's face is covered gauze scarf as a protection against the cold and dust

Centre right: The Chinese love colourf clothing, particularly on young children

Bottom right: The stores are full of bri plaids and prints, but these colours are usually concealed under a drab outer la

Recreation

Top left and above: Skating is a popular winter sport

Below left: Ice Hockey

Top right: Children prefer to use a homemade wooden sled on the ice. It consists of a piece of wood, metal runners and two steel rods to propel them

Centre right and below: Some, like the man on the right, fish from a rubber tyre, while others even swim in winter

Above left: A family outing may include a picnic; or (centre left) a ride in a boat on one of Peking's many lakes

Below left: Peitaiho is a favourite summer seaside resort for foreigners. It is also a place where selected Chinese rest and relax

In their free time, Chinese visit scenic places such as the Temple of Heaven (right) or relax in parks (below)

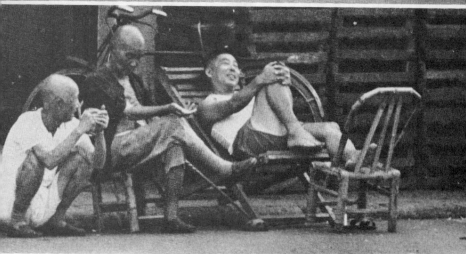

Above: To remain healthy . . . physical fitness is important. So during work hours, there are exercise breaks

Centre: But no less important is regular rest

Left and above right: The passion for card playing begins with the young . . . and continues through old age

Bottom right: The school girls' favourite game is Chinese jump rope

The Park

In the early summer mornings the parks are full of young and old people doing traditional Chinese sports

Above left: Two old retired men playing the **erh-hu** (two-stringed fiddle) in a park pavilion

Left: Young people practise sword dancing

Above right: A man shadow-boxing

Below right: On an early autumn morning a child was sitting on a bench in the park practising on her **erh-hu**

School

Above: Schoo[l] begins for s[ome] children at a[ge] three, althoug[h the] majority start [at] school at age [six] or seven

Left: There is [no] school unifor[m] and most chi[ldren] go to school [...] wearing brig[ht] coloured jack[ets] and carrying [a] khaki bag

Above: The school programme includes doing acupressure. The children are pressing certain parts of the face in order to relax the eyes and to avoid nearsightedness.

Right: Students start learning a foreign language in the fourth grade, at the age of ten or eleven. The teacher has asked me to speak to her class so that they will hear my American accent

Welcome, dear friends! You are warmly welcome [?]isit our class

Family Life

Above: Three generations usually live together in a two room flat

Left: Often the husband and wife share household chores

Below: The grandparents are very important members of the family. They care for their grandchildren while both parents are working

Above right: Family ties are very strong. Chinese relative living abroad are having a reunion with their family living in Peking

Centre right: The family care for them when they are old and sick

Below right: After leaving Peking I returned one year later to enjoy my family reunion. From right to left: Mr. Gu, our interpreter; Mrs. Shu, my teacher; Mrs. Lee, our cleaning woman. Missing are the driver and the cook, who were not in Peking at the time

Chao Yang
It is cleaning day in
Chao Yang. While
the old people are
sweeping the streets
(left) the young are
weeding the grass
(below) and
washing the
school windows
(above right)

Hua Hsi
Centre right and
below right: In the
Hua Hsi brigade the
young women and
men are doing the
hard field work

Ching Ming

An annual festival fo
commemoration of t
dead. In April 1976,
however, it develope
into a demonstration
eulogising the late
Chou En Lai

Above: People left
wreaths at the Marty
monument and white
paper flowers, the si
of mourning, on the
bushes nearby

Left: They wrote poe
and pasted them on t
monument

Below: The crowd
over 100,000 people
the square

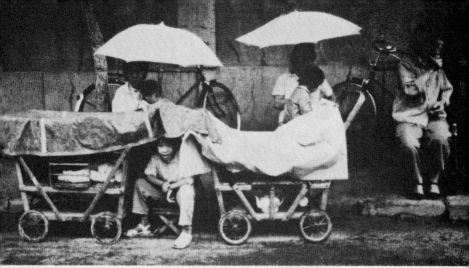

Earthquake

Above: When the earthquake struck at 3.45 a.m. July 28, 1976, the people left their homes with few belongings. It was raining and they remembered to bring rain gear

Centre and below: As soon as they learned that they would not be able to return to their homes, they started building outdoor shelters and used whatever materials they had on hand

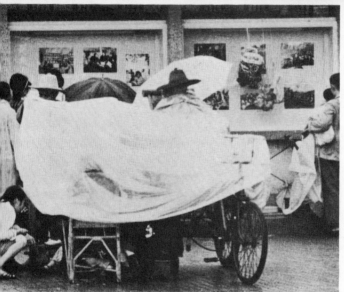

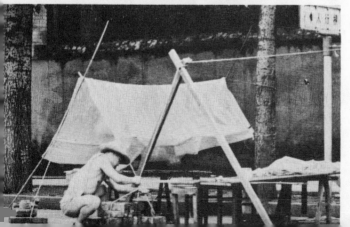

When they learned that shelter life might go on for weeks they started improving their homes and adding more household possessions

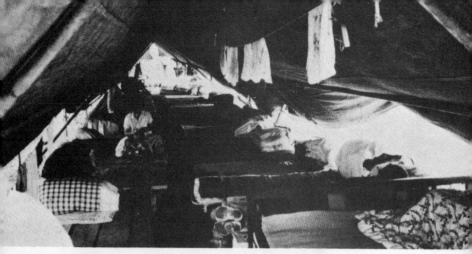

Shelter living
became more
comfortable and
the dwellings
improved. Some
(above and below)
were communal,
while others (left)
were family homes

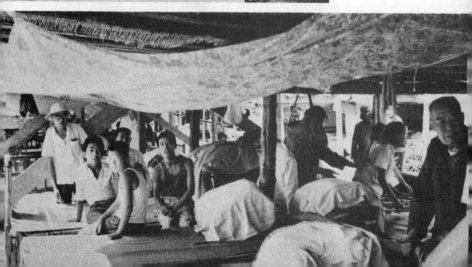

There were outdoor clinics (above) . . . barber shops (centre left) . . . kitchens (centre right) . . . classrooms (below) . . . offices (above right)

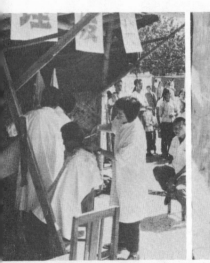

Centre: When the earthquake recovery work began, everyone in the neighbourhood participated

Below: The middle school students were enlisted to carry bricks

Death of Mao The announcement of Mao's death in September 1976 has just been broadcast. These people are standing on Tien An Men square and are facing the large picture of Mao which hangs on the entrance to the Imperial City. In the background is the Great Hall of the People where Mao's body lay in state.

and grain products are rationed for them, but not for us.

Eating in a restaurant is a special occasion for most people. A Chinese friend told me, 'It costs at least three times more to eat in a restaurant than to eat at home, and this is an extravagance. But the food at home is different from the specialties a restaurant offers.'

There were two 'masses' restaurants that featured only Western dishes, and they, like the restaurants with Chinese food, were always crowded. The Chinese called one the Moscow Restaurant, because it was located in the large Exhibition Hall the Russians had built during the fifties.

This restaurant had two sections, one for foreigners and the other for Chinese. A Chinese friend loved to go there on Sunday with her family, and she often described the dishes she ordered. 'I had pork, mashed potatoes, and peas, and also a hamburger platter with bread, potato, and vegetables.' When I told her she had ordered two meals, she said. 'It was too much to eat at once, and so I put the leftovers into an aluminium tin and had them this morning for breakfast.'

The Peace Café had the atmosphere of a university café or pub. Young people with books in hand sat and drank beer. While some of the customers speared sandwiches with knives and balanced a piece of cake on a fork, others were familiar with the foreign way of eating. One elderly distinguished couple, who looked like a professor and his wife, sipped cups of coffee and ate apple pie, habits they had not acquired in China.

MR YU EXPERIMENTS WITH NEW DISHES

When Mr Yu returned from his New Year's leave he was anxious to make new dishes. He decided he was going to prepare his version of Peking duck.

In restaurants the famous Peking duck, which has been force-fed to increase its fat content, is prepared by filling it with water and hanging it inside a wood-fed oven above burning fruit logs. The water heats up and cooks the meat from the inside while the fire makes the skin crispy.

Not having such an oven at home, Mr Yu wanted to create a similar effect by immersing the whole duck in oil and frying it. But we did not have a large-enough wok. He told me the proper size wok would cost twenty yuan. This was about one third of an average worker's monthly salary, and a very steep price to pay, I thought. But I didn't want to disappoint him, and told him to go ahead and buy the wok.

When Mr Gu, Mr Liu, and Mrs Lee heard this, they opposed the idea immediately. Mr Gu said, 'We have figured you will use this wok at most five times, and that is too much to spend. Can't you borrow one from a friend?' Almost all my friends had Western-style cooks and no one I knew made Peking duck at home. I then left the problem to our staff to resolve.

They spent the entire morning discussing it and by late afternoon Mr Liu returned with a wok in hand. 'It cost only two yuan because the metal is cheap,' he said. Placing it on the burner, he saw it did not fit, but remarked, 'We'll make it fit.' The following day everyone took turns hammering the wok down to the proper size in order for it to fit on the stove.

The preparation of the duck required that it hang in front of a slight breeze. After another lengthy staff discussion, Mr Yu and Mrs Lee resolved the problem with a wire clothes hanger.

That evening I heard the dog growling outside the dark kitchen. Thinking someone had broken into the flat, I cautiously approached the kitchen with a book in hand. A duck swinging gently in the breeze greeted me. The next day the duck was a complete success, and I asked Mr Yu if he would prepare it for guests. But I knew he would not make it for just any guest. When we had guests Mr Yu was always interested in knowing who they were.

One ambassador once joked to us, 'My cook (who was known for his excellent Chinese food) always asks who is coming for dinner and their rank before he decides about the menu.' On one occasion we had a private lunch with this ambassador and the food was disappointing. I remembered the joke he had made several months before, and realised where we stood in the cook's esteem.

We loved Mr Yu's cooking and were delighted when a guest from the Foreign Ministry said, 'He is only twenty-seven and so talented!'

He was always eager to make new dishes and there was no end to his surprises.

Although his specialty was Chinese cooking, Mr Yu asked if I would teach him a few Western dishes, and I agreed at once. He was a quick learner, but as soon as he was left on his own to make a 'Western' meal, Chinese cooking habits interfered.

Instead of serving goulash, carrots and potatoes together, he brought each dish as a separate course. And then, thinking that three courses were not sufficient, he added another meat course. When I explained to Mr Yu that we ate our dishes together, this presented a problem.

In Chinese cooking all the ingredients are finely chopped and prepared ahead of time. This cuts down the cooking time to a few minutes so that one can cook a dish, serve it, and then go on to the next dish. This was not possible with Western cooking and so Mr Yu, like many other cooks, made each dish ahead of time and at mealtime rewarmed everything. The result was often over-cooked or dried-out Western food.

'FIFTH AVENUE' PEKING—SHOPPING AND FASHIONS

Besides spending the winter months eating and watching Mr Yu in the kitchen I did a lot of browsing in local shops. Sometimes I went to Wangfuching, Peking's main shopping street, which I nicknamed 'Fifth Avenue'. Its street sign was written in Chinese and pinyin, the phonetic translation of Chinese characters into the Latin alphabet. As the years went by, I noticed an increasing number of streets and shops with signs in both Chinese and pinyin, which is now being taught in schools.

A policeman stood at the entrance to the street, forbidding bicycles from entering it. Wangfuching was open only to bus and automobile traffic.

The displays in store windows verged on pop art. Rubber hot water bags of different colours formed a design to look like one big water bag. Forty of fifty handkerchiefs were displayed to resemble a big fan. Tubes of toothpaste and jars of skin cream were arranged in the shape of a flower.

Baihuadalo, Peking's largest department store, is located on Wangfuching, and like all other stores it is government owned.

From the outside it looks like a Macy's of the 1940s; its six storeys tower over neighbouring stores. Instead of elevators or escalators, it has narrow staircases with enamel spitoons, and its interior has neon lighting.

Almost all the items in the store are made in China, with the exception of one-yuan Cuban cigars, which were too expensive for most Chinese and very popular among foreigners. In addition there were 900-yuan Swiss Rolex watches, which only people in high positions could afford.

The range of merchandise was enormous. There were departments for canned food, different types of clothing, sports equipment, kitchen utensils, records and musical instruments, school supplies, radios, etc.

The merchandise seldom changed, but when there was a long queue, this was the signal that something new was on the market, and customers would rush in that direction, stand in line, and discover a little later what was being sold.

When I was shopping in Baihuadalo blue and red glass fish had just gone on sale and created great excitement. They had coloured bulging eyes and smiling expressions on their faces. Each fish stood on its tail in a mermaid pose. 'How beautiful,' people remarked, as they stood impatiently in the queue, worrying that the supply of 2.50-yuan fish would run out.

The Chinese specialised in kitsch and my favourite piece

was a fat black-and-white panda bear made of wax. He was about six inches high and was in a sitting position. His lips were red and his black paws with manicured white nails held a yellow, red, green, and blue striped ball.

The candy counter was always crowded, reflecting the Chinese sweet tooth. The fifty-foot-long counter displayed at least thirty different kinds of hard candies and toffee, but chocolate, which customers could afford only on special occasions, was the favourite.

Once I saw a commotion at this counter and joined the excited crowd. They had gathered in front of a new automatic scale that lit up and registered the weight and price of the candy. This had replaced a hand scale and abacus, but the wooden box for collecting money was still present.

Chinese were fascinated by new automatic labour-saving devices, but at the same time they were sceptical about their accuracy. I had seen this in the bank when hand calculators were introduced. For the first months both the abacus and hand calculators were used for each transaction, until the employees had confidence in the calculator's accuracy and their ability to use it.

In another bank in China I saw a machine sorting and counting bills. At first I thought this was a practical invention, because the largest Chinese bill is ten yuan and when a foreigner wanted to exchange a lot of money it would sometimes last a very long time. The main reason was that two men would have to count the pile of money two times each for accuracy.

Unfortunately, the employees operating the sorting and counting machine treated it as though it were replacing two people. They made the machine count the same pile four times for accuracy, thus losing the time it should have saved.

While the Chinese were becoming accustomed to mechanical devices, I was fascinated by an ingenious system of payment in one small store. A cashier sat in a booth with overhead wires from different counters leading to her. Clerks used a clothespin or metal clip to attach the customer's money and a sales slip to the wire. Then they gave it a shove in the cashier's direction and waited on someone else until the cash and receipt came back on another wire. Months later, I saw a modernised version with a wire that moved mechanically.

Next to the candy counter was the popular cigarette counter where men were the main customers. There were over twenty brands to choose from, and sometimes the same brand was displayed in different wrapping. A package in cellophane cost twenty-five fen more than one in paper.

Packaging was about one third of the cost of some items. So everything from ink to sauces and oil would be poured or spooned into the customer's own vessel.

The fabrics department of Baihuadalo occupied half of a floor and offered a vast assortment of material. Wool, velvet, corduroy, silk, cotton, and polyester were shown in solid colours, prints, checks, and floral patterns. During successive winters and summers the colours and prints became bolder and more people were buying them.

When a customer wanted to see a particular cloth, she would ask the clerk to put the roll of material on the counter. At that point not only the customer would examine the material, but everyone around her would feel and discuss it.

Customers were always interested in what other people were buying and they sometimes became involved in my purchase. On one occasion I was looking for a solid coloured material for a blouse that had to match a skirt I had brought along. The clerk put several shades of blue cotton on the counter for me to examine, and at the same time the customers who had gathered behind me moved closer to feel the material.

Turning to one woman who looked my age, I asked her which shade she thought would match my skirt. She did not reply, but an older woman next to her spoke up. The first woman then forgot her shyness and agreed with the older one that one shade of blue was the prettiest. I thanked them for their help and followed their advice.

In a store that sold clay pots for marinating vegetables, I asked the clerk for the recipe for this dish. She started listing the ingredients and then the crowd surrounding me interrupted to make additions and corrections. As they talked I wrote down the ingredients, and suddenly there was silence around me. 'How can you write with your left hand?' a woman asked. It then occurred to me that I had never seen a Chinese writing with his left hand. Later a friend told me when children enter school and begin writing the teacher does not permit them to write with the left hand, but she did not know why.

During our first winter, Baihuadalo sold ready-made blouses only in solid white and blue cotton but in the following years printed, checked and striped polyester blouses were sold. In addition, women's jackets were shown in printed cotton and silk fabrics, instead of only blue or grey.

There were no fitting rooms in stores, but sometimes a rack had used jackets in different sizes that a customer could try on to determine his size. Clothing was cut squarely and shapelessly and people were mainly interested that the garment was large enough. We soon learned that this meant there should be room for layers.

When Gerd went to a tailor to have a winter suit made, he brought along a summer suit to be copied. From previous experience we had learned that the Chinese copy every detail exactly, even when a seam was crooked. Therefore he was very surprised during the first fitting to find that the jacket was enormous. When he brought this to the tailor's attention, the man said, 'I have left room for the winter layers you will be wearing under the jacket.'

The Chinese loved colour, which was not always visible to the inexperienced, foreign eye. Women wore checked and striped gloves and flashy socks they knitted. The woollen scarf department in Baihuadalo was also full of checks and plaids. In the wool long underwear department, I once saw several customers reaching for the last two pairs of underwear the clerk had in her hand. Their colour was red, white and green and they looked like a candy cane.

My eye was trained to focus on the ankle. As the weather became colder people wore more layers, which made their pants shorter. Layers were then showing, and the combinations were striking. One young man wore blue, burgundy and orange underwear, which looked like different pairs of athlete's training pants.

I noticed that older women wore only dark colours, such as grey and black, and teenage girls liked reds and green and bright colours. I learned the hard way what a woman in her mid-thirties should not wear. When I appeared for my Chinese lesson in a red striped blouse, Mrs Shu said critically, 'That is a very bright colour you are wearing today.' When I asked her what I should wear, she replied, 'I prefer you in blues and beiges,' the colours she usually wore. 'Women of our age usually wear the quieter colours,' she added.

Besides being colour conscious, the Chinese were interested in fashion. The stitching, the placement of pockets, the shape of the collar, the buttons, the cut of the jacket or pants, and the material were important details that no Chinese missed.

The unisex style that was so popular in the West, I noticed did not appeal to the Chinese, who made a clear distinction between men's and women's styles.

Men wore zippers in the front and women wore zippers on the side. All of my pants had front zippers and this attracted attention.

Women wore black cotton shoes with a strap over the arch, and men wore a loafer style. Shoe stores did not have my size in the woman's department and so I bought men's shoes, which made my feet stand out, not only for their size, but for their style.

When I wore blue denim pants for bicycling, one Chinese asked, 'Why are you wearing that material? It is what workers wear.'

Another time I bought a traditional peasant jacket, made of coarse cotton with frog buttons. When I tried it on at the counter, the people around me laughed, and wherever I wore it they smiled. 'Only an old male peasant would wear that jacket style,' a Chinese explained.

In Baihuadalo I wanted to buy a V-neck sweater for myself, but this style was available only in the men's sweaters. When I asked the clerk if he had one in my size, he said, 'You are in the men's department.' It did not occur to him that I would want to buy this fashion for myself.

Noticing that people were gathering around me, I said, 'The sweater is not for me. It is for my husband, who is my size.' Then he was happy to wait on me.

The first sweater he showed me was too small and when I asked for the next size, he said, 'mei yo' (do not have). I had heard this often in shops and had gotten used to this response.

The clerk suggested that I try on a sweater two sizes larger. It was enormous, but he remarked, 'That is the right size,' obviously considering the other layers Gerd would be wearing underneath.

I told him I would think about buying it, and then glanced at the price tag. The larger size was more expensive than the smaller. Later I noticed this was the case with all ready-made clothing and shoes. Price was based on the amount of material used.

When Chinese saw foreigners dressed in Chinese styles, their reactions were mixed. Sometimes they laughed. Another time an old man looked at a German student dressed in a padded blue jacket and baggy blue pants and commented, 'It is interesting. People from other countries wear the same styles at home as we wear here.'

Chapter 5

The Chinese Reaction to Foreigners

THE CHINESE GRAPEVINE

The foreign community was a hotbed of gossip and no one enjoyed it more than the Chinese. What took place in one foreign household was often the topic of conversation in another.

I first learned about the Chinese grapevine when one of our staff whispered to me that a blonde hair of a woman was found on the pillow of a bachelor we knew. Another time I heard that a friend of mine treated her Chinese badly. She never offered them tea and the driver had no place to rest, I was told.

When I wanted to pass on information, I relied on the Chinese grapevine. This was particularly useful when we were going on holiday and a Western family had agreed to take care of Bubbles, providing her *aiye* (the term used for cleaning woman and nanny) was not frightened of the dog. I knew our people would pave the way for Bubbles' reception. When we were about to leave and deposited Bubbles and her basket with our friends, the *aiye* would welcome her and ask if we had brought her ball along.

We also used the grapevine to air our complaints, hoping they would be included in the 'family' report that other foreigners told us the interpreter made weekly.

We unwittingly played an important part in our staff's life by influencing their standing among colleagues. On one occasion a neighbour, whom we didn't know very well, asked to borrow our ladder, having learned from her *aiye* that we owned one. Another friend said that her *aiye* recommended that she buy a floor waxer on her next trip to Hong Kong. Her *aiye* knew another *aiye* whose employer had this machine, and she did not want to lose face by not having one.

An *aiye* who took care of a blond, blue-eyed child seemed to be envied by other *aiyes*, who thought blond hair and blue eyes were a beautiful and exotic combination. Wherever I went I watched Chinese fuss much more over blond children than over brunettes.

A cook who worked for an ambassador was deferentially referred to by other cooks as 'master'. A driver who sat behind the wheel of a Mercedes was often more arrogant than one driving a Toyota.

THE LANGUAGE BARRIER

Although our staff always spoke to me in Chinese and usually understood, with occasional help from Mr Gu, what I was saying in Chinese, the clerks in local stores on remote side streets had a mental block as soon as they saw my face. Any attempt I made to say the simplest thing about what I wanted to buy would result in a blank stare. This frustrated me because I had worked so hard to learn Chinese. But I was persistent.

After repeating myself several times, someone in the crowd surrounding me understood what I was saying and told the clerk. I was convinced I had said the same thing, but the clerk's reaction was different and his face lit up with understanding.

One time I asked for an item in Chinese and the clerk went to fetch it. When she brought it back I asked how much it cost. She disappeared for a few minutes and brought back a paper and pencil. Assuming I would not understand her, she wrote the sum on a piece of paper.

Although the written language is the same throughout China, the pronunciation differs according to province. For example, Cantonese is a different spoken language from mandarin, the northern Chinese dialect I spoke. To be understood in shops in Canton one had to speak Cantonese. In Peking I felt relieved when I saw Chinese from other provinces using their fingers to draw characters on the palms of their hands because even they had difficulties being understood.

A British friend who spoke fluent Chinese said it was some-times impossible to be understood because some Chinese were unwilling to believe that a foreigner could speak their language. He was on his way to the Ming Tombs one day and was un-certain about the route, so he stopped two old men who were walking together.

'Is this the way to the Ming Tombs?' he asked. They stared at him as though they were deaf and said nothing. He repeated the question several times, but still received no response.

While walking back to his car, he overheard one say to the other, 'Strange, it sounded as though he asked us, "Is this the way to the Ming Tombs?"'

A German friend who spoke Chinese had a different experi-ence. She was invited to join an American delegation for sight-seeing and a lunch when Chinese were present. Not realising that she spoke Chinese, they carried on a conversation about the eating habits of the Americans. 'That man looks like a wolf the way he eats.' 'The fat man next to him doesn't stop pushing food into his mouth.' She wisely remained silent.

I assumed Chinese could not understand German, but, through a blunder, I found out differently. The first time Gerd went to have his hair cut at the International Club I accom-panied him, fearing that without my assistance he would come home with the Chinese cropped look. After the barber started clipping his hair, I said to Gerd in German, 'If he cuts any more hair, I will kill him.' At that point the barber turned to me and said politely in German, 'Is it the right length?' Later I found out that he had worked in a German-owned barber shop before the Liberation and spoke at least five languages.

SPECIAL SHOPS FOR FOREIGNERS

It was easier to establish contact with Chinese in shops that were open to foreigners. Gerd had a special relationship with an old clerk in a scroll shop. They had spent hours together looking at scrolls, discussing painting techniques and artists.

He knew Gerd's taste, and when we entered the shop the old clerk would go to closed drawers to fetch scrolls Gerd had not seen and he thought he would like. If we could not decide whether to buy a scroll, he would put it aside until we made up our mind.

The Friendship Store was only a three-minute bicycle ride from our door and this was where the majority of foreigners did their daily shopping. It was a department store and supermarket and had a dry cleaners, watch repair service, shipping office, bank, florist, tropical fish section, and tailoring department. In addition, it had an office that bought used articles, which were later sold in Chinese second-hand shops.

Some of the local stores sold similar products that were sometimes a little cheaper, but their quality was different. One clerk in town even advised me to go to the Friendship Store, where he said the merchandise was of a better quality.

The Friendship Store was different from local stores. Here all clerks could speak some English and there was always an interpreter on hand. The rooms were spacious, clean, and well lit. Food was refrigerated, sizes catered to the foreign figure, and there was elevator service to the three shopping floors. In addition, there were no staring crowds.

Some of the food sold here was not available in local stores. It had warm bread daily, lean beef and pork, butter, German-style smoked cold cuts, French pastry, cream, and even inexpensive sturgeon and black and red caviar. Mr Yu and I bought most of our food here but, when I had time, I preferred to shop for vegetables and fruit in town where they were fresher and the choice was often larger.

At the Friendship Store I formed the closest ties with Chinese outside my home. Very often while I was doing my shopping, clerks who knew me asked for help in English pronunciation or grammar. An older man in the scroll and carpet department always greeted me with a broad smile, and then pulled out of his pocket a list of English questions that he regularly saved for me.

At some counters I felt as though I were conducting an English class. When one person asked me a question, all the others would gather round and we would repeat words in unison together.

Some departments were known for their unfriendly clerks, but I had few difficulties with them. A foreigner who lived in China over thirty years taught me an important lesson. 'Everything depends on your attitude, tone, and the way you talk to the Chinese. If you are nice to them they will be nice to you.'

In the fish department there was seldom fresh fish. The frozen fish was displayed on the counter and often it defrosted and started to smell. Many customers protested that the fish was not good, and either refused to buy any or tried to persuade the clerks to fetch frozen ones. The clerks were often insulted by this treatment and refused to do anything.

Remembering what my friend had told me, I went up to the fish counter one day and asked if there were frozen fish available. The clerk pointed to the defrosted fish in front of me and said, 'These are good.' I agreed with her but said, 'I have come on my bicycle and am afraid that the fish will spoil on the way home. If it spoils and I eat it, I will become sick.'

When the subject of health entered the discussion, the clerk became sympathetic. She offered to look in the storage room to see if they had frozen fish. A few minutes later she returned with a selection of fish. In the future, when I shopped at the fish counter, all the other clerks immediately recognised me and fetched frozen fish.

PROTOCOL

The Chinese were extremely conscious of rank and protocol, and when a foreign delegation arrived, social and political differences were put aside. A head of state, even if he came from a tiny country whose name people did not remember, or from a world power, would be welcomed at the airport

by 5,000 primary and middle school students dressed in colourful costumes. The Chinese prime minister would greet him and
then accompany him into town, where the flag of the visiting
country could be seen flying along main streets in the city.
And coloured silk pennants and banners, welcoming the
foreign guest in his native language, were strung across Chang
An.

That evening the premier would host a banquet in the Great
Hall of the People in honour of the foreign guest. Ambassadors,
their wives, selected Chinese, and journalists were invited.
Journalists' wives, however, were excluded. 'The journalists
are here to work, not to enjoy themselves,' a Foreign Ministry
spokesman explained.

The seating was done according to protocol, with the most
senior ambassadors sitting at the tables with the fewest people
and highest-ranking Chinese. The journalists sat in the back
row, nearest the military band, which played both Chinese
and foreign pieces.

During a banquet for the former Australian Prime Minister
Gough Whitlam, the band played 'Waltzing Matilda', the
unofficial Australian national anthem, and when Chancellor
Schmidt was in Peking the band played German folk songs
and works of Beethoven.

The dinners ended with speeches by the Chinese premier
and head of state, and they were usually remembered more
for length than for content. The guests were very pleased with
the ten-minute specials, and were incensed at the head of state
who spoke for fifty-five minutes.

One evening an ambassador of a friendly country rose to
leave at 9:45, in the middle of dinner. The Chinese thought
they had done something to offend him. When they asked him
what was wrong, he said, 'I have a bad heart and live on the
tenth floor in my building. Unless I am home by ten o'clock,
when the elevator operator goes home, I will have to walk up
the ten flights.' After that evening elevator operators were on
duty around the clock in his building.

When a delegation of owners and heads of some of the biggest firms and industrial organisations in Germany came to Peking in 1973 to negotiate trade possibilities between Germany and China, the Chinese made an error in protocol. They had misjudged the importance of the group, and treated them like just another trade delegation of businessmen who wanted to sell their products to China.

The government sent minor officials to the airport to receive the group and assigned the chairman of the delegation a Shanghai car, instead of a Red Flag, the Chinese-made black limousine reserved for important people. On the way into town the Chinese were surprised to learn that the chairman of the delegation had seen Brezhnev, Nixon, and Brandt in the last month.

On the following morning the Chinese made amends. A Red Flag car was waiting to pick up the chairman. Realising the blunder they had made, the Chinese started talking about the possibility of the delegation seeing Chou En-lai. Then a long waiting period began, during which the group was kept in suspense. The Chinese would not say whether they would or would not see the premier. They only told them to stay together and that no one should stray.

Many of the members of the delegation were accustomed to having scheduled appointments with government heads when they asked for them, and this treatment was something new and disagreeable. They were angry and protested at not being told something definite. But this was the way Chinese did things and they had to accept it.

Twenty-four hours after they had been instructed to stay together, they were ushered into a room and told they would see the premier immediately. It was ten P.M. and the vigil was not yet over. They had to wait in the hotel another ninety minutes without explanation before being driven to the Great Hall of the People for the meeting.

It finally began at 12.00 midnight. At one in the morning it ended, but Premier Chou En-lai asked the delegation head to remain behind. The German returned to the hotel after 2 A.M., satisfied with his visit to China and perhaps a little humbler after the Chinese lesson in protocol.

FOREIGN ENTERTAINMENT

Protocol matters did not affect the life of the majority of foreigners, whose rank did not entitle them to invitations to banquets or receptions. But they could go to Peking opera, acrobatics, and sports or cultural programmes. We usually had advance notice when a foreign group was coming to Peking to entertain, but tickets for foreigners were always limited. The group, we were told, was there to perform for the Chinese.

We were very excited when we were able to attend a concert the Vienna Philharmonic was giving in Peking. The setting for the concert was an indoor sports stadium accommodating eighteen thousand people, and not a seat was empty. The more than one hundred musicians were placed on a green carpet in the middle of an area the size of a football field, where they looked very lost.

At the beginning of the concert the audience could not settle down. While Mozart's *Eine Kleine Nachtmusik* was transmitted over an excellent loudspeaker system, people squirmed, chatted, looked around, ate apples and cookies, drank lemonade and went out to buy more food, as they would do at sports events. The spectators were obviously bored with the quiet, peaceful music.

Only when the second part of the programme was announced did the audience awaken. The Philharmonic was going to play 'The Blue Danube' waltz, a familiar piece to the Chinese, and a ripple of excited buzzing and then spontaneous applause erupted before the music began.

For this selection the people sat up straight in their seats, listening to every note. A foot tapped, a hand directed, a head kept beat with the music. When the piece ended everyone wanted to hear more. Even two encores did not satisfy them.

The only other time I saw Chinese displaying emotional involvement was at sports events. From early school days, children learned the motto, 'Friendship first, competition second'. This slogan hung in all stadiums and was repeated several times on the loudspeaker during athletic programmes.

In international competition the audience was expected to applaud and cheer for both sides, and they usually did. When Chinese played against African teams, the Africans often won and everyone seemed happy.

The atmosphere was different, however, when the German national amateur football team played in Peking. The Chinese were under the mistaken notion that this team was the world champion and a victory for the Chinese would mean a world victory.

We attended the soccer match, and it was clear who the favourites were. Although 'Friendship first, competition second' echoed in the background, there was a dead silence in the stadium when the German team scored their only goal of the game. But when the Chinese scored, the spectators shouted and jumped up and down. The game ended as a tie, but from the elated faces of the Chinese, one would think they had won.

The American field and track team had an unprecedented experience in Peking. For the first time in their history, they encountered a team that had no competitive instinct or will to win.

One American shotput thrower was so baffled by the non-competitive attitude that he called in an interpreter to translate a pep talk. 'This is not a passive sport,' he told his opponent. 'You must put more emotion into your effort.' Then he demonstrated this by throwing the shot and uttering a loud grunt at the end of the throw. After some coaxing, the Chinese imitated him and threw the best throw of his career.

The audience seemed far more interested in the diversified appearance of the Americans than in the events. They laughed at the full-bearded long-haired men, who weighed over 250 pounds. Hairy bodies are ugly to the Chinese, who have little body hair.

Some blacks wore neat rows of short pigtails on their heads, and the Chinese approved of this. 'The pigtails are very practical because they keep the hair out of their face,' one Chinese friend remarked. 'Why don't the others do the same?'

Only one team left Peking unhappy about their experience. The German callisthenic team had been victorious in all Chinese cities before arriving in Peking. According to protocol the Chinese must give a banquet for every delegation visiting Peking. The only chance they had to entertain the callisthenic team was at lunch on the day of an evening performance. The meal was held at the Big Peking Duck restaurant. The Germans, perhaps over-confident, ate and drank their way to their first defeat, which they later blamed on the luncheon invitation.

LEARNING CHINESE STYLE

The Chinese tried to help foreign parents resolve schooling problems for their children by opening an international elementary school in March, 1973. Until then parents could send their children only to embassy schools or Chinese kindergarten and nursery school. There they had Chinese classmates and learned the same lessons together.

An Italian friend told me about one of the lessons her son had learned in nursery school. He returned home from school one day and asked her to give him all the dirty handkerchiefs in the laundry. When she asked why, he said, 'Today my teacher taught us to help our mother by washing handkerchiefs.'

From the beginning the Chinese authorities at Fen Caodi, the new elementary school, indicated an awareness of the problems involved in teaching their ideology to foreigners. At a meeting of parents that took place in the Service Bureau, an official said, 'Since the students come from various countries, we will not teach the Chinese ideology and social system, because it may not be suitable for their countries. We will follow Chairman Mao's teaching that "We shall not impose on others" and will avoid teaching ideological matters.'

It was difficult to stick to this commitment as long as English was taught from textbooks used in Chinese schools. A typical text in the first-grade book read: 'Tom is an American boy. His father is a worker. His mother is a worker, too. Tom has a little sister. Tom's father and mother are out of work now. The family is poor. Tom cannot go to school. They live a hard life.' In addition, the pupils had to learn a vocabulary that consisted of such words as 'little red soldier', 'peasant', 'commune', and 'revolution'.

The teaching language in the school was Chinese, because the majority of children came from non-English speaking countries. Although Chinese attended the school, classes were not mixed. The only time Chinese and foreign children saw each other was during recreation periods.

A Canadian mother of two boys attending the school felt the Chinese educational experience was beneficial to her sons. She wrote:

> The school applied Chinese standards of discipline, which are strict. Foreign children did not seem to mind the Chinese rules about standing up when answering a question, greeting teachers when they entered the room, refraining from talking during class, resisting temptation to fight, etc. As applied to foreign children, Chinese discipline was characterised by understanding, encouragement and guidance, rather than by authoritarianism.*

The educational programme for elementary school children was different from that of foreign students who lived together with Chinese room mates at institutes in cities like Shanghai,

* 'A Chinese School and the Foreign Community: a Canadian family's experience in Peking' by Tama Yagai Copithorne in *Outlook 21*, Autumn 1976.

Nanking, Canton and Shenyang. In Peking we became friendly with German students who were attending the Peking Language Institute, which was opened in 1974 to students from thirty-seven countries. The students visited us on weekends and sometimes they invited me to visit them on the campus. There were separate dormitories for the Chinese and foreigners, but some foreigners had Chinese room mates.

The students' day began with a trumpet blast at 6 A.M., followed by news on the loudspeaker system. While foreigners turned over and tried to catch a little more sleep, the Chinese jumped out of bed, washed, and then gathered outside for morning sports. 'To strengthen the body' was an important part of their educational programme.

Although there was central heating in the dormitories, the rooms were draughty, and in winter students wore padded jackets and many layers of clothing in the classroom. Chinese and foreign students attended separate classes, but the canteen provided a meeting place for all students on campus.

The menu took into consideration the Chinese students' limited budget and so served soup, rice, steamed bread, vegetables, and soy-bean products. More hearty and expensive meat and chicken dishes were offered to the foreign students.

Plates and chopsticks were not provided, and so each student brought his own. They lined up cafeteria style, selected their food, and sat where they chose. The Chinese customarily ate in five minutes and then left, whereas the foreign students talked during their meal and were always the last to leave the dining hall.

After lunch the students returned to small and spartan rooms. Each room had two beds, a desk, a chair, and very little space to hang or store clothing. The Chinese had only one change of clothing and so the storage space was ample for them.

The communal shower had hot water only during certain hours of the day, and then it was full. The Chinese showered regularly and also used the hot water for washing their clothes.

One student described the shower as always looking like a laundry. The Chinese changed and washed their underwear daily and washed their cotton shoes and caps at least once a week.

The practice among the Chinese was to share the gifts of food received from home. When a Chinese and foreigner lived together the Chinese would accept a gift, such as tea or cigarettes, only when he could give something in return.

Every Chinese student who had extra money would send it home, rather than spend it on himself. His only extravagance in a month might be to go out to eat with six classmates. Each chipped in sixty fen a head for a five- or six-course meal.

Living habits were different and room mates took time getting used to each other. One Chinese room mate was so shy he dressed and undressed in the morning and evening under his covers. Another strung a clothes-line across the middle of the room and hung his drying laundry and clean clothes on it.

Conversations between room mates never involved politics, a subject Chinese, in general, refused to discuss. They might talk about their family and, if they grew close to their room mates, personal subjects, such as a girl friend, would be introduced.

For the most part, some foreign students told me, there was little interest in life abroad. On occasion a room mate asked, 'How many beggars do you have in your country?' or 'Do you have starvation at home?' These questions seemed to relate to the texts they were reading.

The foreign students had few complaints about the living conditions, but they objected strongly to being treated like children. At 10 P.M. the trumpet blew, signalling bedtime. When students came home late, the gatekeeper gave them a lecture. When they did not come to class a teacher checked to see if they were sick.

The feeling that people should be cared for and instructed in daily life was a national policy. We experienced this often on our train trips. The same announcement was broadcast every time a train approached a station : 'Take all of your things with you, do not forget anything, do not go to the toilet anymore, pay attention when you disembark.'

Independent thinking or expression were not a part of the educational system. Repetition and memorisation were the learning and teaching methods. To discuss a topic meant to confirm an already accepted principle and conclusion. To contest it was wrong.

A German student asked his Chinese room mate to correct the composition he had written about a factory where he had spent a few weeks working. The room mate's idea of correction was to introduce his own preconceived ideas into the composition.

For example, when the German wrote, 'I worked in a factory,' his room mate would write, 'I worked in a beautiful factory where the workers were following the revolutionary line of Chairman Mao. . . .' When the German said to his room mate, 'You never visited this factory. How do you know so much about it?' the Chinese replied confidently, 'Because this is true of all factories in China.'

'FOREIGN EXPERTS'

While foreigners in the diplomatic community had little contact with Chinese, 'foreign experts' worked with them daily. This was the title Chinese gave to all foreigners who were under contract with the government, either as teachers in institutes and universities, or as editors and translators in foreign-language publishing houses.

These foreigners fell into different categories, depending on the length of time they had spent in China and their ability to conform to the regulations guiding their lives. Many were 'old friends' who had arrived in China before and during the war years and had settled here. The Chinese had been generous to them. They earned much more than their fellow workers. Their full wage continued during sickness, when they were on holiday, and when they were too old to work regularly. After a three-year absence, one woman returned to find her entire salary waiting for her.

Their medical costs were taken care of by their work organisation and they were treated in the foreign section of the hospital, where the care and treatment is much better than in the Chinese section. Drivers picked them up to bring them to work, and cars with drivers were available at a nominal fee for private purposes. In summer their work organisation sometimes sent them on an all-expense-paid holiday to Peitaiho, the seaside resort, or to another city for a rest.

Many who returned to their native country for a visit found the adjustment so difficult that they hurried back to the security of China. One woman, who had lived in China thirty years, went home for a few months and came back saying, 'This is the country where I want to die. In the West it is a sentence to grow old. Here it is an honour.'

Although the foreign experts enjoyed material security, life was not always easy for them. During the Cultural Revolution every foreigner lived in uncertainty about his fate. In order to prove their loyalty to the Chinese, some over-reacted.

A journalist who was living in Peking at that time remembers seeing an American friend of the Chinese wearing more Mao buttons on his jacket than the Chinese. During the Cultural Revolution foreigners were visible in the front row at the demonstration in front of the British Embassy just before the Red Guards burned it down. Later, Red Guards accused two of the active participants at this demonstration of spying, and they were sent to prison for several years.

Coincidentally we encountered this couple in Lhasa, Tibet, the most difficult city for foreigners to visit in China, and their presence there meant they were back in good standing. But they went out of their way to avoid us. The Chinese had set the dining table for four, but they decided to eat their meals privately.

They behaved like many other foreign experts who were worried about having contact with the resident foreign community. One expert told me confidentially that the Chinese had warned her she would jeopardise her relationship with them if she maintained contacts with the foreign residents. Therefore she severed all ties with foreigners.

Those who did speak privately to foreigners were very careful about what they said and would not discuss Chinese politics. When they talked to visiting tourist delegations, they did so with the consent of the Chinese. After listening to an expert speak for an hour one foreigner commented, 'What he said could have come out of *Peking Review* or *China Reconstructs*,' two magazines the Chinese government published.

In spite of their daily contact with Chinese, these people led a lonely existence. When work was over, they went their separate ways. The experts lived in flats in the Friendship Hotel compound, where they did not dare to mingle with guests. On occasion we saw them at official functions or in the Friendship Store, where they stood out in their Chinese attire and only spoke with the Chinese staff.

The young foreign experts, who have a two- or three-year contract with the Chinese, were often not as cautious, grateful, or uncritical as the older set of expatriates who have made China their home. Many of them were young Maoists who had studied Mao's teachings abroad and were interested in seeing how they are practised.

One young man was working for a publishing house in Peking when the campaign against Teng Hsiao-ping was raging in the early part of 1976. Finding the campaign one-sided, he protested by putting up a picture of Teng on his working desk. The director called him into his office and asked him to take it down. He refused, saying he wanted to hear an explanation from the Teng side. Only after his colleagues secretly gave him a long written series of quotes from Teng, indicating that they were supporting him, did he take the picture down. More than a year later, when Teng was back in office, I heard that this man received a coloured autographed picture of Teng.

A twenty-three-year-old Australian teacher had an experience in China that I thought was impossible. While teaching at the Foreign Language Institute in Sian, she fell in love with a young Chinese, and they wanted to marry. Knowing that contact between Chinese and foreigners was carefully observed, I was amazed she could spend time with him.

Unofficial regulations prohibited a foreigner from marrying a Chinese. As soon as the school authorities heard about their involvement, they banished the young man to the north of the province and forbade him to write, meet, or phone her. In the meantime, the wilful young woman had sent a letter to the Foreign Minister requesting permission to marry.

When she received no answer to her letter, she asked Prime Minister Fraser, who was visiting China, to give a letter to Hua Kuo-feng. Fraser supported her request but received a firm no from the Chinese. Still, she did not give up hope.

A few months before her visa was to expire she and two Chinese girls were attacked by a madman wielding a cleaver. He fractured her skull and injured the other girls even more seriously. The Chinese paid for her parents to visit her, and at the same time she applied for an extension of her visa, saying she wanted to recuperate in China and couldn't go back to Australia before her hair grew.

The Chinese agreed, and after she recovered, they sent her to teach at the Shanghai Foreign Language Institute. Then she applied to the Shanghai Revolutionary Committee to marry. In the meantime, the Chinese had been telling the young man that she was no longer interested in marrying him, and she was hearing the same story about him not wanting to marry her.

She wrote more letters to the leadership, referring to Chou En-lai's statement, 'If China seeks foreign experts, they should be permitted to marry and live as Chinese.' While her application was pending, a French student in Shanghai, who had also fallen in love with a Chinese classmate, gave an interview to a French journalist and discussed the Chinese refusal to let them marry. This made front-page news in newspapers throughout the world, and after adverse international publicity the Chinese granted the French woman permission to marry. A short time later the Australian girl also received permission.

Had both women talked with foreigners who had married Chinese and remained in China they might have had second thoughts. One of my friends commented, 'No matter how long I live here, the Chinese will treat me as a foreigner. After thirty years I am still an outsider.'

He was married to a Chinese woman and worked as a language teacher at a university. They lived in a lovely old Chinese-style house they had bought eighteen years ago. The house was registered in the name of the Chinese son, because a foreigner cannot own property in China. Their neighbours were Chinese, but they had little contact with them, because there was a foreigner in the family. The wife's relatives had severed ties with her because of her husband, and he had little contact with foreigners because of his wife.

When he shopped in the Friendship Store his wife accompanied him, and the Chinese doorkeeper, who had the authority to stop her, let her pass. But she could never enter the store alone. When she was sick she went to the Chinese section of the hospital, where she had to wait a long time to be examined. When he was sick he went to the foreign section of the same hospital and was attended to immediately. When she went out alone to buy vegetables, she had to wait in line. When her husband was with her, they were sent to the head of the queue and were given the choice produce. When they rode on a bus together, passengers would rise to offer them seats. When she was alone, she had to stand. When they entered restaurants, they were ushered into a separate room to eat. When she was alone she stood and waited for a table to be free. His institute did not offer them paid holidays to Peitaiho because the hotel accommodated only foreigners.

Their children suffered the most. They went to Chinese school but their classmates would not visit them at home. When they were with their father they were treated as foreigners, and when they were with their mother or alone they were regarded as Chinese.

Living marginally in two worlds caused them psychological and personal problems. When they were older the only solution was to live separately from their parents. This was the only way they could have a life of their own and not suffer the stigma of having a foreign parent.

Chapter 6

Life in an Urban Community

NO LONGER A STRANGER

During that first year I felt like a stranger in Peking. The surroundings and way of life were different from anything I had ever known. The sights and sounds were new. The manner of speaking, thinking, and reacting was often confusing.

Rather than refuse a request, the Chinese would not respond to it. This frustrated me because I was accustomed to a direct answer. Sometimes they gave answers that were evasive. When I went to a local tailor to ask if he would make a simple apron for me, he said, 'Now we make only pants.' The next tailor said, 'We only repair garments.' Another said, 'That is too complicated to do.' Fed up, I finally asked the fourth tailor, 'Will you make anything for me?' He said quietly, looking down, 'Why don't you go to the Friendship Store tailoring department? They make everything.' No one was willing to tell me that local tailors were not permitted to make clothes for foreigners. They were refusing me without saying 'no,' but I had missed this point.

Laughter often left me perplexed because it had so many meanings. Was something funny, embarrassing, or sad? Was the person afraid, angry, or nervous? After I proposed a solution to a problem, and the Chinese laughed, did this mean they agreed or disagreed?

It took me a long time to understand Chinese humour. Slapstick appealed to them. I had seen this on stage and at home. When I told Mr Yu to make less food because Gerd was gaining weight, and then showed him in pantomime what Gerd looked like before and now, he laughed and called everyone into the kitchen to enjoy the joke.

A foreign teacher told me about an experience in her classroom that made all the Chinese laugh. A student was writing
a phrase on the blackboard, and suddenly the entire class burst
out in laughter. She asked them what was funny. One girl
replied, giggling, 'That student is so tall and his writing is so
small.' The naiveté and subtlety of their humour left me with
the same blank expressions they had on their faces when I
told them a simple joke.

What Chinese said was not necessarily what they meant.
At the end of a visit to a factory or commune, our host would
always say, 'We would like your criticism.' Once I made a
few suggestions in a factory, and these were received with
giggles and cold stares. The next time I praised their efforts,
and this was obviously the correct response.

Direct criticism of a Chinese was insulting. When an American friend gave a cocktail party for forty people and the
cook made too much food, she told him he should make less
food the next time. He replied defensively, 'You invited too
few people this time.'

The Chinese form of directness sometimes surprised me. For
example, people often asked me, 'How old are you?' When a
grey-haired friend responded that she was forty-nine, the next
question was, 'How old is your husband?' who was very youthful looking. When she said he was fifty, the Chinese replied,
'But you look so much older than he does.'

When I returned after shopping, often someone in my
household would ask, 'How much did that cost?' Once I overheard the remark, 'That was too much to pay.'

Another time, when I came home with what I thought was
a lovely vase, everyone giggled instead of praising it. I didn't
understand this, so I asked a Chinese friend if she liked my
vase. Laughing, she said, 'That is a man's chamber pot.' Everyone else was too embarrassed to tell me this.

The Chinese were very modest, and often they disguised
this modesty in phrases that confused me. When I thanked
Mr Gu for helping me and he responded, 'That is my duty,' I

thought, mistakenly, that this was a complaint. When I com-plimented Mr Yu on his cooking and he said, 'I did not do it well,' I didn't know at first if he felt he could do it better or if he were just being modest.

It took me a long time to learn how to ask a question and what questions to ask. Once I asked Mr Gu where he lived. He replied, 'Ten minutes from here.' 'Where?' I said inno-cently. A giggle and an awkward silence followed. I wondered what I had done wrong, and then it occurred to me that there might be some regulation against his giving me this informa-tion.

Through my working experience in Washington I had learned how to weave my way through difficulties, but China imposed a feeling of impotence on me. Situations controlled me and I had no impact on them. The helplessness I suffered the first year often made me consider giving up and returning to a society where I felt at home. Something inside me, how-ever, refused to admit defeat.

During that painful breaking-in period it never occurred to me that I was creating my own adjustment problems by trying to do things my way instead of accepting the Chinese method.

During our second year a subtle and gradual development began to take place in me. Without realising it, I was changing from being impatient and wilful to becoming more tolerant.

An incident in the Bank of China first made me aware of this change. While I was sitting in the bank waiting for my cheque to be cashed, a well-dressed Western diplomat briskly walked up to the counter and said he wanted to cash some money. There were already several customers ahead of him and I knew that such transactions often took as long as thirty minutes.

Several minutes later my number was called and I went to the counter. The diplomat, who had been sighing and pacing back and forth almost from the time he entered the bank, followed me. When I picked up my money he shouted at no one in particular, 'I have been here a long time and don't have all day.' His outburst met with silence, as though no one had heard him.

When I saw the look of frustration on his face I remembered how often I had felt this way. I had learned there was nothing I could ever do to hurry up the Chinese, who worked at a slow, regular pace. Whenever I showed irritation in a store because the clerk was a study in slow motion, she remained calm and unhurried, and so I learned through experience that patience was the only answer.

When I first arrived I resented the preferential treatment Chinese reserved for foreigners. I thought it was unfair in local stores to be served before the people who had been there earlier. Once I refused to go to the head of the queue, and, to my surprise, the queue suddenly stepped behind me.

Another time a woman who was being waited on objected when the clerk pushed her aside and asked me what I wanted. I said I could wait, but the other people in the queue shouted at this and forced her out of line. I was extremely embarrassed and apologetic about the situation I had created.

But the experience of an English friend helped me to understand why we were given preferential treatment. While buying tomatoes at a local stand, he overheard a man behind him say, 'Why is the foreign devil given priority?' Another man replied, 'If he is a foreign devil the clerk should wait on him and get rid of him quickly. If he is a foreign friend he should be given priority.'

Through my refusal to accept the traditional custom of special treatment to foreigners, a Chinese friend told me, I was insulting them. This came as a startling revelation to me.

As my understanding deepened, my attachment to Peking and the Chinese grew. I wanted to see how they lived and meet their families, but such contact, outside our home, was forbidden. I always hoped these rules would be relaxed because I wanted to have a more personal relationship with the people around me.

THE INVITATION TO VISIT CHAO YANG

During our first year, Gerd wrote a letter to the Information Department asking to spend some time living with a Chinese family in a city and in the countryside. The request went unanswered, but Gerd persisted, and repeated his wish many times.

Finally we were permitted to visit a Peking family for three hours, but this was hardly enough time for us to see how people lived in a community.

It wasn't until our third year that the Information Department responded to our request. It arranged for us to spend a week in Chao Yang, Shanghai's first workers' residential area, where no other foreigner had spent more than a few hours.

When we arrived we had our first disappointment. Our Chinese hosts apologetically told us that Chao Yang had no suitable accommodation for us. They asked if we would mind staying in Shanghai's Peace Hotel. We agreed and soon realised that the programme planned for us was so full that we didn't mind sleeping in a hotel for foreigners.

SURROUNDINGS

Chao Yang looked at first glance like a typical suburb, one which could have belonged to many cities in the world. The only difference was that bicycles, instead of cars, occupied the road.

When we took our first walk through town, I was struck by its physical difference from Peking. The commercial section was centrally located and built with the idea of making shopping easier for its seventy thousand residents. Everything from a bank and post office to a department store, cinema, and other facilities were within a block of each other. In Peking these shops and services were more spread out and looked drabber. Undoubtedly it was also the grass and trees, instead of dry, parched Peking soil, that made Chao Yang more cheerful and pretty.

After passing the shopping complex we came to a shop that collected waste materials. In Peking I had seen only three-wheeled bicycles parked on street corners, buying scrap from customers, and I was interested in seeing what kinds of things the Chao Yang shop bought.

When we stepped inside, we saw a few customers waiting for stacks of newspapers to be weighed. The clerk stopped what she was doing and said, 'We buy everything.' On the wall was a price list for feathers, cloth, shoes, jute bags, glass, aluminium, hair, and woollen goods.

Here, as in Peking, much road and building construction was taking place. Both men and women participated in the work. A team was digging up a road in order to put pipes underground. A new storey was being added to the neighbourhood hospital and a five-storey apartment building was under construction.

Red banners were flying in front of the new Neighbourhood Workers College, which had its official opening on the day we passed by. The booming of drums and the clashing of cymbals accompanied processions of people walking toward the college.

In each group the future students, who were 'barefoot doctors (paramedics), workers, teachers, and housewives, could be distinguished from their friends, colleagues, and family members, who were walking with them. The students carried red paper flowers, and rolled-up red certificates.

Everyone was laughing and enjoying himself on the sunny autumn day. People appeared to be more outgoing and better dressed than in Peking. The women wore fitted pants that had no room for layers, and their blouses were tailored. More people showed off bright prints and stripes. The jacket pockets had special stitching, a Shanghai fashion that was to reach Peking two years later.

Many in the procession were wearing leather shoes rather than the black cotton ones that were still very common in

Peking. Hair was longer and women looked much more attractive. The variety in appearance and the relaxed, friendly atmosphere contrasted sharply with Peking.

After leaving the processions behind I saw a typical Peking sight. Two women wearing white surgical masks and caps were sweeping the streets at a pace that seemed extremely slow. A few blocks farther a woman sat on a small sweeping machine, brushing the streets with a rotating broom. I had seen these machines in Peking and wondered how long it would take before they would replace the manual sweepers.

The residential area was lined with trees. Once again I thought how pretty this community was. It was a welcome change from Peking not to have high grey walls obscuring everything. New five-storey apartment houses in the background towered over old two- and three-storey apartment houses.

Within the residential area was a local food market, which was open only between 5:30 and 7:30 A.M and 2:30 and 5 P.M., according to the sign posted on the door. The hours were arranged, I thought, to accommodate the working people.

At the end of the street was a park with green meadows, trees, a pond, and even an empty outdoor swimming pool, which I had never seen in a park before. As in Peking, old men and women were relaxing and doing exercises and traditional sports under the trees.

After leaving the park we returned to the residential area and walked through the yards of apartment buildings. Bamboo rods, serving as clothes-lines, hung between tree branches. There was no litter on the ground and the surroundings looked as though the people were proud of where they lived. Balconies were full of plants and each building had a carefully groomed garden with chrysanthemums and dahlias in bloom. It was a luxury to see flowers grown merely for beauty. In Peking we only saw sunflowers, which were planted because their seeds contained valuable oil.

OUR HOSTESS MRS CHEN

At the entrance to a three-storey apartment house, we saw a round-faced, sturdily-built woman standing and knitting. When she saw us, she hastily put aside the half-finished blue sweater, gave a tug to her grey jacket, and straightened out her matching pants. This was Mrs Chen, who was our hostess that day. She shook our hands and greeted us, then led us through a dark hallway to the ground-floor one-room apartment where she lived.

A tall, good-looking man was waiting for us. This was her son, who lived next door with his family. Pointing to two hard-back wooden chairs, the finest in the room, Mrs Chen asked us to sit down and then went to get tea. This gave me a moment to glance around.

A double bed occupied about half of the floor space. The rest of the room contained three stools, two benches, three locked wooden trunks piled on top of each other, and two chests of drawers, one with a mirror and the other with a carved edge.

Mrs Chen returned with the tea and sat down in a wicker chair that was just large enough to contain her bulk. She then pulled it closer to the square table we were sitting around. Noticing that my eyes had settled on one of the chests in the room, she said, 'That was the first piece of furniture we bought.' And then she started to tell us the story of her life.

In 1952 the Chens were one of the first families selected to live in the new workers' residential area, which provided workers with housing and shopping conveniences near their factories. Like the other thousand selected families, the Chens came from 'most crowded and difficult circumstances', Mrs Chen said.

At first Mrs Chen told us that she was reluctant to accept the offer because she had no furniture and felt that a family could not move into an empty flat. But her factory persuaded her to buy furniture later. And so she, her husband, and their young son moved into the flat with only a cotton quilt and wooden board. 'Now we have two quilts for this season and another two for winter,' Mrs Chen said proudly, and I could see that the room had no space for another piece of furniture.

Mrs Chen described how difficult her life had been before the Liberation. 'We lived in a thatched hut,' she said. 'When it rained outside, it rained inside too.' Her parents were unemployed and at the age of eight she went to work in a silk factory where she said, the machines were so high she had to stand on a stool.

When she was twenty-five the Japanese-Chinese War forced the factory to close. Soon after, her house was bombed and the family moved to a shelter for homeless people. Their new quarters had a mud floor, and everyone lived together in one room covered with reeds.

'Poor people married poor people,' she explained. She said her parents chose her husband, assuring her, 'He is honest.' Mrs Chen met her future husband on their wedding day, when the matchmaker introduced them in the refugee home and pronounced them married.

They were too poor to invite friends to the ceremony, and only an aunt was present. 'The only gifts I received were two pairs of shoes from my sister,' Mrs Chen said. Two years later, after having given birth to a son, the factory opened and she went back to work.

Until Mrs Chen mentioned her son, he had been sitting silently and attentively next to her. Then he began talking, like his mother, in an animated way. 'We moved here when I was only twelve years old. Then my mother worked and my father was unemployed. I had never used sanitary facilities before and found them interesting.'

In primary school, he wrote compositions about how happy he was to be living in new housing with lovely surroundings. After graduating from middle school in 1962, some of his classmates went to the university and others were assigned to work. He went for a year to a technical school run by the Bureau of Chemical Industries before starting work in a pharmaceutical factory, where he was presently employed.

In 1968 his future wife, who had just completed four years at the College of Chemical Industry, was assigned to his workshop in the factory. 'At first we worked together and discussed production. Through work we got to know each other better. We got along well and worked hard. Sometimes we took walks in a park. I asked her to visit my house and she invited me to visit her house. Boys take the initiative and I asked her to marry me. She was shy but agreed, with the consent of her parents,' he said.

Before marrying, he gave his future wife a watch and she saved money to buy a set of furniture. 'I contributed more money toward the furniture, which cost six hundred yuan, because my family earned more than hers,' the son added.

Two years after meeting, they married. There was no special marriage ceremony or dress. They went to the office of the Revolutionary Committee in Chao Yang to fill out a form expressing their intention to marry, and had a physical examination. Later they picked up the marriage certificate.

The Chens celebrated the occasion by inviting fellow workers for tea and candy, and twenty close friends and relatives for dinner. The father, relatives, and retired friends prepared the food and the banquet lasted two hours. Guests brought gifts of a thermos bottle, clothing, bedding and sheets, and their parents gave them quilts.

The Chens had a three-day marriage leave, which they spent at home in the new apartment the Housing Management Bureau had assigned them. It was located in a different apartment block from where the parents lived, and the older Mrs Chen was unhappy about this arrangement. She wanted the family to live closer together. Later, when Mrs Chen learned that her next-door neighbour was going to move out, she applied to the housing bureau on behalf of her son.

Although both families had separate flats, it was as though they were living together as a single unit. The older Mrs Chen was in charge of the money, amounting to a combined income of 193 yuan every month. The son earned 51 yuan and his wife 58 yuan. Mrs Chen had retired from the factory at the regulation age of fifty and her husband at sixty and both were receiving 70 per cent of their final wage, amounting to 42 yuan each.

We were interested in how Mrs Chen spent the money each month and she was only too pleased to tell us in very great detail. Rent for the two rooms cost 6.30 yuan, electricity 1.50 yuan, running water five fen a head, gas for the stove 4 yuan. 'Our gas is high because we have to cook a great deal for the baby,' Mrs Chen explained.

There was no charge for heating because the building had no heating. The average temperature in winter was about 10 degrees C. 50 degrees F., although at midnight, Mrs Chen mentioned, the temperature could go down to minus 2 degrees C. 29 degrees F. 'But we have plenty of quilts to keep us warm,' she added.

The four Chens spent about 15 yuan a head for food, while the baby's food bill was 25 yuan because she needed glucose, milk, and cod liver oil. On holidays and when relatives came, Mrs Chen pointed out, the food costs would be higher.

The young couple ate one meal daily in the factory, where the most expensive dish cost 20 fen. For breakfast they all had rice made the night before or fried dough bought in a store. At dinnertime the older Chens preferred eating more vegetables than meat, 'for health reasons,' Mrs Chen explained.

Each month the daughter-in-law gave her parents ten yuan and the young couple put eight yuan into a Mutual Aid Fund in the factory. This fund was set up for factory workers who needed money for an emergency or to buy a necessary article, such as a bicycle. Then they paid it back as soon as possible. 'If I want to buy a television set, I must save for it myself,' the Chen son pointed out. Once a year they were given back the money they had put into the fund.

They did not have to worry about medical expenses, because,

as factory workers, they were entitled to free medical care. The neighbourhood health station would take care of their minor complaints and the Neighbourhood Hospital or District Hospital would treat the serious problems.

From the remaining money, which added up to around 80 yuan, Mrs Chen put 25 yuan into a family savings account, from which anyone could withdraw money when he wanted. Two years ago the son and his wife had withdrawn money to buy a radio for themselves, and this had caused a family quarrel Mrs Chen was eager to air.

She sat up in her chair and, looking like a scolding teacher, she began, 'I have different opinions from the young couple. I had a radio and told them they could use mine whenever they wanted. They refused and then bought their own for 135 yuan.' Her voice started to rise with excitement and she talked faster. 'Two months after they bought it, the price was reduced and a radio of the same quality now costs 90 yuan.'

I wondered how often the son had heard his mother repeat this story, but he said nothing. The smile on his face, however, revealed embarrassment.

'Last year we bought a sewing machine and now we are saving for a television set, costing 300 yuan. We have 400 yuan in our savings,' Mrs Chen said. The pleased look on her face and her tone of voice told me she would decide when to buy the television.

We had visited a Peking family with about the same basic costs per person as the Chens, but they had four workers and earned considerably more money. Already they owned a television set, sewing machine, and camera. Now they were saving for more furniture and were putting money aside for their parents, who lived far away. They had to prepare for the long and expensive journey they would have to make when their parents died.

While Mrs Chen was adding more water to our cups to freshen our tea leaves, her husband appeared for the first time. Mr Chen was a slight and timid man. He was wearing a blue apron over a brown knit sweater and had obviously just come out of the kitchen. 'I never had a chance to meet foreign friends before, and would be happy if you would eat with us,' he said quietly. We accepted the invitation at once and then he disappeared.

I heard the sound of chopping and smelled food cooking since we entered the Chen flat. I asked if I could visit the kitchen. It was located at the end of the dark hall and was shared by the two Chen families and a neighbour on the ground floor. The kitchen was equipped with three gas burners, each with two flames, one wash basin, a cupboard, and a lot of cooking utensils. Other floors had the same communal arrangement for three families, and each family knew what the other was eating daily.

Next to the kitchen was the communal bathroom, which had only a toilet. When the older Chens wanted to bathe, they could go to a public bathhouse in the neighbourhood. The younger Chens could shower at work.

Mrs Chen, who was obviously used to monopolising the conversation, spoke about her husband when we returned to the flat. He loved to cook, although she occasionally cooked for the family. He took walks in the park, napped after lunch, and went to the cinema. In addition he did some gardening work on the patch of land belonging to their apartment house.

When we commented on how beautiful the garden was, Mrs Chen said, 'We plant flowers in the garden instead of vegetables, which would need fertiliser, and that is unhealthy. Vegetables are cheap anyway,' she added.

While we were talking a pretty, well-dressed young woman walked in. She was the twenty-nine-year-old daughter-in-law, and she was wearing narrowly-cut blue pants and a freshly pressed matching jacket. Underneath the jacket the collar of a white blouse was folded over a grey cashmere sweater. She, like her husband, had on black leather shoes. The older Chinese wore cotton shoes.

The younger Mrs Chen had just returned from the factory. She excused herself for a minute, and came back carrying her eighteen-month-old daughter. The baby was dressed in a green-and-yellow knit sweater and green pants her grandmother had made. A squeaking plastic doll attracted her attention at once, and this gave the mother a chance to talk.

She was a shy woman. When I asked her if she wanted any more children, she said, 'I will think about that in three or four years.' Then she added, almost as an afterthought, 'More children are too much trouble.'

The arrival of Mr Chen, who carried steaming dishes, turned the conversation to food. The first of the eight pork, vegetable, fish, and egg dishes was on the table and it was time to eat. The food was delicious and every time I complimented a dish I was rewarded with another heaped spoonful, so my plate was never empty.

During the meal we rarely saw Mr Chen, and then, just before finishing, he rushed in out of breath with a plateful of white bread. 'I heard that foreigners like this and went out to buy it,' he said. I had never seen this kind of bread in local stores and imagined that someone had gone to our hotel to pick it up.

When lunch was over the younger Chens invited us to visit their flat next door. The ornately carved matching double bed, wardrobe, chest of drawers, and night table contrasted sharply with their parents' simple furniture.

A neon light was hanging from the ceiling. The night table had mostly technical dictionaries on it. A rubber goose was on top of a wardrobe. The main table was covered with a white tablecloth and pictures of the wife and child, protected under a sheet of glass. The controversial radio was in a yellow plastic case on a table.

The typical Chinese bric-a-brac I had often seen in Peking stores was scattered throughout the room. There were plastic flowers, a red-and-white glass penguin, and a plastic pine tree with shells in the background. Their favourite object was a small crane made of real feathers, and this piece had a glass cover.

The walls were decorated with a Mao poem, an embroidered picture of Mao playing ping pong, a poster of a young peasant girl, and travel pictures of the Nanking bridge and Hangchow lake. When we asked if they had visited these places, the young Mrs Chen said quietly that she had travelled to Sian, Peking, Soochow, Hangchow, and Nanking during the Cultural Revolution.

The younger Chens worked on different eight-hour shifts in a factory that produced raw materials for medicine. They told us of the benefits they received as factory workers: a 3-yuan transport allowance each month, which they saved because they preferred to bicycle the twenty-five minutes to work daily; work suits, shoes, face masks; free hair cuts once a month, free showers, free birth control pills and contraceptives, free medical care for themselves and a 50 per cent reduction for their daughter; a day care centre, which they did not use because their daughter was looked after by the grandmother.

They had one day free a week and enjoyed spending it with their daughter. Sometimes they would take walks in town and occasionally they would go shopping in the department stores in Shanghai where the choice was larger than in Chao Yang.

Twice a month the younger Mrs Chen visited her parents, who lived 20-minutes away from the apartment by bus. Her father worked as a cameraman and her mother had already retired from an embroidery workshop.

We had been with the Chens most of the day, so when the older Mrs Chen entered the room and asked if the younger couple had answered all our questions we took this as a sign that it was time to leave. While we were shaking Mrs Chen's hand and thanking her for her hospitality, she said, 'I was thin before, now I am fat. I have no worries.'

THE WOMEN'S LEAGUE AS MEDIATOR

The older Mrs Chen had mentioned that she belonged to the Women's League in Chao Yang. We met its director, Mrs Li, a forceful, outspoken woman like Mrs Chen. Mrs Li proudly told us about the League's family planning successes in Chao Yang.

'As a result of our effort, women between twenty-five and thirty-five have an average of two children, and those between thirty-five and forty-five have around three children. Having too many children is not good for the health,' she said.

But not everyone listened to the League propaganda. 'There are still some people influenced by the ideas of Confucius, who preached male domination and superiority,' Mrs Li explained. And she told us the tale of a woman with two daughters who did not want another child, but whose husband and mother-in-law insisted that she try to have a boy. 'In the past women wanted sons who would take care of them in their old age,' Mrs Li said. The League stepped in, talked with the mother-in-law and had the husband's factory talk with him, and settled the dispute.

Although Mrs Li did not discuss the persuasion technique, I had heard in Peking that teachers who wanted to have a child had to request permission from their department heads, who in turn consulted their superiors. If the request was granted, the woman would be given permission to become pregnant during that year. Those who had children without permission were criticised.

The Women's League also became involved in resolving marital disputes. Mrs Li told us about a couple who had been quarrelling for one year because 'the husband had ideas of male domination.' The wife was the only daughter in the family and visited her parents often. Sometimes she had no time to do housework and the husband, who refused to do household chores, complained, 'You cannot leave the housework for me to do.' She replied, 'Men and women are equal.'

The Women's League criticised his Confucian idea and settled the problem. 'Now the husband also does housework,' Mrs Li said rather smugly.

When young people wanted to marry much before the government-recommended marriage age of twenty-five for girls and twenty-seven for boys, the Women's League was once again called in. If the two refused to change their minds, the League consulted the factory, school, and family, and finally the younger people had to agree.

I was surprised to learn that everything from conception to marital problems could become a community concern and no one seemed to object.

UPBRINGING AND EDUCATION

The younger Chens were fortunate to have someone at home to take care of their daughter until she reached school age. Other families had to put their babies into a day care centre until they were eighteen months old, then into nursery school for the next two years, followed by kindergarten until they were six and a half years old. Removing babies at such a young age from family life and the home must have been difficult for many parents. From the time I arrived in China I noticed that children under six are the favourites in the Chinese society. It first showed in their ready-made clothing, which was more expensive than that which their parents wore. The second thing that struck me was that children seldom cried. It took me a long time to discover that the reason was they were never left alone. The grandmother constantly fondles, touches, and carries the child. She conducts a continuing con-versation with him regardless of his age or ability to talk or understand. In the family he is the centre of attention and can do what he wants.

I had noticed that spanking was not the usual method of discipline. On one occasion I saw a mother strike her young child in a store and another customer intervened, soothed the child's feelings, and rebuked the mother. Education, not physical discipline, is the Chinese method of training the child.

After seeing how indulged the children were, I was amazed to see how obedient the children were in the kindergarten we visited in Chao Yang. They were sitting up straight and looking attentive, instead of squirming and talking, or even crying, as I expected from children of this age.

The picture in front of the class showed a tug of war, with the losers on the ground being picked up by the winners. After the teacher asked the class if they knew what the picture meant, she said, 'The lesson is to help each other and to love each other.' Everyone then repeated the lesson several times.

In another classroom young children dressed in eye-catching blue-and-white sailor shirts, dresses with sewn-on embroidered figures, and corduroy pants came running up to us, shouting, 'Welcome aunt, welcome uncle,' a typical greeting to foreign guests. Then they took our hands and led us round the room. The children had many plastic and wooden toys, worthy of a model kindergarten class. The poise and confidence of the children astounded me, especially because my foreign face often frightened children in Peking.

In the third classroom the children, dressed in Tibetan and Mongolian costumes, sang and danced for us. They performed like dolls, but their robot-like programmed movements disturbed me. What I missed was the spontaneous, or even silly, behaviour I associate with children under six.

Later, when I asked a Chinese friend why children appeared so serious, he said, 'From an early age children are instilled with the idea that they must be responsible members of society. Workers, peasants, and soldiers are their heroes, and there is no place for lessons without a political meaning.'

In one classroom four children were standing at a table with a basin in the middle, washing towels. 'They are learning about the dignity of doing physical labour,' the teacher commented. In every classroom we had visited in China, the lesson was the same. By the time students graduated from middle school at the age of seventeen or eighteen they were prepared to go to work in a factory or in the countryside for an indefinite period of time. Students did not choose jobs, they were assigned them by the government. When I asked children from six to sixteen what they wanted to do after they graduated, everyone gave me the same answer. 'I will go wherever the government sends me and do whatever job the government assigns me.'

In Peking I had the most difficult time convincing a Chinese friend that I had applied for a job after graduating from college and been accepted. 'If the government did not assign you work, then your father probably arranged for you to have a good job,' she said. She was obviously reflecting the method sometimes used in China, but never discussed.

THE TREASURED MEMBERS OF SOCIETY

In Chao Yang the only time one has a choice of work is after retirement, when there are many volunteer jobs for people like the Chens. The community relied on retired workers to serve many different functions.

When we visited the children's centre, 'Welcome to Mr Wang, old retired worker' was written on the blackboard at the entrance gate. The centre was open to primary and middle school students after school, and retired people ran it. Children could play ping pong, read books, and listen to old people, like Mr Wang, tell stories about the past.

On the day we visited the centre he was sitting in front of a full classroom of students, who had to strain to hear his quiet voice. 'You students are lucky. At seventeen and eighteen you are in middle school. When I was nineteen I was a beggar. My family had been beggars for three generations. Six out of eight members in my family died before Liberation.'

As Mr Wang spoke his voice grew in strength and became

more excited. 'We had no house to live in. Our home was a pit. In cold weather I covered my body with straw.'

Suddenly a student in the audience interrupted him and shouted, 'We shall never forget class bitterness and we shall always remember our suffering.' Then all of her classmates repeated the same phrase, which was the lesson they learned that day.

A recently retired man described another role the old people play in Chao Yung. 'We educate children from childhood about the glory of turning in the things they find. To keep things is sinful.'

He told us about a fourth-grade pupil who had found a watch in a theatre and handed it in to the management. Later the old people told the teacher about the child's deed and posted signs in classrooms and in the neighbourhood praising this girl for her behaviour.

After hearing so much about the girl's good deed we asked about crime in Chao Yang. Seven people had committed minor crimes such as stealing or fighting. Three of them had reformed themselves and were already active members of Chao Yang, again, we were told.

In the case of petty theft, when the offence is the first one, the case is settled in the neighbourhood, and this is not referred to the Public Security Bureau, which handles serious cases. 'It is the job of parents, community officials, and retired people to work together and educate the offender,' a leader in Chao Yang said.

The old people tell the person that he is born into a new society and that he does not appreciate it. Then they might ask him to write a pledge that he will not steal again. A retired man said, 'It is not good to discriminate against the offender when he tries to reform himself. Sometimes it is necessary to point out his shortcomings, but he should be praised for his good deeds and be given work.'

On Thursday the old people were called on once again to work with the young. It was clean-up day in Chao Yang, and from 6 A.M. until the time people went to work they cleaned windows of their homes, swept streets and sidewalks, and tidied up their surroundings.

In front of the department store employees and staff, who were dressed in work clothes, washed floors and windows and did gardening and raking. Near them a class of kindergarten children stood holding pink flags in their hands with slogans written on them. 'Pay attention to hygienic work.' 'Don't spit on streets.' 'Keep the surroundings clean.' 'Pay attention to drinking water.' 'Throw things in trash baskets.' 'Everyone must take part in wiping out pests.'

The Thursday clean-up was a community-wide activity, involving occasional house inspections. If a flat did not meet the hygiene standards, the neighbours would come in and 'educate' the family. If old or sick people were alone, children helped to do housework.

During Mrs Chen's free time we saw her at the Chao Yang cultural centre, singing in a choir. Older people played chess there and young workers and students used the centre for sports and music activities.

One retired worker told us, with tears in his eyes, 'Before Liberation we were treated like dirt. After Liberation we have been valued like a treasure.'

Chapter 7

Life on a Commune

We had visited many communes during our stay in China, and I was always sorry when our brief two- or three-hour tour came to an end. I enjoyed the countryside, the peace, the simple life, and the openness and warmth of the peasants. Usually they received us in their one-storey homes, which were made of stone and clay and had two or three sparsely furnished rooms. Chickens ran freely in the courtyards and sties had been built for privately-owned pigs. Often the family had a small plot of land not far from the house. There they grew vegetables for their private consumption. I yearned to spend time in these surroundings and leave the crowded city life behind.

After our Chao Yang experience Gerd renewed a long-standing request he had made to live on a commune. He was interested in comparing city life to peasant life. It wasn't until our last spring in Peking that we received permission from the Information Department to live with the Hua Hsi Production Brigade, located between Nanking and Shanghai.

THE SURPRISE OF HUA HSI

As soon as the Information Department approved of our travel plans, everything proceeded like clockwork. We took an overnight train to Wushi, a beautiful southern city located on Lake Taihu. There we were met at the railroad station by a man from China Travel Service, who recommended we spend a few days sightseeing 'to rest up' for our commune experience. I was eager to go directly to the brigade, but knew that a recommendation in China should be followed. Two days later we finally started on the one and a half hour car journey to Hua Hsi. The drive took us through hilly green countryside with rural housing, similar to what I had seen on other communes.

We then turned off the road and stopped in front of a group of five whitewashed row houses that looked newly built. I couldn't believe my eyes. I had never seen this kind of housing in China before, and did not envision that two-storey homes with balconies existed in the countryside.

'This is your home,' our China Travel guide said as a smiling welcoming committee walked out of the house clapping. This was the customary way the Chinese greeted foreign guests, and we responded in the appropriate manner by clapping also. Our interpreter Mr Gu, who had accompanied us, made the introductions.

I was so excited that I did not listen to the names and titles and missed even that of our hostess. She had black sparkling eyes, a short boyish hair cut which looked becoming on her, and a bright warm smile showing off perfect white teeth.

Taking my hand she started to show me through the newly-built house she and her husband and in-laws had moved into the month before. It had six rooms plus a tiny kitchen located in an alcove off the living room. The kitchen had a three-burner stone stove heated from below with sticks and straw piled in a corner. Adjoining it was a cramped pantry where two men were chopping food.

I assumed these were brigade members but later learned that the county guest house had sent three of their staff—a cook, his apprentice, and a housekeeper—to take care of us during our stay. There were no charges for the many courtesies we received, except for the food, which, according to our final bill, cost two yuan a day for each of us, but only one yuan for Mr Gu.

During our stay the in-laws went to live with other children on the brigade in order to make room for our party. Mr Gu, the China Travel guide, and our driver occupied a ground-floor room that contained three cots. We stayed in an upstairs room belonging to our twenty-six-year-old hostess and her husband, who had moved across the hall to the in-laws' bedroom.

On our floor there was also a dining room and a bathroom, which had no running water and resembled no bathroom I had ever seen before. It contained about a dozen bright orange lacquer buckets, which served a variety of purposes. We could wash our feet in one, our hands in another and our clothes in a third. There were two round buckets with lids which were to be our toilets, and two deep oval wooden tubs for bathing. A row of thermos bottles was lined up along the entire length of one wall, and our housekeeper explained, 'That is your bath water.' There were also two white enamel basins with soap and towels next to them.

When I walked into our bedroom I was overwhelmed by the amount of massive furniture cramped into so little space. It all had a red lacquer finish, like the door, and was ornately carved. The double bed had stone flowers and birds embedded in its wooden frame. At first I could not see the top of the bed because it was concealed behind red silk embroidered curtains. Our hostess then pulled aside the curtains and told me to sit on the bed. I liked its firmness and with the curtains drawn and the canopy overhead I felt as though I were in a cosy house.

The rest of the room was cluttered with bamboo chairs, cupboards, trunks stacked on top of each other and a desk in front of the window, which opened onto a balcony. The books, carefully arranged on the desk, looked as though they had been chosen especially for our visit: *The Thoughts of Mao*, works of Lenin, a sociology book, and a volume of short stories about Chinese heroes.

The balcony was the part of the room I liked most. In the following days, I would stand there early in the morning, watching the peasants walk by on their way to the fields. And often I wished I could join them.

Pictures of Mao decorated the walls and the familiar assortment of plastic flowers, a wooden clock, and other bric-a-brac
was scattered about.

After the house tour, our hostess disappeared and the
housekeeper invited us to sit down to a lunch of fish and local
specialities. I was disappointed that we ate our first meal alone,
but later we ate with other families. Lunch was followed by
the usual rest period and then our intensive programme began.

Our fourteen-hour day was full of discussions, visits, and
evening entertainment. Meanwhile, our hostess and her husband were busy in the fields. They left the house at the crack
of dawn (around five thirty) and didn't return from the fields
until six thirty, except for a one-hour breakfast break and
two hours off at lunchtime. After the evening activity we all
came home exhausted. There was only time to exchange a
few words before our housekeeper emptied the thirteen thermos bottles into our tubs and I could relax in the luxury of the
only hand-poured tub I had had in my life.

TOURING THE BRIGADE

The Vice-Chairman of the Revolutionary Committee, Mr Wu,
was our principal guide during our visit. He was surprisingly
young, only twenty-nine, for the high position he held. It
seemed as though there was nothing he did not know or
could not answer, and when he spoke he usually had a cigarette
burning in his nicotine-stained fingers.

Mr Wu told us that Hua Hsi Production Brigade was one of
twenty-six brigades belonging to the Hua Sih Commune. It
was made up of 258 families, and had a total population of
1,000 but a work force of only 450 people. The brigade's main
work was to grow wheat and rice. It also raised pigs, geese,
ducks, fish, chicken, and rabbits; grew vegetables and fruit,
and maintained workshops that produced small farm tools and
simple machine parts for state factories.

Mr Wu's introductory speech sounded like many we had

heard on other communes. 'Before Liberation poor peasants lived on this land and landlords exploited them. Some of the year they had to eat pig and dog food and survive from wild plants.

'In the past eleven years peasants, through their struggle and toil, transformed this poor soil into rich fertile land. This brigade moved over one million cubic feet of earth, levelled 57 hills, filled in 48 old creeks, erased 104 footpaths and built 3,000 feet of underground canals in an eleven-year period.

'The toughest years on the brigade were between 1964–1970, when the brigade members had only seven free days a year.' At that time a story spread, Mr Wu said, about a mother from another brigade who did not want her daughter to marry a man in the Hua Hsi brigade—'They are only dried-up old frogs,' the mother had said.

After more background information, Mr Wu suggested that he take us on a tour of the brigade. As we passed our housing, he mentioned that this was the only housing development of its kind in the brigade, and it would replace all other brigade housing by 1985. Now most families lived in one-storey rustic farm-houses that had been built between 1965 and 1972.

Unlike city families, who lived in small rented flats, rural families owned their houses, which were often four times larger than an average city flat.

It was the busy season and there was much activity in the fields. The wheat was ripe and the peasants cut the stalks with sickles and tied them in bundles. Others waited nearby with bamboo shoulder poles to carry the heavy load to a storage place where it would remain dry.

In the fields students from the brigade middle school worked with the peasants planting rice seedlings. Their pants were rolled up to their knees and dry mud caked their legs. Everyone was in a bent position that made me ache just looking at it. The work appeared to be exhausting and backbreaking, but they seemed accustomed to it.

I often wondered whether those living in the city appreciated how hard the peasants in the fields toiled to provide them with food. While the urban people worked an eight-hour day, six days a week, the peasants rose with the daylight and went to bed when it was dark. The seasons and weather, instead of the clock and holidays, directed their lives.

While walking around the fields and through the rows of housing we could not escape the familiar blare from the loud-speaker. It awakened us in the morning with news and music from the radio and kept the peasants company all day in the fields. In the city people owned their own radios and could listen to different stations, but here a private radio was still too great an extravagance.

As we returned from the fields and passed by our housing development on the way to the shopping centre we saw several pigs lying on the ground with their feet bound. Three men heaved the hundreds of pounds of meat and fat onto a truck that would later transport the pigs into town, where they would be sold to the state.

Before the brigade shopping centre was built peasants had to walk at least a mile to reach the nearest shop located at the county seat. Now brigade members could buy almost every-thing here, at considerably cheaper prices than in town. The food store served also as the local post office. Inside there was a telephone that brigade members could use; there were no private phones. (In the city people also had to go to a local store to telephone because private phones were rare.) Outside there was a mail box for posting letters.

The brigade barber shop with three barber's chairs was next door. As in most urban factories, hair cuts were free for brigade members, but visitors had to pay. 'The rationing of hair cuts is not necessary,' the barber said, 'because everyone knows when his hair is too long and would not cut it when it was too short.' I chuckled because I had never seen a Chinese in need of a hair cut. In fact, I tried to encourage our staff to grow their hair longer, but no one wanted to look different.

The administration headquarters, where we held our discussions, was above the barber shop and food store. It also had a reading room with newspapers, books by Marx, Lenin, and Mao, and a popular television room that was open evenings to brigade members.

Other stores sold materials, ready-made clothing, shoes, and even watches, which cost as much as 247 yuan. The choice was much smaller than in the city but no basic item was missing.

Unlike city women, the women of Hua Hsi brigade relied much more on their own skills and handicrafts. The women made hemp soles for their shoes, which our interpreter, Mr Gu, carefully examined in the shoemaker's shop. 'These are very good soles. You couldn't find them in Peking,' he said. Women also brought along the black material for the upper part of the shoe so the shoemaker only had to put the shoes together. For this he charged twenty fen. The same ready-made shoes would cost at least two yuan in a city store.

There was also a tailor shop that made clothes at half the price charged in state shops. And there was even a scrap shop, similar to the one in Chao Yang, that bought old materials, including human hair for 22 yuan a pound, and goose feathers, for 21.50 yuan a pound.

We knew that fowl were not raised privately, so we asked why goose feathers were on the list. The clerk explained that the feathers came from the birds people had eaten.

Unexpectedly Mr Wu grabbed the clerk's hand to show us it was crippled. I winced at this insensitivity, but the clerk showed no embarrassment, nor did the crippled clerks at the shoemaker when Mr Wu did this. 'They have been trained to do this job so they would have a job,' Mr Wu explained.

During our tour of the brigade, we were not alone. Hundreds of Chinese tourists from schools, factories, and other communes were also visiting the brigade. I asked Mr Wu what they were doing here. 'They have come to learn from our experience,' he said. 'Last year we had between ten and twelve thousand visitors. But you are the first foreigners invited to live with us.' Based on what we had heard and had already seen, it was clear that the Information Department had selected Hua Hsi Production Brigade because it was a model of what communes would be in the future.

EATING WITH THE CHINESE

On our second day we did not have to dine alone. Mr Wu arranged for us to have lunch with a family who had been living in this area for generations, and could tell us of the differences between their past and present life.

The Chaos lived in the older-style housing and their house was in a row of one-storey houses that looked like white-washed barns. They had a square garden in front where herbs and walnut trees grew. Next to the garden, clothing, fish, and shoes were hanging from an intriguing contraption. Bamboo poles were set up like tripods and the legs were weighted down with stones so the wind could not topple the poles.

The seven members of the Chao family greeted us at the door and led us to a large wooden table in a long narrow room that had no other furnishings. This was obviously the dining room. I was used to the size of urban flats, but this room alone, if it were in the city, would have been home for at least six people.

There were the older Chaos and their twenty-five-year-old unmarried daughter as well as the younger Chaos and their two children. Two young children of another son were also living here. As we chatted the older Mrs Chao, who seemed shy and nervous, poured tea. Then she put handfuls of roasted peanuts and dried pumpkin seeds in front of us. Since peanuts were rationed in the city, I wondered where she had bought them. 'They were grown here,' she said proudly, as she dropped more peanuts on my growing peanut hill.

The Chaos were eager to show us the rest of their very spacious house. Two long narrow rooms were partitioned to form two kitchens and two bedrooms. The grandfather and his grandson slept together in one bed and next to them was an empty cot for a guest. The grandmother, granddaughter and unmarried daughter slept in the other room.

A third room housed two angora rabbits, two goats, and food provisions. In the new housing development, where we lived, animals were not permitted.

The next room belonged to the absent son who had left his two children with his parents. He worked in a commune factory some distance away, and only used this room when he came to visit on weekends.

Half his room looked like a furniture storage area. A chest, small wardrobe, four backless wooden stools and four wooden tables, a wooden bathtub and buckets were standing together. When we asked to whom they belonged, the mother said her unmarried daughter had bought these with the parents' help. 'Buying furniture was an old custom girls followed before they married.' The mother's remark made the daughter so uneasy that she hastily offered Gerd a cigarette, although he was already smoking one.

When we asked if she were planning to marry soon, she turned scarlet, took a deep breath and then spoke in a clipped manner: 'I have a friend now, but we have not discussed marriage yet. I must learn and study more before marrying. When I am twenty-seven years old I might marry.'

Mr Wu had told us that the average age to marry was twenty-five. This was younger than in the city, where the shortage of flats, I had heard, often forced young people to wait longer until their work organisation assigned them a place to live. But in families where older people needed support because there were not enough working members, Mr Wu told us, the children were allowed to marry earlier.

The married Chao son lived with his family in a large room furnished like ours, but he had more elaborate knick-knacks. Besides a poster of Mao, he had a map of China, papercuts and two porcelain teapots of cats whose paws stuck out for pouring.

We were curious about two bottles of wine that seemed out of place among the kitsch. Mr Chao explained that this was 'health wine', given to brigade members during the busy seasons.

The label on the wine bottle was so long that we asked Mr Gu to translate it. Soon I had the feeling he was reading the directions on a medicine bottle. 'Health wine is good for the blood, stomach, virility, and nerves. When the eyes blur, there is buzzing in the ears, when you have no appetite, suffer from forgetfulness, are easily frightened, then take two or three spoonfuls daily in the morning and before going to sleep.' Mr Chao added, 'The wine increases the working strength.'

I thought Mr Chao must certainly need his strength. He was an energetic talkative man, who had considerable responsibility in the brigade. Besides being in charge of the pumping station, he repaired radios, watches, and tools for the brigade members.

I had the opportunity to try the health wine at lunch, but discovered it was too sweet for my taste. The meal began with a sweet soup filled with sticky rice balls. Gerd gulped down his portion and immediately received a second helping. I was not as enthusiastic about this new taste, and ate slowly in order to avoid a refill. Realising that all eyes were focused on my slow progress, I asked how the rice balls were made. 'Yesterday I prepared them with glutinous rice and yeast and then let them rise for twenty-four hours,' the younger Mrs Chao said. 'This is a favourite food we give to friends and relatives when they visit us.'

As I struggled to empty my bowl the other courses started arriving: a chopped green vegetable resembling spinach, a cold bamboo and vegetable salad, fish in a pungent sauce, eggs fried whole in a sauce, cooked peanuts, water chestnuts, bean curd, and *jao-tze* (dumplings) filled with vegetables. This was not the everyday fare, I thought.

I loved vegetables and did not miss meat, but Gerd, the

meat eater in the family, noticed its absence. We had heard of a meat shortage in China and knew that in most cities families were rationed to about a kilo or less a month. But I was surprised to find that in the countryside, where pigs were raised, the shortage seemed even greater than in the city.

During the meal the older Mr Chao pointed out that everything we were eating was produced in the brigade. In the city, I thought to myself, people might have more meat, but they could never eat such freshly picked vegetables, a fish that went from the pond into the pan, and eggs laid that morning.

In Hua Hsi all brigade members received daily a pound of vegetables and soy-bean products free. In addition, melon, peanuts, pumpkin and sunflower seeds, water chestnuts, and red beans were distributed free when they were in season. The brigade also grew peaches, pears, kumquats, plums, apples, and walnuts for its members in its five-acre orchard.

The older Mr Chao was in charge of the vegetable planting team. It was made up of older people who were assigned the lighter work, and were responsible for cultivating the collective vegetable plot belonging to the entire brigade. Unlike many other communes, Hua Hsi had eliminated private family plots of land in favour of a collective plot.

'Now we do not have to worry any more about taking care of our own land,' a member explained. The brigade members had also decided to ban private chickens and pigs, which they said damaged crops and were unsanitary. Brigade members received a small ration of eggs a month, but old people and those sick or disabled had an extra ration and received free poultry.

On holidays, the Chaos told us, the brigade gave each family mutton, chickens, duck, sticky rice cakes, lima beans, and fish. This system of free distribution did not exist in the city, where incomes were much higher than in the rural areas.

To the older Chaos, being members of the brigade offered them a life they could hardly have envisioned twenty years ago. Mr Chao said, 'While I was growing up there were six members in my family who shared one and a half rooms. When my father borrowed money from the landlord and could not pay it back the landlord sent people to fetch me.' Mr Chao's voice rose, and he showed emotion for the first time. His face muscles became taut as he said, 'The men took me away, undressed me, and tied me to a tree and beat me.' Scenes similar to what Mr Chao described were shown to us in the brigade's permanent exhibition. There, photographs and illustrations showed Japanese soldiers, Kuomintang landlords, and other officials exploiting, torturing, and killing people in this area before Liberation.

Regaining his composure, Mr Chao said, 'I can thank Mao and the Communist party for my six rooms. In 1968 we moved into this house, which was newly built. It cost twelve hundred yuan, but with seven members of the family working we were able to pay for it within two years. Today there are five watches in the family, two clocks, and each person has at least two pullovers. Before Liberation we did not have money for sweaters. Now we no longer wear patched clothing or patched shoes. The children do not want to wear patched things.'

Mrs Chao then pointed to her small feet. 'They began to bind my feet when I was five years old. Sometimes I cried from pain.' As she spoke tears started streaming down her cheeks. 'Every girl had to have small feet. Without small feet you could not go out of the house. The girls with big feet were beaten by the landlord's men when they went out on the street.' Before Liberation, Mrs Chao said, she wore rags. 'When it was cold I did not have enough clothing. Now we have enough clothing and furniture.'

Mrs Chao told us that her marriage was arranged through a marriage broker when she was a small child. At a young age she was sent to her future parents-in-law to serve as house help, and later was considered married. The Chao's son, on the other hand, had been allowed to choose his wife himself. She came from the same production brigade and had visited his home many times. The younger Mr Chao told us that when he asked his parents for approval to marry, they told him he could decide by himself.

Their engagement lasted for three years, until the younger Chaos had saved enough money to buy the furniture and other goods they would need to set up a household. The red lacquer set of furniture in the bedroom, he said, had cost 300 yuan $150 at the time of their marriage in 1968, and the thirteen-piece set of wooden buckets 120 yuan. And he proudly showed us their red-and-gold marriage certificates, which bore the official seal of the Commune Revolutionary Committee.

There was no marriage ceremony. After picking up the certificate they returned home and had friends to dinner. 'It is no longer the custom to receive gifts, but friends brought us the works of Mao,' Mr Chao said.

When Mr Chao's sister married, there would be a special ceremony. The brigade now conducted its own public marriage ceremonies at New Year, during the slack farming season. All members of the brigade were invited to attend the ceremony held in a brigade hall. The couples, dressed in new pants and jackets, sat together in the front row wearing red flowers on their jackets—red is the traditional marriage colour. A leading member of the commune gave a speech welcoming new members to the brigade and bidding farewell to those women who would be leaving to join their husband's families. The brigade then presented the couples with the writings of Mao, Marx, Engels, Lenin, and Stalin, and agricultural tools inscribed with such slogans as 'Never stop on the way to revolution, always go forward.'

The only expense the family had was the special meal, which the canteen prepared for the newly-weds, their relatives and friends. The older Mr Chao was very much in favour of this ceremony. 'Now there will be no waste of money,' he said.

Mr Chao, although sixty-eight, was not retired, for peasants, unlike factory workers, do not retire and receive a pension at a certain age. 'Today I work only when I feel well,' Mr Chao said.

When old people stop working their families are expected to take care of them. Those who cannot work at all and have no children, however, are provided with clothing, food, medical care, and pocket money by the brigade.

On communes peasants are not paid salaries. Their wages are based on a complicated points system based on the principle 'From each according to his ability, to each according to his skills. Those who work more earn more,' Mr Wu had told us. But men over sixty, like Mr Chao, and women over fifty-five do only as much work as they are physically able, and still receive their old work points.

Work points are the basis for determining a peasant's income. Every day a person works he earns work points. The number he receives is based on what he thinks he deserves as well as his colleague's evaluation of his attitude and work. He can earn a maximum of ten and a minimum of 5.5 work points a day. In 1975 ten work points were worth 1.47 yuan and the average per capita income of all brigade members was 185 yuan.

This was much lower than the 60 yuan that the average factory worker was paid each month. But, unlike the peasant, the city dwellers had to pay for rent, food, and other social services.

Like farmers throughout the world, the peasants in Hua Hsi were simple, hard-working people. Although they earned considerably less than their urban neighbours, they seemed much happier and more relaxed. Their spacious quarters permitted three generations to live together comfortably under one roof, and I felt that the closely-knit family life and isolation from material distractions were the reasons for their contentment.

In the Chao family, Mrs Chao took care of her grandchildren and did the housework, while her husband and daughter worked in the brigade. In 1975 they took home 701 yuan. This was after the brigade deducted the cost of the 1,900 pounds of wheat and rice they had consumed and the solid fuel they had used that year.

The older Chaos spent 300 yuan of their income on groceries, clothing, and other miscellaneous things and put 400 yuan into the bank. When I asked how they would spend their savings, the unmarried daughter, said, 'We are saving money for when I marry.'

The Chao son and his wife earned a cash income of 720 yuan. His family consumed 2,020 pounds of grain in 1975, but he said, 'Usually we have more than we can eat and when we cannot eat our supply we store some.'

They were saving for the time they would have a more modern house, like the one we were living in. I asked if they were planning to buy a bicycle. Mr Chao's father answered. 'It would not be practical or necessary. We have our own shops nearby and when we travel longer distances the production brigade truck or tractor takes us.' He did not mind the isolation rural life created, but I wondered if his grandchildren would feel differently.

THE HUA HSI WOMEN'S LEAGUE

In rural areas families tended to be much larger than in the city, mainly because there is plenty of living space and they needed more working hands. The older Chaos had five children, but their son had only two.

The Women's League in the brigade, like in Chao Yang, had been very active in encouraging voluntary family planning, and had influenced the Chaos to have only two children.

After a woman had a child at the brigade, a League administrator visited the mother and suggested that she wait before having another child. 'When one child is still breast fed it is not good to have a second child,' the new mothers were instructed. If a woman had two or three children the League would advise her that more children were bad for her health, work, and welfare.

We learned that 70 per cent of the women in the brigade with two or three children had already been sterilised. 'This is healthy, and the couples can go on working well,' we were told.

Sterilisation is performed free in the commune hospital and has fringe benefits. The woman is given thirty yuan extra pay and fifty free days with full work points. I had heard that on other communes if a woman had more than three children she was penalised and not given coupons for some of the rationed items. But in Hua Hsi, it was denied that such measures were taken.

The growing population in China was her greatest domestic enemy. If the population could not be curbed there would not be enough food to feed the extra mouths. That is why stress was placed on family planning, particularly in the rural areas, which tended to be lax in following the nationally-advocated policy of two children per family.

The Women's League also became involved in solving family conflicts. We were told of their intervention in a dispute between a daughter-in-law and mother-in-law about the upbringing of the baby.

The older woman was supposed to take care of the grandchild while the mother worked in the fields. Sometimes the mother came home from work and heard the baby crying. This upset her and she scolded the mother-in-law for leaving the baby in the cradle alone and not watching and rocking her. The old woman replied, 'You have your work in the fields, that is easy. But I have to cook, do the household chores, and take care of the baby.'

A spokesman for the Women's League told us, 'Neighbours heard the frequent arguments between the two and called on the Women's League to talk with the family. We decided that the main responsibility for the trouble was the daughter-in-law. She was spoiling the baby and did not have enough respect for old people.'

Women's rights were another important concern of the

League. It made certain that the following measures were enforced: women should receive lighter work during the latter part of their pregnancy; extra cotton coupons after the birth of their first child; thirty-yuan nutrition allowance for newborn babies; the same wages as men for the same work.

When the younger Mrs Chao had her first child she received two months' leave without pay, while urban mothers had fifty-six free days with pay. By the time her second child arrived, rural women were receiving some of the same benefits as urban women, and Mrs Chao was given fifty free days and was paid her normal work points.

Now her six-year-old daughter and four-year-old son attended first grade and kindergarten free, and were already participating in the work of the brigade. The children gathered herbs and at harvest time collected wheat ears.

LITTLE TIME FOR ANYTHING BUT WORK

'Love for physical labour' was instilled at a very early age. The Vice-Chairman of the Revolutionary Committee said, 'The combination of practice and learning improves the ideology of the students who are supposed to take the correct attitude toward physical labour and become used to it.'

In rural areas, students spent much more time in the fields than urban students, whose physical labour, for the most part, was confined to school workshops. Beginning in seventh grade, the young people of Hua Hsi had the fields for their classroom. We had seen the eighth grade standing knee deep in the wet rice fields, while the younger Mr Chao showed them how to operate a tractor. Behind them was a blackboard with a sketch showing how a tractor works and how to plough the fields.

After ninth grade the students spent forty days a year doing compulsory work in the fields. Many also volunteered to work twenty days extra during their holidays and Sundays, for which they were paid according to the work-point system.

From the fields we were taken to see the barefoot doctors. If anyone did not feel well, he went to the brigade medical station, which was attended by three barefoot doctors. After thirteen months of theoretical and practical training in the brigade and commune hospital, the barefoot doctors were able to treat, with herbal and Western medicines such common illnesses as flu, colds, backaches, and tonsilitis. They used acupuncture against toothaches and vaccinated children against whooping cough, tetanus, measles, and smallpox.

They also checked drinking water, wells, homes and the surroundings to make certain they were clean. In addition, the barefoot doctors instructed people not to drink unboiled water or eat raw or cold food. As a result of their work, we were told, stomach and intestinal diseases decreased considerably.

When someone went to the medical station for treatment, she would have to pay only for medicine, which cost very little. For example, if she had flu she might have to pay ten fen for Chinese herbs and about sixteen fen for Western medicine.

When the barefoot doctors found the case serious, the patient would go to the commune hospital. There he would have to pay a five fen entrance fee and food charges and, unlike factory workers, who enjoyed free medical care, the peasant would have to pay 50 per cent of all other expenses. For example, a simple appendix operation cost 10 yuan and the brigade member had to pay half of this.

A family with financial difficulties could seek assistance from the brigade. We were told about a family of six in which the mother was the sole support because the father was ill. After the money for rice and wheat and solid fuel for her stove had been subtracted from her income, she had little more than thirty yuan left for all other expenses throughout the year. The matter was brought to the attention of the Revolutionary Committee, and with the consent of the masses, the brigade paid the family 150 yuan assistance.

Costly burial expenses were no longer a family concern in

the Hua Hsi brigade. The nationally recommended policy was to cremate the dead and the brigade had built a building where urns were to be placed. 'The last burial took place in 1969 because the family insisted on it,' Mr Wu said. 'People now understand that cremation is better, more hygienic and more economical because the collective assumes the costs.'

This view, however, was not shared by all peasants in China. One commune we visited had many new mounds of earth where the dead were buried. These, combined with the old graves, occupied about one third of the arable land.

When we asked the leadership there about burials, we were told, 'We are in the process of doing away with outmoded ideas, but the people's conscience has not reached the point of adopting cremation. Before the parents die, they tell their children where their ancestors are buried because they want to be buried there. And the production leadership usually respects the wishes of the parents.'

In cities cremation was strictly enforced, but on communes, as we saw, there was resistance. Hua Hsi was the exception. Its leadership was strong enough to influence its members to accept new ideas.

A brigade member explained, 'We want to occupy the spare time of our brigade members with socialist thought. If socialism doesn't occupy their minds capitalism will.' Therefore brigade members had practically no time free. When the Chao family returned from a long day in the fields, communal activities in the evening were planned.

The Chao daughter attended agricultural courses in her spare time. They were held at the brigade for middle school graduates, and the students met three times in ten days.

Political evening school was held five times in ten days. When we visited a session I observed a few people dozing while the teacher read a newspaper article. In another class I saw several yawns while a classmate read a political composition she had written.

One evening we watched the Chao daughter and our hostess

play in a women's basketball match. I wondered how the players had the energy to run after a long day in the fields. As if they had heard my unspoken thoughts, they gave a cheer in unison just before coming off the basketball court.

'We women hold up half the heavens. We can play basketball and tear the heavens. We can do field work as well as play basketball. . . . We will sweep away the doctrines of Confucianism.'

The peasants had time off only on national holidays and during the slow season in winter, amounting to about forty free days a year. Occasionally the brigade planned trips to Wushi or to the Nanking bridge or Yangtze River bridge, but limited transport kept most people at home.

Hua Hsi was already planning for the future, when mechanisation would give people more leisure time. We climbed up a hill the members of the brigade had built and looked down on a pond. 'Cities have parks, why not villages,' a brigade member said. 'Every park needs a mountain and a river,' and this was Hua Hsi's beginning. 'Perhaps we will even have a tea house overlooking the pond,' he mused.

Chapter 8

The Outbreak of Violence on Tien An Men

April 5, 1975, began like most week-days, but ended leaving me baffled and troubled. I awakened as usual between 6 and 6:30 and crammed for my Chinese lesson, which began at 8:30. After it was over I did a few household chores before my morning bike ride. As I was walking out the door the telephone interrupted me.

The clipped, tense voice of a German friend asked, 'Where is Gerd?' 'He has probably gone to Tien An Men to see the wreaths, and I am just on my way there,' I replied. 'Don't bicycle to Tien An Men today,' he said excitedly. 'Angry crowds have detained a member of the embassy for thirty minutes. They called him a spy and forced him to expose his film.'

It was difficult to believe this story, because only the day before I had been in the square mixing with the friendliest and most relaxed crowds I could ever remember. They were there to celebrate Ching Ming, an annual celebration held to commemorate revolutionary war heroes and family members who had died.

Assuming my friend was overexcited and had exaggerated what he had heard, I started bicycling toward Tien An Men, unprepared for what was ahead of me. I would witness the first violent political unrest since the Cultural Revolution in the late 1960's.

Ching Ming had begun as it did every year. Six days before, smartly dressed school children in freshly-washed white blouses and blue pants had started filing past our apartment. The beating of drums and the sound of their high-pitched voices singing political songs brought me to the window of our apartment. As soon as I saw the paper wreaths that were carried at the front of each group I knew that Ching Ming had begun. Everyone was headed in the direction of the square, one mile away, where they would deposit the class wreath. It was only the beginning of the march and they looked quite perky and fresh. By the time the younger classes reached the square, they would be out of step, weary, and a bit dishevelled.

On the edges of the vast square, teachers inspected their classes. Students had to stand up straight in a double file. Then they were ready to march in step toward the martyr's monument at the back of the square.

Older classes stood at attention there, holding red flags and paper wreaths, while they listened unemotionally to a teacher or student recite a poem or read a text in honour of the dead. Students had blank stares on their faces and the younger classes sat on the ground dozing and looking around as their teachers tried to hold their attention.

After the recitation they raised their fists and repeated in unison a pledge to carry out the teachings of Chairman Mao. They sang the 'Internationale' and, following this, two students brought the class wreath up to the monument. Other students accompanied them and discussed where the wreath should be placed. As the class started on the long walk back to school, they wanted to be able to turn around and see their wreath in a prominent place on or near the monument.

During the first few days of Ching Ming, mainly school children and families placed simple, homemade paper wreaths at the monument. On one occasion I saw a young boy, perhaps ten years old, pedalling across the square on a three-wheel bike. He was bringing his grandparents to the monument where they would deposit a tall green plant they were clutching.

Then wreaths started arriving with pictures of Chou En-lai, who had died three months ago. This was the beginning of an overwhelming tribute that ended unexpectedly as a political demonstration.

Workers, cadre from government bureaux, and women from workshops joined the Ching Ming observance and marched in groups toward Tien An Men. They looked solemn and proud as they walked behind elaborate paper wreaths honouring Chou. When they arrived at the monument, one of the group read a eulogy to the dead premier. Many cried unashamedly.

Trucks from factories in the outskirts of Peking brought workers with their wreaths to the square. Each truck was packed, and as the people poured out they dusted off their jackets, smoothed their hair, and fell into step to walk slowly toward the martyr's monument.

Many men and women came to the square in twos or alone to deposit a white paper flower on the shrubbery flanking the monument. By the end of the week a white veil covered the hedge.

During this time a few Chinese friends urged me to visit the square. 'You must see how much the people loved Chou,' one said. She went daily to deposit a white flower on the shrubs, she told me.

Only after the demonstration, when she said to me, 'Don't tell anyone I was there,' did I hear that certain work organisations had forbidden their employees from going to Tien An Men. She had obviously defied regulations.

Some paper wreaths were designed to look like a hammer and sickle, the sign of the Communist Party. Others contained black and white or colour pictures of Chou in the centre of a magnificent multi-coloured floral decoration. Teams of workers had stayed up all night to create these masterpieces.

It must have been difficult to decide on the proper text that would reflect their love for Chou. The most moving words I saw were, 'The premier loved the people. The premier suffered together with the people. Therefore the people loved the premier.'

Each day the number of people visiting the square grew until it reached the tens of thousands. I was present to hear large crowds cheering when a wreath displaying a picture of

Chou in the middle of a map of China was hoisted up to the top ledge of the monument. This had a political meaning to the Chinese, who knew that until then only Mao's picture had appeared in the middle of the map of China. But I was not aware of this.

Many people had come to the square with poems to Chou, written on pieces of notebook paper that they glued to the monument, its parapet, and the backs of wreaths. Some poems were several pages long and were hung on a string attached to the balustrades surrounding the monument.

Everyone was pushing, shoving, and squeezing each other to get close enough to read what was written. Sometimes a man stood in front of the crowds reading his own text and other times a person nearby read it.

Many young people had brought along notebooks and pens and were writing down the words, using backs and shoulders of friends to steady the papers. Sometimes the crowd would shout to the speaker 'Louder' or 'Read more slowly.' When a word was not clear he would write the character with his finger in the air and then there would be a shout of recognition. No one wanted to miss a word.

Later foreigners told me that, while writing the texts, they had received help and praise from their Chinese neighbours. The Chinese leaned over their shoulders, watching them write the characters. When they stumbled over a word or meaning, the Chinese would try to explain it to them.

Three days before the outbreak of the violence, Gerd brought Mr Gu along to read the texts on some of the wreaths. Mr Gu was amazed to see some honouring the second wife of Mao, Yang Kai-hui, who had been executed by the Kuomintang, but he made no comment. During the previous Ching Mings this had never happened, and it looked like a bold attack on Chiang Ching, Mao's present wife.

Suddenly I had doubts. I had thought this was a moving tribute to the beloved Premier Chou, but it appeared that some people were using it as a political demonstration. I had heard rumours, after the death of Chou, about how Chiang Ching had opposed him. These wreaths made the rumours more credible.

When we went to Tien An Men on Sunday, April 4, the day before the wreaths were removed, it was just like a county fair. It was a beautiful, sunny day, the square was filled with thousands of families, all there for an outing.

Wreaths covered the entire square and families wound their way slowly around them, while admiring some and reading the texts on others. Mothers pushed their babies in bamboo carriages and fathers boosted children on to their shoulders so that they would not be trampled or lost. Groups sat in between wreaths eating bread, fruit, and cookies, and children played hide and seek. Every family with a camera had brought it along to photograph family members. While Gerd plunged into the masses to take pictures, I remained on the outside of the square answering the many *ni haos* (hellos) of the people passing by.

Everyone seemed to be happy that foreigners were there to witness this event. While we stood together in front of wreaths, people talked to us about the weather or a wreath. One couple asked two English friends to pose with them for a picture. The Chinese, who were usually camera-shy with foreigners, relaxed and enjoyed themselves, and for the first time I did not feel like an outsider.

While pedalling to the square on that memorable April 5 I passed groups carrying yet more wreaths. I could not detect a change in the atmosphere. People were laughing and looked as relaxed as they had the previous day. But when I was one block from Tien An Men I did see an old woman standing on a street corner, holding her wreath and looking bewildered. I could not understand why she was not walking toward the square.

A few hundred yards later I was stunned by what I saw. The square did not have a trace of the thousands of wreaths that were there the day before, and a police line was standing in front barring any entrance from the north side on Chang An.

I was on the other side of the street in front of the Forbidden City. From there I saw what appeared to be an enormous blue blanket on the west side of the square, in front of the Great Hall of the People, where the Peoples' Congress meets and political meetings are held. Suddenly I realised that what I took to be a blanket was actually thousands of people. I decided to follow the other cyclists, so I dismounted with them and crossed the street. We then walked past the police line, a few yards away. Every head was turned in the direction of the empty square. Some faces looked angry, while others had confused expressions. I wondered why the wreaths had been removed and who had removed them.

When I arrived at the north-east corner of the Great Hall of the People, crowds of people were pouring into the square. Parking my bike on the sidewalk, I walked slowly with others toward the steps at the east entrance. The steps were covered with people, and remembering the warning of my friend, I decided not to plunge into the masses. Instead, I followed a grandmother and grandchild who went to sit on a ledge on the side of the steps.

Not seeing any other foreigners, I wanted to appear as inconspicuous as possible, so I started playing with the child next to me. The people nearby, who were spectators like me, smiled and made small talk with me. They seemed as unaware as I of what was going on a short distance away.

Only later did I hear from others what had happened before I arrived and what I had missed while I was sitting there, involved with my neighbours. People had tried to storm the Great Hall and gain admittance to it, and during this unsuccessful attempt a few soldiers had been badly injured. Soon after, students were beaten and dragged to the monument, where they were beaten again and forced to bow before the crowds. At the same time, foreigners had been encircled, shouted at, and asked to expose the film in their cameras.

Only later did I find out that Gerd had been one of their victims. He had been pursued by angry young people when he had tried to make an unsuccessful escape from the square into the Bank of China, a block away. They had surrounded him, demanding that he expose his film, but the crush of the crowd had prevented him for several frightening moments from opening his camera.

Not knowing about any of these events, I felt completely secure where I was sitting on the fringe of the crowd. Only when a speaker's voice echoed through a megaphone did I turn my attention to the thousands in front of me. They looked tense and angry, I was certain, because the wreaths had been removed, and I sympathised with them, but I did not think it was a good idea to go any closer. I strained to hear what the speaker was saying but could not catch a word. He was standing in the middle of the blue mass shouting phrases and the people around him were listening silently and attentively. From time to time I lost sight of him as he was jostled back and forth by the crowd. Then the megaphone passed from hand to hand, and there were different speakers.

At exactly 11:30 A.M., the people around me started to leave. It was lunchtime and they were going home to eat. I was a little let down that the demonstration was over and I had seen nothing dramatic happen.

Suddenly I heard shouting from the speakers. Then in the middle of the throng, a group who looked like workers and students in their mid- and late twenties joined arms and started singing the 'International'. This was my favourite melody and so I hummed along with them. After several interrupted starts of the song, they moved slowly in a mass across the square to where the Historical Museum is located.

Wondering why they were moving in that direction, I followed behind, joining the other stragglers who were as curious as I. As they approached the museum the front lines started running toward the steps and people disappeared inside the large courtyard of the museum. I noticed a truck parked next to the steps. Soldiers jumped out of it and ran up the steps. They disappeared in the direction of the first group. Until then I had not understood what was going on, but a feeling of excitement and uncertainty started growing in me.

By the time I reached the sidewalk near the museum the bulk of the people were standing quietly on the steps, not moving any farther. I had not seen that the first group had turned over a steel barrier and gained entrance to the museum through force.

Looking around me, I saw many empty trucks parked on the sidewalk and guessed they had delivered people to the square that morning. Unexpectedly, the crowd suddenly veered in my direction. I had no time to escape. They sucked me in and I was trapped in the middle like a captive. There was nothing to do but march along with them in the direction of a building south-west of the museum entrance, about one hundred yards away.

I had visited the square many times but had never noticed this building. Later on, the newspapers referred to it as an 'army barracks' where the army detail covering the square had their headquarters.

We stopped in front of the entrance to this building, and the same man who had the megaphone on the Great Hall steps was holding it again. He was only about fifty feet away from me and I could see his dark-rimmed glasses, crew cut, and tense, pale face. I did not understand what he was saying, but the crowd kept repeating, 'Mei yo jen' ('No one is there'). The building was empty and I wondered why people were trying to enter it.

Although the faces in the crowd seemed tenser, I felt safe in the group surrounding me. They were men and women who had intelligent, sympathetic faces, and they did not show any concern that I was there.

Suddenly a man with a bloody face grabbed the megaphone, and as he spoke other people supported him. He was the first injured person I had seen and the sight of him troubled me.

What was I doing here, I asked myself? I still could not understand what was going on around me.

Shortly after the injured man appeared, a line of soldiers ran along the side of the crowd in the direction of the building. The army's appearance frightened me and the people around me, and they stepped back and bumped into me.

If the army moved in I did not want to be caught in a stampede from the front, and so I tried to leave the crowd slowly, without drawing attention to myself. I managed to reach a jeep that offered protection, but at that moment the jeep's roof collapsed from the weight of the people sitting on it. This provided a welcome comic relief from the tension that had been building up since the soldiers' appearance. As soon as the laughter was over, I heard shouting and noticed that people were staring at me.

When I turned round, I was shocked. A group of factory workers who were standing in a truck were shaking their fists and yelling at me. The expression on their faces was so menacing that I knew I should leave as quickly as possible. They were telling me to go away and I started walking in the direction of the square. As I moved the crowd separated for me and I no longer saw a single friendly face. I was very frightened but did not want to show it, so I walked slowly, staring straight ahead.

Suddenly I saw familiar faces in front of me, and they were like an island in a rough sea. I steered towards them, while people followed me shouting, but I was no longer afraid.

The crowd behind me saw the foreigners ahead and started screaming, 'This is the business of the Chinese people, go away.' By then I had joined my friends and felt safe. Thinking the danger was over, I relaxed, and to my surprise, could not stop stuttering and shaking for the next minutes.

While leaving, we passed a police squad marching in double file toward the angry mobs behind us. Within seconds our followers lost interest in us. Now they had another target. They surrounded the police, pushed them and knocked off their caps. Soon the bareheaded police were retreating out of step, leaving their caps behind as trophies for people to vie over.

The mood was changing, and we had the feeling we should move as quickly as possible away from the south-east corner of the square. While walking, my friends who were fluent in Chinese began to explain what had been happening at the Great Hall in the morning. The speeches were difficult to understand but they thought they had heard people asking where the wreaths were and who had removed them. The crowd had crossed the square to the museum and then had gone to the army barracks in search of the wreaths and those responsible for removing them.

Once we were away from the crowd, I left the protection of my friends and went to the Great Hall of the People to pick up my bicycle. The steps were now empty and a line of soldiers stood in front of them. I was amazed at the contrast in mood on this side of the square. People were sitting quietly on the sidewalk under the trees eating lunch. As I passed them, they smiled and said 'ni hao.'

Heading in the direction of home, I pushed my bike across the square, behind the police line. An angry crowd caught my attention. They were pushing a man in a police uniform through the line toward me. As he came closer I saw his older, pale face and realised he must be a senior police officer. The tough crowd of young men in their early twenties, who were encircling him, took no notice of me, a few yards away. They were jostling, jabbing, and pushing the poor officer from side to side.

This group looked different from the people I had seen in the crowd earlier. These young men wore their blue workers' caps at a rakish angle and had cigarettes hanging out of their mouths. They wore expressions of defiance and scorn on their faces. I had never seen Chinese hooligans before, but they looked like that type.

While they were manhandling the policeman I glanced with

pleading, desperate eyes at the police line behind him, hoping someone would come to his rescue, but there was no reaction. Their young pale faces were tense and their bodies rigid, but obviously their orders did not permit them to become involved.

The growing mob then knocked the hat off the policeman's head and threw it up in the air. He retrieved it and in a cool, dignified manner put it back on his head again and pulled it down closer to his ears. I admired his control and at the same time wanted him to fight back and defend himself.

The crowd was becoming rougher with their target. They lifted him off the ground and it looked as though they were bouncing him along.

This was the first time I had ever seen Chinese attack a policeman. Sometimes they showed their disrespect by en-circling them and shouting at them, but now their anger was much deeper. Physical aggressiveness was not a Chinese characteristic. On the few occasions that I saw cyclists angry enough to punch each other, the surrounding crowds always immediately separated them. No one was willing to do this now.

Billows of smoke suddenly appeared in front of the museum. Noticing this, the mob abandoned the policeman and ran toward the fire. I breathed a deep sigh of relief, and the police-man adjusted his cap, straightened out his uniform, and returned to the police line.

Then I saw an empty truck speed away from the area of the smoke with four or five men hanging on to its back. I did not know if the driver was afraid his truck would burn or if these men had something to do with the fire.

Other Chinese spectators were moving toward the smoke, and I tagged along. As we walked together, I asked the man on my right side, 'What is burning?' He said, 'A jeep is burn-ing,' but his neighbour corrected him and mumbled, 'It is a Shanghai car.'

Masses of people stood near the smoke, making it impossible

to see anything. When a fire engine arrived it was immediately buried in the crowd. A little later I saw the fire engine being pushed away with children playing on it. Someone had been tampering with the motor, I thought.

As I came closer to the smoke the expression on people's faces became more menacing. I knew that I should not go further, but I did. A middle-aged man approached me and said, 'It is dangerous for you to stay. You must leave.' His firm voice and unsmiling face told me that he was worried and I knew I had to leave.

Turning round, I started pushing my bike across the square in the direction of home. My protector, who I assumed was a security man, and a few other people followed me to the edge of the square to make certain that I was safely on my way. While riding home, I suddenly realised how exciting the last four hours had been, but I still understood very little about what had happened.

Although I was two hours late for lunch, I knew Gerd would excuse me when he heard about my experiences. I rushed in the door of our flat and a pale, drawn face greeted me. Gerd said quietly, 'Where have you been?' I could feel the tension and concern in his voice. During the last hours he had called all over Peking searching for me, and one friend had told him she had seen me racing on my bike towards Tien An Men at around 10 A.M. Since then no one had seen me, and he had been worried that I was in serious trouble.

In the afternoon the Foreign Ministry advised foreigners to stay away from Tien An Men, where they could not guarantee our protection. Unfortunately, a Japanese correspondent awakened very late that day after a long night of *sake* drinking, and, unaware of the warning, went to the square loaded down with cameras. He arrived just before a third car was burning near the army barracks. The crowds descended on him. For one solid hour they beat him, and during this time his cameras, money, and identification disappeared.

At dusk, around six P.M., I took a walk past the square, but remained on the side of the Forbidden City. Groups of workers in their mid-twenties passed me on the street and either looked down when they saw me or gave me a chilly glance. I saw a man with a bloody bandaged head run out to the street from the direction of the square, stop a jeep, and climb in. At the same time smoke was coming from the army barracks in the south-east corner. It had just been set on fire and the crowds were concentrated in that area. The martyrs' monument, which had been the focal point for hundreds of wreaths during the previous few days, now had two small wreaths standing defiantly on its ledge.

A short time later, at about six-thirty, loudspeakers surrounding the square broadcast an appeal from Wu Teh, the mayor of Peking. He said that counter-revolutionary elements had created the civil disorder that day and that people should return to their homes. Few heeded his plea.

At eleven we drove past the square and were surprised to see that all the lights were out. In the darkness I could see people concentrated near the monument, but the rest of the square was empty. Later we learned that the workers' militia, with staves in hand, had encircled the remaining hard-core dissidents and beat up those offering resistance. There were rumours that people had been killed, but this report was unverified.

On Tuesday, the day after the violence, trucks full of workers-militia and army men filed into the city to enforce order. The square was open, and government photographers were standing at the front of the square, as they usually did, taking pictures of tourists.

The following day army men surrounded the square and allowed no unauthorised person to enter. Water trucks washed it down and women scrubbed every inch of its surface, as though they were assigned to remove the taint of Monday.

The atmosphere in the city was tense. Crowds gathered on street corners and harassed policemen. People huddled in groups speaking quietly. The faces of pedestrians and cyclists looked worried. In a store where I frequently shopped, the salesgirl, who always greeted me, pretended she didn't recognise me.

I returned home and was relieved to find my Chinese family as friendly as usual, but I could detect an uneasiness and strange quiet even in our household. I had tried to discuss the events of the last days with them, but no one would comment. Later on, I heard that many Chinese were even afraid to talk at home, because they never knew who might overhear them or who would use this against them in the future.

Around midnight on Wednesday, two days after the Tien An Men violent demonstration, I saw trucks with red flags driving slowly up and down Chang An. People who looked like factory workers were standing in the back beating big red drums and banging cymbals. They were celebrating some occasion, but I had to wait until I arrived home to hear the news. Teng Hsiao-ping, a vice-premier who had enjoyed great popularity, had been removed from office, and Hua Kuo-feng was the new premier.

Although it was after midnight and most Chinese were already asleep, Gerd wanted to return to the square to see if there were any further reaction to the announcement. We picked up our friend, an Italian journalist, who brought along her five-year-old son. He was packed in a blanket and slept in the car until we approached Tien An Men, where the sound of drums awakened him.

Sitting up, he said excitedly, 'Now we must all go out and fight for the revolution and for the heritage of Premier Chou.' He had learned this in Chinese kindergarten, and no one had told him that things had changed.

On the following days organised demonstrations took place in front of Tien An Men. Thousands of people from factories, schools, workshops, and government ministries filed past the square and denounced Teng Hsiao-ping in a dutiful way.

The older housewives were happy to have time off from their routine work. The sun was shining and it was a nice day to be outdoors. Some hobbled on tiny bound feet and others waddled and puffed as they moved in small groups toward the square. They came directly from their workshops, and were dressed in faded jackets and worn clothes. Each carried a pink paper flag condemning Teng. Occasionally their leader interrupted the chatter and rallied them to shout, 'Down with Teng Hsiao-ping!' and then they continued talking.

A young factory worker was having a wonderful time loudly beating a big red drum balanced precariously on the back of a three-wheel bike. As a joke the driver suddenly swerved to one side, and the drum almost toppled over. Everyone around him laughed, and the drummer joined in also.

While bicycling near the Foreign Ministry I saw a long column of people walking down the street. Pedestrians and cyclists were beside them, pointing and talking excitedly. I rode to the front of the group and saw a banner saying, 'Foreign Ministry', with a portrait of Mao next to it. Then there was another banner reading, 'Down with Teng Hsiao-ping'. Directly behind it was Chiao Kuan-hua, the foreign minister, marching in a row next to the other deputy foreign ministers.

In the past I had seen him receiving people at the airport, attending receptions, and hosting dinners, and his smile had never left his face. Now I barely recognised his painfully drawn and troubled face. His relaxed manner was gone and he looked burdened with problems. A grey cap was sitting firmly on his stiffly-held head. His face had a fixed, determined expression and his eyes stared straight ahead.

Unlike the foreign minister, the people walking behind him looked bored. Occasionally they shouted in an unemotional, detached way, 'Down with Teng Hsiao-ping.' The only time I saw a few faces perk up was when they recognised me. Then they waved and smiled.

I knew Gerd would be interested in taking a picture of this group, so I went to the nearest store with a telephone. After reaching him, I rushed back to the group. Minutes later Gerd arrived with camera in hand. Upon seeing him, a deputy premier nodded in recognition, but Chiao Kuan-hua, who knew him, avoided looking in the direction of the camera.

Some weeks later, a friend spoke with Chiao Kuan-hua's very attractive wife, who said, 'It was nice Mr Ruge took pictures of the Foreign Ministry passing Tien An Men. He was the only foreign journalist there to take this picture.' She was obviously pleased by the turn of events.

Six months later, when Teng Hsiao-ping's enemies were arrested, the foreign minister and his wife were removed from their posts in the Foreign Ministry. Some people said she was too close to Chiang Ching and caused his downfall, while others were unhappy about how Chiao Kuan-hua, a close friend of Chou En-lai, had lost his position.

One year later it was rumoured that Chiao Kuan-hua had committed suicide, and the Chinese, without denying this rumour, suggested that journalists not print the story. I felt sorry for the former foreign minister. He was a victim of an internal dispute and had obviously joined the wrong faction at the wrong time.

In the weeks following the Tien An Men violence we learned about the texts on many of the posters. The majority were eulogies to Chou En-lai, but some were political attacks on Chiang Ching and her colleagues. These were obviously the reason all wreaths were removed.

No Chinese ever discussed the events of that day with me, and when I brought up the name Chiang Ching after this incident, the response was cold, angry silence. Only when I returned to China eighteen months later did the Chinese reveal to us that she had forbidden students and teachers from going to Tien An Men during Ching Ming. But many had defied her orders and later been penalised. They told me that the outbreak of hate against Chiang Ching resulted from her attempt to prohibit students and teachers from wearing white flowers and black armbands during the mourning period following Chou's death. 'Her attempt to undermine the premier resulted

in people rising up to defend his memory during Ching Ming,'
a friend said.

But many questions still remained unanswered about
April 5, 1976. Who had authorised the removal of the wreaths?
Was the violence planned or spontaneous? Three years later
the Chinese were still waiting for an official explanation.

Chapter 9

Earthquake

The vibrating floor and shaking bed jolted me out of sleep. I had been dreaming that I was in a train rumbling along on a bumpy track. Instead of being in a train, however, I found myself sitting upright in bed with everything moving around me. Our clock showed 3:45 A.M. and I was still in a stupor. 'Do you think this is an earthquake?' I asked Gerd sleepily. The sound of the word 'earthquake' and the crash of a splintering vase in the living room brought me to my senses and propelled me out of bed.

I dashed past the living room, where the chandelier was swinging violently from one side of the ceiling to the other, and joined Gerd, who was having difficulty awakening the children. They had just arrived for their summer holiday and were indignant that we were disturbing them in the middle of the night. 'Stop kicking my bed, Papi, I want to sleep,' Lischen protested.

The continued rippling movement of the earth and our excited voices awakened Bubbles, who stumbled into the children's room, yawning and stretching. Grabbing the children and Bubbles, we sought shelter under the arch of the living room doorway.

The Chinese had advised us to go to this secure place after an earthquake scare a year and a half ago. At that time the tremors from an earthquake in Liaoning, a neighbouring province, made our pictures and chandelier sway back and forth as though they were on a gentle sea. But now the sea was angry and I was petrified that seven storeys might collapse on our head.

It seemed like hours from the time we got out of bed until the tremors subsided and we could dress. But in fact the earthquake, whose epicentre was one hundred miles away in Tangshan, lasted only two and a half minutes. During that time many other foreigners had left the building. We were the last stragglers to join them outside. Everyone was exchanging earthquake stories and I soon realised how lucky we were to be living on the ground floor. German friends, whose flat was on the thirteenth floor of a newly built building behind us, were still looking a little green. Their washing machine and refrigerator had slid from one side of the kitchen to the other and their liquor cabinet had emptied its contents on the floor. Their building had swayed slowly from side to side, like a boat on a stormy sea, and they had been certain that it would at any moment topple to the ground.

Guests living on the fifteenth floor of the Peking Hotel told us later that they did not dare to leave their beds because they were afraid of being struck by furniture crashing from one side of the room to the other. Others reported kitchen cabinets opening and pouring dishes onto the floor, mirrors breaking, pictures falling down, and new cracks in walls. There were no casualties among foreigners, but many were in shock.

The wives of our African neighbours huddled together outside as though they had seen the devil. One had had the presence of mind to grab her most precious possession, a fur coat, before fleeing, while an English couple had remembered at the last moment to clad themselves in towels. The Japanese, old earthquake hands, were the calmest group. We drove out of the compound, but they returned to bed, leaving speechless those who had vowed never to enter their flats again.

When we drove through the streets of Peking everything was quiet and under control. Large groups, who seemed to have assigned places, were gathered silently in the middle of streets or on sidewalks, a safe distance from buildings. Older people were sitting on low wooden folding stools, or squatting on the ground. Some had brought bamboo fans with them and were fanning themselves on this muggy, humid summer morning. Men had remembered their cigarettes and the burning tips looked like fireflies dotting the grey dawn.

In the fading darkness, the only sign of damage was in old residential quarters. There, small piles of cement, stone and ornamental pieces from corners of roofs lay on the streets and sidewalks. We tried to get a glimpse of the condition of housing, but walls and closed doors blocked our view. Although we saw no injured, friends living in the Hsin Chiao Hotel reported seeing people with head injuries and broken bones brought on three-wheel bicycles to the hospital across the street.

Within a short time traffic policemen were at their posts and the roads started to fill with jeeps, trucks, official cars, and bicycles. Some of these people were part of the work force the Hsinhua news service later described in detail. It reported, 'Within half an hour after the earthquake, some thirty thousand repair workers in the city returned to their work posts, organised into groups, and went from street to street to check the condition of houses and do necessary repair work.'

We returned home thinking fallaciously that Peking had suffered minor damage from the earthquake. The admirable calm and discipline of the Chinese people in the face of disaster had prevented us from knowing the truth, which became evident several weeks later.

The earthquake did not keep our staff from appearing at their usual time in the morning. After seeing that we were well, they asked, 'How did Bubbles behave before the earthquake?' According to a Tientsin radio broadcast peasants had noticed that animals had behaved strangely before the previous earthquake. It reported that swans and turtles had left the water and gone ashore. The Manchurian tiger became unconscious. The Tibetan yak lay on the ground and pandas put their heads in their paws and screamed. A poster warning of earthquakes said that pigs behaved like 'hooligans' and dogs barked.

Our Chinese friends were disappointed to hear that Bubbles was sleeping before and during the earthquake. But Lisa, a Labrador retriever, saved Bubbles' face. She made front page news in the British newspapers because she barked shortly before the earthquake, giving her owners warning.

Although new cracks appeared in the walls of Mrs Lee's and Mr Liu's flat, the structures still seemed sturdy, and their families were fine. Our cook Mr Yu was the most concerned. His family lived on a commune near Tientsin, which is sixty miles from Peking and sixty miles from Tangshan, the city that was completely devastated. He had no way to contact them, and had to wait for news from people returning from that area to Peking.

The first reports came from foreigners. The Australian Prime Minister Gough Whitlam and a small delegation had been in Tientsin and, although they escaped serious injury, their hotel was badly damaged. The Japanese and French embassies were informed that members of Japanese and French delegations had died in Tangshan. In addition, Hsinhua reported that Tangshan had suffered 'extremely serious damages and losses,' but did not give any figures of the number of injured and dead. It would take several months before unconfirmed reports stated that about 75 per cent of Tangshan's population (over three quarters of a million people) had died during the earthquake, and that the entire city had been devastated.

Soon after our staff arrived, I asked them to go home, where they had families to care for and outdoor shelters to build. More severe tremors had been forecast and orders had been issued that all Chinese must start living on the streets.

Only reluctantly did our people leave me, and as they shook my hand and told me, 'Please be vigilant and alert,' our anxious eyes revealed our fears. Would we ever see each other again?

Nature was cruel on the earthquake day, July 28, 1976. Continuing rain soaked everything and hampered emergency building efforts. But the Chinese were unrelenting. With water dripping down their faces and rubber sandals sinking into mud, they set up shelters out of whatever materials were available at home.

Bamboo poles and ropes supported overhead covers consisting of umbrellas, raincoats, striped bed linens, towels, straw mats and plastic tablecloths. Inside there was only enough room for a double bed.

One man had settled his housing problem very simply. He used the back board of his three-wheel bike as a bed and his raincoat as a roof.

While the Chinese were preparing for a long stay outdoors, the foreigners living on the higher floors in buildings were moving their families into embassies. Further quakes were expected, and the Foreign Ministry warned us that we should be ready to leave our flat at a moment's notice.

The Chinese radio was at first silent about the earthquake, but foreign broadcasts heard on shortwave radios confirmed the gravity of the situation. The earthquake was one of the most severe recorded in history, and it would take many weeks before the earth settled down.

Anticipating more trouble, the Service Bureau distributed and put up large army tents at every embassy and the International Club. The preparations did not begin too soon. Fifteen hours after the earthquake, a second strong tremor hit Peking, and this did more damage than the first.

When the second tremor came, I was visiting friends in a Chinese neighbourhood of crowded one-storey houses, surrounded by courtyards. We were sitting and drinking tea in the courtyard when the grapevines started to move and a lamp hanging from the roof swung violently back and forth. Until then I had admired the calm and control the Chinese had exhibited. But suddenly I heard a wave of shouts, howls, and wails from people running out into the streets. I grabbed the wife of our host and held her firmly against me, comforting her while the earth trembled and rumbled.

On the way home I noticed that Baihaudalo, the largest department store in Peking, had lost a large corner of its fourth and fifth floor. The falling pieces had broken one of the picture windows. Two large cracks appeared on the east side of the Great Hall of the People. During that day the rain weakened already-shaken structures and roofs, and walls of houses collapsed. The only buildings left undamaged this time were the new ones and the very old.

The next day our staff once again came to work. The dark shadows under their eyes revealed their exhaustion and anxiety. After the second large tremor, they expected more, and so sleep was difficult. Mr Yu had spent the night sitting under an umbrella outside. Mrs Lee and her three children had sat in a hot and humid bus with crying children, and Mr Gu had fought mosquitoes in his shelter. I asked them to go home and rest, but Mr Gu said, 'It is our duty to remain here. As long as you stay in the flat, we will come to work.'

That day wet bed covers, straw mats, and clothing were hanging on bamboo poles all over the city. Peking looked like a refugee camp. While the sun was out, people took a break, played cards or chess, and tried to catch up on sleep lost during the last two nights.

Meanwhile, we were making preparations in the event of sudden evacuation orders. Mr Liu filled the car with gas and helped us put emergency supplies into the trunk. Fresh water, food rations, a change of clothing, and essential documents occupied all of the free space. Then we parked the car outside the gate next to a long rectangular tent the Chinese were erecting.

This tent would house the team assigned to guard the compound during the next weeks. The Chinese were busy lugging in boards, setting them up on wooden frames, and then putting their bed rolls on the makeshift beds. A telephone connected with the earthquake command post was rigged up. A loud 'hello' came from inside the tent and then my teacher Mrs Shu emerged. To my delight, she would be taking care of us for the next few weeks.

Inside the compound men were setting up a smaller tent,

which later became the bicycle parking lot for the twenty or thirty people who worked in shifts around the clock. In addition, twenty-four empty buses were lined up in the parking lot of the Friendship Store, a two-minute walk from our door. The Chinese had taken every precaution for our safety, and all we had to do was sit and wait for the worst.

That evening we heard a loud pounding on our door. It was Mrs Shu, who said, 'You must leave at once. We have received word that there will be another large tremor in the next few hours.'

Gerd, in the middle of typing a story on his telex, told us to go to the car, promising he would follow soon. When he did not come immediately, Mrs Shu became worried. 'Where is he? He is the last person left in the compound. Any minute something terrible could happen,' she said. The sight of workers walking in and out of the gate with bamboo construction helmets on their heads added to the tension, and I kept glancing at the entrance to our building. Finally Gerd appeared, and we drove on empty streets to the Germany embassy.

Nothing happened during the next five hours, and so, at one A.M., tired and nervous, we decided to return to our apartment. As we started to walk through the partially closed gate to our compound, the guard said, 'Where are you going?' 'We are exhausted and want to go to bed,' Gerd replied. To my surprise, he let us pass.

At four o'clock in the morning the ringing of the telephone and the banging of aluminium pots awakened us. Once again we were told to leave the flat, and we stayed away for several hours. But nothing occurred, and so we returned.

By now we were the last family to remain in a complex housing five hundred people. On the insistence of their ambassadors, staffs and families had moved into embassies. In addition, the Foreign Ministry encouraged everyone to leave their apartments. Elevators stopped functioning and there was no hot water on the upper floors.

Gerd was willing to move, providing he could set up his

office outside with a telephone and telex, but that was too complicated. Recognising the advantageous location of our flat on the ground floor next to the gate, the Chinese did not put pressure on us to move out. Instead, they called often and assigned a team of at least thirty people to take care of us and the compound in the event of an emergency.

On the fourth day after the earthquake, we had visitors. Three important members of the Information Department came to see how we were and to inquire about the living and working conditions. We assured them that everything was fine and that we were taking all the necessary precautions. They left telling us, 'Be vigilant and alert. The danger is not over.'

While the people from the Information Department were with us, senior members of the Foreign Ministry visited embassies, where they saw chaotic conditions. Families had spread out in halls, living rooms, and dining rooms, and every bit of floor space was cluttered with suitcases, mattresses, and people. Babies were crying, youngsters were bickering, and mothers were complaining about the living situation and asking when they could return to their apartments. Everyone's nerves were on edge and ambassadors reported that little work could be done under the present circumstances.

The following morning, the Information Department called and a spokesman read an ominous report. He said:

After the earthquake in the Tangshan-Fengnan area there have been continuous post-quake tremors. According to our knowledge a post-quake tremor may take place in the coming days and the epicentre is possibly moving toward Peking. Take into great consideration the safety of yours. The Foreign Ministry wishes to notice as follows: if Mr Ruge and his family hope to leave China temporarily, the Foreign Ministry is ready to provide possible convenience. If Mr Ruge and his family hope to leave Peking for Canton temporarily please go through the relative procedures according to the travel formalities and we shall provide possible convenience. For safety reasons those who remain in Peking we advise to leave their houses and stay far away from any construction. If he is going to leave Peking or China tell us, then go to the police bureau to get a travel visa.

While we were listening to this message it was being transmitted to every embassy, and within hours ambassadors had received permission from their governments to evacuate women, children, and all but necessary staff from Peking. Pakistan International Airlines sent for a special plane to fly Pakistanis home at government expense. Japanese Airlines arranged for a chartered flight to pick up their nationals, who complained that they had to pay out of personal funds. CAAC scheduled more flights from Peking to Canton, and other governments granted paid family leaves in Hong Kong and Japan and paid for transport home.

The uncertainty of the situation and the frightening warning convinced Gerd to send the children and Bubbles back to Germany. Within a few hours the Information Department gave the children clearance to leave that evening. Two hours before the plane departed the Service Bureau arranged for Bubbles to be examined in a veterinary clinic according to departure regulations.

Within a few days every compound looked like a ghost town. The embassies were islands of occupation. A feeling of camaraderie had grown among the survivors, and this was strictly along national lines. Small staffs ate, worked, and lived together and seldom left their closely knit 'family' quarters.

Thinking a British friend would like a change of company and scenery, we invited him to dinner. But he refused, saying, 'The others would be hurt if I deserted them.' An Australian came to see us secretly, making us promise that we tell no one he had been there.

When we went to visit embassies, however, we were welcomed like honoured guests and treated to games, films, and dips in pools. Everyone asked sympathetically how we were surviving in our solitude. As time wore on, people started to envy our way of life, but I felt like a prisoner.

The remaining businessmen, who had been living in hotels, were evacuated to the most beautiful location in Peking, the Forbidden City. There, the Chinese built a tent city under the cypress trees and between majestic sixteenth-century ceremonial halls that had been untouched by the earthquake.

The day we visited this settlement, the businessmen dined outside at tables set with white tablecloths. Waiters dressed in white jackets served them dishes from a menu offering mushroom soup, goulash, roast chicken, and tomato and cucumber salad.

Unlike the diplomats and businessmen, we had to follow a strenuous routine that left us with little sleep. At night we stayed up in shifts, so that one would always be awake to alert the other in the event of danger. And during the day sleep was not possible. Gerd was constantly running from the telephone to his telex to report on the situation and I was too restless to lie down while the earth moved continually under my feet. Struggling to keep my eyes open at night, I left the lights burning in the living room and sat in an uncomfortable wooden chair. I went outside every hour to get a reviving breath of fresh air and talk with those Chinese who had the night shift. These gestures assured the Chinese protecting us that we were being 'vigilant'.

In addition, we impressed them with our home-made earthquake alarm system. We balanced two beer bottles nose to nose on top of each other and placed the lower one on an aluminium pan. In the event of a large tremor the upper bottle would fall and the crashing noise would wake us up. Fortunately this system never went into effect.

The Chinese felt that people were least alert in the early morning hours, and so the Information Department called regularly between four and six A.M. to report on the number

and gravity of the tremors on the previous day. Every conversation ended with the sentence 'Continue to be alert and
vigilant and take measures to ensure your safety.'

By morning I looked forward to the arrival of our staff, who
provided a distraction for me. We compared the reports and
warnings received during the night and discussed personal
problems.

Mr Yu had still not received word about his family, and he
was frantic. Public transportation had broken down outside
of Tientsin where his family lived, and so we all sat down one
morning to discuss how he could reach them. His bicycle
provided the best possibility. The distance was seventy miles
and we figured it might take two days to make the trip. 'What
will happen if it rains or I get a flat tyre? No one will be able
to repair it,' he said. We did not want to think of this even-
tuality and so discussed the food he should take along in order
to keep up his strength. I wanted to give him chocolate, meat,
and cookies, but he refused. 'I must travel light. Apples, a loaf
of bread, and a bottle of water will be enough.' The next day
Mr Yu did not appear and we all hoped he would find his
family well.

Anxious to know if he had arrived safely, I asked a friend
of his if he had heard from him. He told me I should not worry.
'If he arrives and finds that his family died during the earthquake he will hurry back to Peking. If he finds everyone fine,
you will not see him for a while.' Happily that was the case.

The emergency situation continued in Peking and the stress
of waiting and expecting something disastrous to occur was
wearing me down. When nothing happened, I started to think
that the threatening movement of the earth under me was my
imagination. At times like these I called the German Embassy
and asked if there were still ripples or small waves in the
swimming pool. That was the best barometer of the earth's
activity, and the answer was always 'yes'.

After a few weeks we became inured to our new way of life,
and were even able to joke about it. When one Chinese said,

'If another earthquake comes, go under your beds. Then we will know where to dig,' we all laughed, and felt that perhaps the worst was behind us.

The Chinese in our neighbourhood prepared for a long outdoor stay. Every day people improved their shelters. Now pipes, large logs, wooden planks, rope, and wire supported tar paper, rubber, canvas, cloth, and straw roofing. Cement blocks held down the sides, and floors were made of bricks, to protect against dampness from the wet ground.

Some of the building materials were procured from factories, but others came from construction sites. Across the street a high wooden fence, about five hundred feet long, disappeared in one morning as people dismembered it and helped themselves to the strips of wood.

All shops had been closed since the earthquake. Sidewalk stands were set up in front of the shop doors. Around the corner the vegetable stand had a plentiful supply of cucumbers, peppers, celery, pumpkins, tomatoes, and eggplant, all grown in Peking's outskirts. The smell of fish and marinated vegetables came from another counter. People lined up nearby to buy meat and soy-bean products, and those purchasing eggs and oil showed their ration books. Restaurant staff were outside serving customers lukewarm beer from tea kettles, while other people waited at the door to be handed soup, steamed buns, and other simple dishes. A man riding a three-wheel bicycle sold cigarettes and matches, and a woman passed by distributing cold tablets and herbal medicine from the back of her bike. A young mother examined rubber bottle nipples that were displayed next to mosquito incense, clothes-pins, soap powder, flash light batteries, and umbrellas on a cart.

While walking through our neighbourhood we saw that normal life was resuming. Locked bikes were parked inside or next to shelters set up in front of modern four-storey apartment buildings. Clothes-lines with underwear, long pants, shirts, and blouses drying on them were strung between trees. A woman scrubbed her laundry with water that ran out of a pipeline along the curb. Down the street a truck was being utilised to empty out latrines people had dug.

In shelters children played cards on the beds, while their grandparents dozed. Parents who were not needed at home to care for children or the sick went to work. The damp earth provided a drawing board for a group of boys making designs with sticks. A middle school girl combed her freshly-washed waist-length hair, and a young child brushed her teeth with water from a basin.

Families had solved their food problems in a variety of ways. One family sat around a table eating rice, vegetables, and fish that they had cooked on a nearby gas burner attached to a propane tank they had removed from their kitchen. Other people were permitted to return to their flats at mealtimes to make quick dishes for their families or the entire floor, while someone stood outside on guard.

One very large tent we passed housed about fifty people. When we asked how they had come together, a grey-haired energetic woman said, 'We belonged to the same socialist courtyard,' and then added that the tent had come from a government institute where one of the members worked.

A group of older women sat outside a large army tent in comfortable bamboo chairs, fanning themselves and drinking tea. Nearby a similar tent housed a nursery school and kindergarten where babies slept in cribs.

We then came to a first aid station with a white flag hanging outside the tent. Members of the Residents' Committee, responsible for organising this neighbourhood, sat inside. They invited us into their office to discuss their work.

We had already seen that the Housing Administration had provided the old, sick, weak, and injured with spacious canvas tents. Until now there were no injured among the over eighteen hundred families in this jurisdiction, and the two-year-old apartment buildings in the background had suffered no damage.

During the last few days I had noticed more army patrols

in the city. In addition, shelters started appearing with wooden doors and locks on them, and signs saying, 'Never forget class struggle and remain vigilant against disruptive activities of class enemies.' Mrs Lee had a lock on the zipper of her purse.

At the same time jokes circulating among the Chinese referred to theft in Tangshan. 'A man buried under a house stuck his hand out waving for help, and someone passing by stole his watch.' 'A rescue worker, who had been very active doing relief work, was found buried with several watches on his arm.' There was no way to know if these jokes had a factual background, but they indicated that this was a deep concern of the people living on the streets.

We asked the Residents Committee about any cases of theft in their neighbourhood. A perky, attractive forty-year-old teacher responded. 'There has been no theft here, but militia patrols are on duty around the clock to ensure that no bad elements take advantage of the situation.' In addition, she brought to our attention an article in the newspaper which said, 'The workers' militia-men in the capital . . . are maintaining order in traffic and public security in co-operation with the people's police. They patrol the streets day and night, doing propaganda work among the masses and protecting them.'

Parks and large open areas were also the sites of large settlements. We visited one sportsfield located on Chang An, the main avenue, where six thousand people lived in a place that looked like a shantytown. It had its own canteen, barber shop, grocery stores, repair shops for clothes, bikes, and flashlights, and an area to show films. It also had a medical station, where we asked to speak with the nurse.

'People are generally healthy, but very tired,' she said. She had treated cases of colds, insect bites, chronic diseases and high blood pressure, but no dysentery because prevention was the first goal of her work. 'People must clean lavatories, the inside and outside of their tents, and remove garbage daily,' she stressed.

The hygiene campaign was intensive not only here, but

throughout the city. Posters hung on every street, reminding people about sanitation measures: 'Keep the place clean and kill flies;' 'Wash raw vegetables and fruits before eating!' 'Boil water before drinking.' As a result of these efforts, no epidemic broke out in Peking throughout the emergency.

On the eighteenth day after the earthquake, we asked the leaders of this settlement how long they expected to be living on the street. One man said, 'We will have no problem with weather until October.' Another said, 'Ideologically we are prepared to stay a long time.'

The very next day the Information Department called to say that 'The abnormal phenomenon that existed in the Peking area in the last several days has in the main disappeared and no strong earthquakes will occur in the near future.' The Chinese received this information a few hours later, and the encampment that had taken eighteen days to build was dismantled within a few hours.

Those who remained on the streets were those who had no safe quarters to return to, and for the first time, we realised that the earthquake had left several thousand Peking residents homeless. But they had adjusted well to the difficult living conditions. That night, when most families were preparing *jao-tze* in the comfort of their kitchen and celebrating the end of the emergency, I saw mothers and children making *jao-tze* outside tents. They obviously felt very much at home, although home was in many cases only a shelter made of plastic sheets and matting.

Chapter 10

Death of Mao

During our last weeks in Peking my life was like the spinning cycle in a washing machine. First we experienced the earthquake, followed by nearly three weeks of uncertainty and tension, while we waited and feared the unknown. Then, no sooner had we started to pack and attend farewell parties than the parties were interrupted by the death of Mao, and the arrest of the 'Gang of Four'.

Mao died six weeks after the earthquake. This news hit our household harder than nature's wrath. Mr Yu was cleaning up the kitchen after lunch on September 9, and as usual he was listening to the programme blaring from the pocket-size transistor I had bought two years ago at Tokyo airport.

It was exactly three P.M. when he darted from the kitchen into Gerd's office, where Mr Gu was sitting. Rarely had I seen him move this quickly, so I followed him to inquire what had happened. A flash announcement had just come from the radio telling all listeners to tune in at four P.M. for an important broadcast.

Within seconds the faces of everyone in our household became drawn and solemn, their eyes showing worry. When I asked Mr Gu what the announcement meant he said, 'I do not know,' while shaking his head back and forth almost mechanically. 'When was the last time you heard such an announcement?' I inquired. 'Just before Chou En-lai's death was announced,' he answered almost in a whisper. 'But maybe there will be good news,' he added as an afterthought.

Between three and four o'clock everyone in our household found a way to keep himself busy. Mrs Lee took out the ironing board and started pressing handkerchiefs in a robotlike manner. Mr Liu sat opposite Mr Gu, holding a newspaper in front of his face, but he was not reading aloud as he usually did. Mr Yu started cleaning cupboards he had just recently cleaned. Mr Gu sat at his desk staring ahead. Feeling useless in the flat, I went outside to tell other people about the announcement.

A few minutes before four, I put the radio in our front hall and opened the door so that the elevator operator would hear the broadcast too. Quietly she thanked me. Then we all crowded nervously around the radio with the faint hope we would hear good news. But this was not to be. Mao had died.

Although our people had spent one hour preparing themselves for this announcement, the news stunned them. Mr Gu stood immobile as tears ran down his cheeks. Mrs Lee embraced me and burst into tears, and I suddenly realised that my cheeks were also wet. Mr Yu and Mr Liu stood in front of the radio, frozen in place as though they did not believe what they had heard.

After the announcement, a eulogy was read and then funeral music was played. For ninety minutes we listened to the same broadcast, repeated continually, and finally each person reluctantly tore himself away from the radio, put on his jacket, picked up his black handbag, and walked out of the door with head lowered.

Gerd had left the flat immediately after the announcement to see how others reacted to this news, and I was too restless and upset to stay alone. I followed the others as they left the flat, walked toward my bike and, without any idea of where I was going, started riding down Chang An toward the centre of the city.

Instead of throngs of people weeping on the streets as they had done after Chou En-lai's death, I saw only a few people displaying deep emotions. A truck passed me with an old woman sitting in back crying, while a younger woman tried to comfort her. Several construction workers, who had been busy with earthquake relief work, walked down the street supporting a young worker wearing a bamboo helmet on his head. In a daze he was unable to stand or walk without help.

An eerie silence descended on the city. Those who spoke, spoke in a whisper. Even young children stopped playing and laughing. Only the sound of car horns, bicycle bells, and funeral music broadcast from loudspeakers interrupted the quiet.

Everyone seemed to know what he should do, as though he had rehearsed his role before. Each family hung the red Chinese flag with five gold stars at half mast before their front door. In fabric shops clerks were busy cutting up black material, and customers left these shops pinning black armbands on their left arms. Many carried several strips of black cloth for other family members. Every Chinese would wear the black for one month.

Long queues stood in front of paper shops, which remained open on that day longer than usual. People were waiting to buy white crepe paper, which they made into paper flowers— another sign of mourning. Already some pedestrians had these home-made flowers in their buttonholes.

On a street corner near Mao's residence army guards changed posts. Those being relieved from duty wore red 'on duty' armbands, but their replacements already had the black armbands on.

At Tien An Men square a soldier lowered the flag and hundreds of people formed a semicircle around him, watching silently. After rolling it up he crossed the street and walked toward the Forbidden City. The crowd followed him, but then suddenly stopped in front of the Gate of Heavenly Peace. Everyone stared up at the large picture of Chairman Mao hanging above the main entrance to the Forbidden City. Cyclists on their way home from work dismounted in front of the gate and joined the crowds who were looking up at the Chairman's picture. Older people lowered their heads or made a deep bow, a traditional sign of respect, while a few young students broke the silence by raising their fists and reciting a pledge to carry on Mao's heritage.

As I approached Chung Nan Hai, the residence of Mao, cyclists slowed down or dismounted and pushed their bikes past the high red walls surrounding the compound. When they passed the decorative Chinese entrance gate there was little to see but soldiers standing at attention, as they always did. Today, however, people kept their eyes glued to this gate even after passing it.

On my way home, I once again had to pass Tien An Men, where people were gathering. I joined the many who were walking toward the monument to revolutionary heroes. Four pine branches lay at its base, and on each branch were white paper flowers and a strip of paper with Chinese characters I could not read. This was the first time anyone had dared to place a sign of mourning at the monument since the April violence that year. I hoped Mao's death would not lead to a similar event.

A few hundred yards in front of the monument a group of people, their heads bowed, sat on the pavement. An old worker had put his small transistor on the ground and they were sitting around him listening to the death announcement.

Overnight the city dressed for mourning. The pictures of Mao hanging outside official buildings were bordered with black and yellow silk. The giant coloured portrait over the Gate of Heavenly Peace was replaced by a picture in black and white. The colourful exhibits of merchandise were removed from the shop windows and a black background with large white paper flowers, wreaths, and a picture of Mao filled the space. On the sidewalks the photo display windows were empty. All entertainment was cancelled. Theatres and movie houses were closed. Banquets and cocktail parties were postponed. The Chinese even gave up their greatest passion, card playing.

During the first week of mourning beautiful paper wreaths

appeared in courtyards. After Chou En-lai's death people had brought home-made wreaths to Tien An Men square.

A few mourning gestures looked spontaneous. Some middle school girls wore white ribbons entwined in their braids. Old-style Mao badges, prized by collectors, appeared on a few jackets. Elaborate white paper flowers adorned trucks, tractors, buses, and jeeps.

For the first time I saw *The People's Daily*, the party newspaper, being sold from sidewalk stands. Usually a man or woman, dressed in a green uniform, delivered the paper on a bicycle to each door. Crowds of people stood near the stands reading the story of Mao's life and studying the pictures of him from youth to old age.

A few days after Mao's death, his body was placed in the Great Hall of the People and thousands of specially-chosen Chinese were permitted to view him lying in state. Those selected waited hours as the long queues slowly moved from Tien An Men square to the northern entrance of the Great Hall, a few hundred yards away.

Even before I had gone to China I had wanted to see Mao. During my working years in the White House under President Johnson I had seen many world leaders. But Mao, the leader who was the most mysterious and fascinating to me, never appeared.

When we arrived in China in 1973, Mao no longer made public appearances, except to receive foreign visitors of high rank. And so I gave up hope of ever seeing him. It was only after his death that this became possible. The foreign community was invited to the Great Hall of the People to pay last respects to the Chairman.

When our Chinese heard that we were going, they became very excited. But I was torn between two emotions. I felt badly that I was invited instead of them, and at the same time wanted nothing to interfere with this opportunity.

Mrs Lee helped me pick out what I was to wear. She chose a simple two-piece black blouse and skirt and then took them away to iron out the hardly noticeable creases. After I dressed, Mr Yu and Mr Liu carefully inspected me and removed a little lint from the back of my blouse. Although Mr Gu was not supposed to come, we took him with us, knowing it would be more meaningful for him to be there than for us.

Just before leaving the house Mrs Lee pinned a beautiful white crepe paper flower on my collar and put another in Gerd's buttonhole. Then she started to weep and talk at the same time, and I could only piece together what she was telling me. She had made these for Chairman Mao, whom she loved. He had done so much for the Chinese people and for her. Although she would not be able to see him, I was to leave her flowers with him. Then she embraced me. I took a deep breath to clear my blurred eyes.

As I stood in line at the entrance to the room where Mao was lying, I heard the loud wailing of Chinese who were passing by the body. This same wail would haunt me every night during the television broadcasts that portrayed the grief in the Great Hall of the People and other parts of China. Nowhere else had I ever witnessed such an outburst of emotion.

The wailing distracted me as I was shuttled with hundreds of other foreigners past the glass-encased body resting under the Chinese flag. It was all very theatrical, and the bright lights spotlighted on the heavily made-up face of Mao helped muffle my emotions. My only thoughts when I saw him was how pink and swollen his face looked and how large the famous wart on his chin appeared.

Within ten days after Mao's death, his teaching 'turn grief into strength' became the work motto for the entire nation. This is the way the Chinese people paid tribute to him.

Until that time, earthquake shelters and the high grey walls surrounding housing had hidden the earthquake's impact. Now the gates leading to courtyards were open and one could look in. The extent of damage was shocking. I saw many houses with collapsed roofs, crumbling façades and cracked walls.

Within twenty-four hours, the impact of the work motto was visible. Peking looked like a construction site. One truck after another filed into the city carrying bricks, sand, lime, and wooden poles, which they deposited on sidewalks in stricken neighbourhoods. Other trucks then came to remove the rubble from fallen structures. The dust made me choke but the Chinese knew what to do. They wore white cloth masks to protect their noses and throats.

Grandmothers, nursery school children, middle school students, soldiers, cadre, and factory workers made up the work force. They sifted sand, mixed cement, carried bricks, combed through the remains to select out the still useable material, shovelled debris onto the sidewalks, and built new housing. One morning I watched sixteen young people construct an entire two-room house. Work throughout the city was non-stop, with no time for tea breaks or idle chatter, and at night construction continued under spotlights.

Although Peking's population was hard at work, I detected an uneasiness in the atmosphere. I was used to seeing solemn faces during the mourning period, but they also looked tense and troubled. Sometimes groups huddled together on street corners, speaking quietly. At home our staff whispered to each other.

Feeling excluded, I tried to engage Mr Gu and Mrs Shu in a discussion which was of interest to everyone. Who would be Mao's successor? When I suggested that Chiang Ching, Mao's wife, might play an important role in the decision, this met with stony silence and even more concerned expressions.

Then photos of Mao's life and the mourning ceremonies in the Great Hall of the People went on display in the sidewalk picture galleries. The photo of Chiang Ching attracted much attention. She was wearing a black veil on her head, and people were pointing to this.

During this period, a Chinese friend asked me, 'Is wearing a black veil a Western custom? Madame Chou En-lai wore nothing on her head after her husband died.' Some days later another friend remarked, 'Chiang Ching sent a strange wreath to honour the Chairman. Madame Chou En-lai brought a small bouquet of fresh flowers to her husband's body every day.' These subtle remarks left no doubt about people's feelings.

At the same time there were many rumours circulating in the foreign community about the line-up of the new leadership. Since first-hand information was rare, it was difficult to determine whether a rumour stemmed from a reliable Chinese source, or if it was the conclusion of diplomats studying the problem. Foreigners believed that Hua Kuo-feng and Chang Chung-chiao, a close colleague of Chiang Ching, would share the leading roles.

Exactly one month after Mao's death, the first wall posters appeared in Peking hailing the appointment of Hua Kuo-feng as chairman. But some hours later they were removed. We didn't know what this meant and waited two long days before things became clear. Then we heard that government bureaux had been informed of Hua Kuo-feng's appointment as the new chairman. Although this news did not become official for several hours, the behaviour in our household had changed so rapidly that I knew it had to be true. Everyone was smiling, laughing, and joking. This mood was contagious and soon all of Peking seemed to be smugly relaxed and grinning.

A few days later the newspaper published a front-page article about the arrest of Chiang Ching and her three close associates, Chang Chun-Chiao, Yao Wen-yuan, and Wang Hung-wen. At that point many who had not dared to discuss politics before broke their silence. It was as though a balloon had burst.

My teacher's first words hinted at the significance of this development. 'Now the future of China will be great. We are all jubilant today.' These same phrases echoed through the households in the foreign community.

Nasty stories about Chiang Ching started circulating, and both foreigners and Chinese compared the different versions they had heard. 'Chiang Ching wears a French wig and has Japanese false teeth.' 'She was married seven times.' 'Her guards spat at her when she was arrested.' 'She dirtied her underpants when her hands were put into handcuffs.' The more exaggerated the tales, the more the Chinese enjoyed them.

We considered postponing our departure. Our Chinese friends in the Foreign Ministry said we would have to wait several months before we could understand what had happened. But we did not have much time, because Gerd was already late for a one-year fellowship at the Harvard East Asian Research Centre. And so he confirmed the departure date a few days later.

I stayed on ten days after Gerd had left, in order to help an old and sick German-Chinese couple, who had been close friends, depart for Australia. After waiting many months and almost giving up hope of getting permission to leave, they had finally received their exit visas, following the fall of Chiang Ching and her associates.

At last, however, the time came for me to leave. During my last lesson Mrs Shu, realising how unhappy I was, tried to perk me up. 'The next time I see you you will be speaking fluent Chinese,' she said. Thinking she would never leave China and not knowing then that I would ever be able to return, I replied quietly, almost to myself, 'I hope there will be a next time.'

As we walked to the door together, her eyes, like mine, were full. But she did not want me to see this. She looked back and waved to me only once after she was on her bike and her face had regained its usual composure.

Chapter 11

Epilogue

THE SHOCK OF AMERICA

From the day I left Peking until my return one year later China had a firm grip on me. Old friends said I had changed. I was quieter and less outgoing, they thought. But I knew the changes were much deeper. I felt more settled inside. I was no longer restless, hectic, and competitive. Obviously the Chinese calm had influenced me.

I tolerated different opinions and accepted advice readily. I was not eager to win a point and cause the other person to lose face. The most unforgiveable offence in China was to humiliate a person, and my newly learned 'diplomacy', as a friend called it, was the lesson the Chinese had taught me.

People's obsessions with material possessions bored me. I was content to wear jeans, take walks, and live a simple life without frills, which was not the case before I went to China. The Chinese had the minimum, and they showed me how happiness stemmed from things money could not buy.

China had taught me to be frugal, and America now shocked me with its excessive waste. Garbage cans were heaped with food people could not finish at the table. Many products were packaged in reusable plastic containers, but no one felt they were worth keeping. I was indignant that no place would accept our glass bottles and newspapers for recycling. Only after they filled our garage did I reluctantly throw them away. I had learned to use tin foil, plastic bags, and wrapping paper more than once, but this was a bother for most people. America had a rich mentality, and people felt they did not have to save.

I missed the Chinese warmth and close family ties. A father

and married son would never walk down the street in Cambridge, Massachusetts, holding hands. While Chinese children rarely opposed their parents, American children were disrespectful and then were rewarded with gifts.

Old people seemed to be a burden to their families. They were sent to old people's homes because the children were too busy with their lives to take care of them. In China children were responsible for caring for their parents until they died. I found that some of the Chinese respect for age had rubbed off on me, and it deepened my relationship with my own parents.

When I had been in China my Chinese friends had spent several months coaxing me to slow down, rest more often, and take better care of my health. Gradually I gave in, and saw the advantages of their relaxed, unhurried lives. In this mood I returned to the States, and was forced to go into training immediately to keep up with the pace of life. People did not saunter. They moved with a determination and purpose. It was as though everyone was late for an appointment.

When I stood in a queue in Cambridge, patiently waiting, the people ahead and behind me sighed deeply, shifted from one foot to the other, and murmured about the slowness of the cashier. Meanwhile, I admired the efficiency of the system with a cash register that did all the mathematics, a packer who quickly put the items into bags, and a cashier who knew most prices of articles by heart. These people needed a dose of Chinese slowness!

In a few areas the Chinese influence lingered. While walking down streets I wondered why no one was staring at me. Instead, I was gawking at the outlandish costumes people were wearing and thinking how silly they looked. In stores I would invariably say 'hsie hsie'—thank you—or 'tui pui chi'—excuse me—when I bumped into someone.

When I left my purse hanging on a shopping cart in one store, another customer came running up to me and said, 'Lady, where do you think you are? You are in the highest crime area in the country!' It did not take long for me to learn the hard way. Twice within three months our house was broken into, and I yearned for the days when I could leave the door unlocked in Peking.

The absence of bicycles on the roads did not impress me as much as the driving habits of Americans. I was surprised to see drivers smoking, eating, and using one hand to drive. Such offences would earn the driver a long lecture from an irate policeman in Peking. On the other hand, I used my horn every time I wanted to pass and other drivers' unfriendly expressions reminded me that this was not necessary. Unlearning Peking habits was not as easy as I had anticipated.

As months passed, instead of Peking fading into the background, it grew in dimensions. Everyone wanted to know about life in China, and once I started talking, it was difficult to restrain myself. At Chinese New Year I sent a letter and family picture to each member of our staff, hoping they would receive it, but knowing they would not be able to respond. Friends in the foreign community kept me posted on developments, and their information was much more complete and regular than the scanty reports that appeared in the press.

When German friends from Peking came to stay with us, they suggested that I return for a visit, and there was nothing that I wanted to do more. They then wrote an invitation for me to be their guest, and I anxiously waited for weeks to hear whether the Chinese would issue a visa. Finally I received the news that I could return.

For several nights I tossed in bed, planning everything I would do in Peking. I wanted most to spend time with our old staff and friends from the Foreign Ministry, but they would have to receive official permission from the organisation where they worked in order to visit with me. I knew exactly what dishes to order in my favourite Szechuan restaurant, but had forgotten the names of the specialities in the Fukien restaurant. I thought about which shops I would visit and could envision the clerk who would be standing behind the counter when I entered. Each face was clear, but would they still remember me?

PEKING, ONE YEAR LATER

On the first evening of my return to Peking the overwhelming reception I received set the tone for the entire visit. A German film was being shown at the International Club and Chinese were invited. Hoping to see my teacher and interpreter again, I attended.

Nervously I stood at the entrance to the auditorium waiting for the right faces to appear. Many Germans greeted me and welcomed me back, but these were not the familiar faces I had waited so long to see. Then Mrs Shu grabbed my hand, and we stood beaming at each other, speechless. Still holding my hand, she led me to the section where her colleagues were sitting and told me to sit beside her. 'This is my old student, the wife of Mr Ruge, formerly the West German journalist for *Die Welt* in Peking,' she explained excitedly. When they heard the name Ruge, many nodded and repeated to each other what she had said. They knew the name because many had read Gerd's articles in an internal publication available to cadre. Some had even used his reports as teaching material in classrooms.

News of my presence reached our former interpreter Mr Gu, who was sitting several rows ahead, and he came running over to me. He pumped my hand, and several seconds passed before we spoke. During that time his eyes seemed to fill up with tears. Or was it my imagination, and my sight blurred from emotion?

During intermission Mrs Shu stayed by my side. Every time a foreign friend interrupted us, we both considered it an intrusion. So much had happened in the last year that she wanted to discuss. In addition, she was anxious for me to go out on my own again to observe the changes. Shortly before we separated that evening Mrs Shu said what I had been waiting to hear. 'Come and visit me where I am teaching whenever you have time.'

Mr Gu and Mrs Shu had never before displayed publicly their feelings toward me. Formerly every Chinese had been careful not to appear too close to any foreigner because of possible repercussions. And I had been careful to conceal my closeness to my Chinese family when I met them outside our flat. Now they showed me that things had changed, but the extent of the changes struck me only when I went to the Friendship Store.

As I walked up the steps of the Friendship Store, the usually disgruntled grey-haired man, who still monitored the entrance, saw me. His pinched face broke into a smile. I had never seen him in such a friendly mood before.

The lobby now had a new addition. A service counter had been set up prominently in a corner. 'Your suggestions and criticisms are welcome,' stood in bold black print on a sign with an open notebook and pen beneath. I had heard this phrase so often, that I wondered what it meant now.

One of my favourite clerks, who spoke excellent English, was standing behind the counter. When she saw me she came over to shake my hand and welcome me back to Peking. 'I have missed you. Where have you been?' she asked. After I told her she said, 'Have you noticed changes in Peking since the smashing of the Gang of Four?' I would hear this question many times during my stay.

When I asked her about the suggestions customers had made, she discussed quite openly how the store had responded to a few 'criticisms'. The vegetable and meat department was no longer closed during lunch hours, and butter and pork sausage were being sold at separate counters. She added, 'The Pakistanis had made this suggestion.'

As she spoke, another employee came over to listen to our conversation, but she continued talking. Never before had I had a discussion with a clerk about store matters, and my old worries returned. I was afraid of making trouble for her by talking longer, and so I broke up the conversation and started wandering through the store.

Familiar clerks greeted me and welcomed me back. They wanted to know where I had been and whether I would now stay. It was astonishing that they had remembered me and had noticed my long absence.

During different phases of our life in Peking I had learned to feel when the Chinese were under political pressure. Then their relations toward me became strained. The smiles and greetings were fewer and those who spoke with me tended to weigh every word they said. But now the atmosphere was relaxed and congenial. I hoped this would continue.

Foreigners no longer complained of bitter confrontations with store employees. The customers also seemed to be behaving themselves better. In the toy department a clerk was scratching the head of a young African boy, while trying to teach him how to operate the abacus. In the tailor shop, the former scene of regular temper tantrums, everything was calm. When I went shopping fifteen minutes before closing time one day, the clerks went to the storage room to fetch things for me. Previously, they would have insisted that I come back the following day because it was too late to fill my order.

All the clerks now spoke better English, and this led to fewer misunderstandings. The Chinese were making a visible effort to maintain friendly relations with foreigners, whose numbers had multiplied since I had lived in Peking.

Judging from the number of buses parked outside the Friendship Store, the tourist trade was booming. The year before the pace in the store had been leisurely and there had always been time to chat with clerks or to answer someone's question about an English word. Now this was impossible because of the amount of traffic passing through the store.

Most of the day the Friendship Store looked like Macy's before Christmas. But it provided services Macy's could not offer. A Japanese tourist group, numbering at least five hundred, descended on the store one late afternoon. The group had probably just come back from a long day of sightseeing and was weary. The store, therefore, quickly set up a milk, juice, and yogurt counter in the lobby.

Once while I was in the shop the guide of a German tourist group came up to me and greeted me like an old friend. We had met him briefly when he had accompanied another delegation. 'This year I have travelled in China with over five tourist groups, and next year there will be many more. Isn't that wonderful?' he exclaimed.

This news was very upsetting to me. China was opening its doors to masses of tourist groups and I felt, selfishly, that the Peking I remembered and loved would be spoiled.

The Friendship Store had already changed its prices and expanded its merchandise to keep up with the world market and demand. I was disappointed the shop no longer offered the bargains I had enjoyed. But tourists, who had not paid lower prices before, found everything reasonable. Often I heard the phrase, 'That would cost much more at home,' and I thought, if you were not here, the price of cashmere sweaters would not have risen 40 per cent in one year. Now a cardigan cost 34 yuan instead of 21 yuan, and black caviar was 14 yuan a pound instead of 7 yuan. Even postal costs had increased 30 per cent.

With the growth in tourism, the quality of goods declined. Shadow puppets were now of very flimsy leather and were painted with gaudy colours. The suede pants were thinner and less durable. Ornamental objects and jewellery were mass produced and the wonderful craftsmanship which used to distinguish many pieces was lost. Well-made old objects like the ones I had bought were very rare.

I was pleased to see that the choice of merchandise, colours and sizes was taking foreign taste and figures into consideration. Some silk patterns imitated Pucci and Hermes. The ready-made Chinese jackets, blouses, and sweaters were stylish and well cut, instead of being squarely shaped with sleeves that were too short. Glass objects had a Swedish flare and leather wallets had credit card compartments.

In addition to foreigners, there were also high-ranking Chinese customers doing their shopping in the store. In the silk department I stood next to an army officer, his wife, and daughter, who were looking at silk. When I went over to the glove department, they followed me and tried on different pairs of gloves. Formerly, I had had the impression that the Chinese permitted to enter the Friendship Store were there on official business only.

At the same time that the Friendship Store was crowded with enthusiastic buyers, the Chinese stores were full of serious customers, intent on buying instead of looking. During the last year the range of products had expanded and prices for new items were higher. A large shipment of children's tricycles was being unpacked in one store. They cost between 20 and 40 yuan, but this did not seem to dampen the interest of customers who were eagerly trying to get close to them. In another store I stood behind an elderly couple who paid 160 yuan for a down blanket. This new luxury item cost almost three months of an average worker's salary. Earlier, such extravagance would have attracted a great deal of attention, and might possibly have been criticised. But now I was the only person who was impressed with this purchase.

Stores were cleaner and more orderly. The floors were constantly being swept and the shelves were no longer layered with dust. Windows had a scrubbed look and the supplies were arranged according to an orderly system instead of being scattered and haphazardly displayed.

The clerks seemed more polite to Chinese customers, and service was better. As a result, the people were nicer to each other and there was less shoving and more queueing. I even saw a group of primary school girls help a man pick up brooms and baskets that had fallen off his three-wheel bike. I had waited to see this scene for many years.

Women were more fashion conscious, and their clothing showed it. Bright colours now began at the neck. Printed silk scarves were tied around the neck and the collar of the blouse was folded over the outer jacket. This style of collar was popular before the Cultural Revolution, a friend told me.

Many women were wearing printed cotton and silk outer jackets, which had formerly been hidden under a blue facade. The turtle-neck sweater was now in fashion. A Chinese friend pointed out that the pants were narrower, although I barely saw the difference.

I marvelled at the number of pretty faces on the streets and then realised that the hair styles had changed. Instead of having short chopped hair or hair plastered down with bobby pins, women were wearing their hair longer and loose, and this made their faces look softer. Some even had waves and curls.

Men were also letting their hair grow a little and some had short sideburns. The fashion among young men was to wear the cap at a slight angle, making them look dashing. Men were always conscious of where pockets were placed, and a Chinese woman complained to me, 'Now I must change all the pockets on my husband's old pants.'

The shoe stores had many leather shoes on display, and anyone who could afford leather was wearing it. The black cloth shoe had become much more a sign of a simple worker and peasant. In one store a black leather ankle boot, similar to a short riding boot, was available only to those with coupons, and many people went away grumbling and disappointed.

The latest 'in' object was the transistor radio, and this reminded me of America during my teens. Boys in their early twenties could not be separated from their pocket-size toy. They walked down streets and went through parks with the radio glued to their ear. This was hardly necessary, because anyone within half a block could easily hear the programme.

Many more cameras were slung over shoulders, and I wondered if these were rented or owned. Seeing a man with a

Hassalblatt, probably the most expensive professional camera in the world, I asked if it belonged to him. 'That is our camera,' he responded, and to this day I do not know if he meant it belonged to his family or to the institute where he worked.

When I talked to people, they no longer shunned me or seemed afraid. Sometimes they even began the conversation. We walked out of a restaurant one night and a young couple passing by spoke to us in French. At the Great Wall another couple asked a foreigner if he would take a picture of them with their camera. While walking down sidewalks and shopping in stores I no longer attracted as many stares and crowds. In fact, I was doing the staring now. I was surprised and delighted to see young couples walking down streets during the day-time arm in arm or hand in hand. Previously I had only seen couples close together at night-time. Children frequently shouted 'Hello' as I rode by. Formerly such a greeting was an important happening in the day for me, but now it was routine.

The relaxed atmosphere and openness toward foreigners carried over to the field of music. Upon entering one store I was surprised to hear Beethoven being played. He and other Western composers had been condemned as being bourgeois when Gerd and I had been in China. In fact, the Chinese people had been warned that Beethoven's spirit of rebellion should not be confused with the revolutionary spirit of the proletariat. Now Western music was once again acceptable.

Cultural life had also undergone a great change. The one Peking opera I saw when I returned featured old mandarin costumes, and the plot was no longer the familiar one of a bad landlord exploiting the labouring class or a counter-revolutionary sabotaging the farm work in the countryside. Instead, it focused on the Boxer Rebellion, when the Chinese rose up against Western domination. The greatest attraction for both the Chinese and foreign audience was seeing Chinese on stage dressed up as Westerners with long noses and blond and red wigs.

When I arrived in Peking everyone was talking about the

performance I had just missed. The Oriental Dance Ensemble, which Chou En-lai had organised in 1965, had been revived. Their show must have been spectacular. A Chinese cast sang songs, performed dances, and wore costumes of foreign countries, and foreigners who watched African, Sri Lankan, Mexican, and Argentinian songs and dances being performed by Chinese said their countrymen could not have done a more polished job.

The most noticeable change in Peking was its facelift. The anti-earthquake shelters now beautified the landscape with their different architectural designs. Some were A-shaped and others were rectangular, square, or round. They were made of bricks, stones, cement, and wood, and looked as though they were there to stay. Many had glass windows and wooden doors with large locks. I named my favourite house the 'villa' because it had a garden and fence surrounding it. At night this house was lighted, indicating that it was lived in, while the majority were dark and empty.

Slogans were posted everywhere telling people to keep the city orderly and clean and to obey the traffic regulations. In line with this campaign, I noticed a decline in litter-bug offences and at the same time noted that the number of automatic street sweeping machines had at least doubled in the past year.

It was the cabbage season when I was in Peking and the area had just experienced unseasonable rain, causing the cabbage to wilt and rot. At first the city was a mess. Leaves were strewn all over the streets and sidewalks, and children were having cabbage wars. Then an emergency order was handed down from the Peking authorities. Within twenty-four hours the cabbage mountains and green litter had disappeared and were replaced by cabbages neatly arranged in rectangular piles in rows.

Although buildings were in construction throughout the city, the materials were no longer loosely scattered over a large area and the dust was not as oppressive. People painted the facades of their houses for the first time in many years, and courtyards looked very tidy.

The traffic on the roads seemed to have doubled since I left China. The drive to the Great Wall was a harrowing experience because the roads were flooded with trucks travelling at reckless speeds. Disregarding oncoming traffic, drivers would overcome smaller vehicles, sometimes forcing them off the road. The narrow roads had originally been built for horses and bicycles. Now they could not accommodate the truck explosion, especially when each driver was intent on passing the next.

Sometimes a line of traffic at least half a mile long would have to wait ten or fifteen minutes before a red light changed. At such times I was grateful to be back on a bike, which often got me to my destination faster than a car could.

For years cyclists had not respected or obeyed traffic rules and did whatever they wanted on the road. With the increase in motorised vehicles, they presented a greater hazard. Finally a traffic safety campaign was launched to educate the cyclists and pedestrians, and the people in charge of enforcing it were the traffic policemen, who had formerly had little power and had often been the target of angry crowds.

When the campaign had begun in summer, cyclists had been fined for offences, I was told, but this penalty no longer existed. Instead there were other punishments. At one intersection I saw a cyclist ignore a red light and ride through it. The policeman stopped him, and, after an exchange of words, a truck drove up and took away the bike of the cyclist. To my surprise no crowds gathered to shout objections or taunt the policeman. The offender had to write a self-criticism before he was allowed to fetch his bike on the outskirts of the city the following day.

Freshly-painted white lines indicated where cyclists should stop before a red light, and the bicycle lane was clearly marked with a white line. Young, rosy-cheeked policewomen with pigtails stood on these lines reminding cyclists where to stop and ride. When cyclists did not take these girls seriously, an authoritative policeman appeared, and no one dared to challenge him.

During the early-morning and late-afternoon heavy traffic hours middle school students stood on Chang An and acted like a fence, enclosing the bicycle lane. Their numbers alone prevented any cyclist from entering the truck and bus lane. At the same time, primary school students entered police booths at main intersections and read in high-pitched voices the traffic rules over loudspeakers. In addition, cars with loudspeakers toured the city, repeating the regulations.

The pedestrians were also expected to obey traffic rules and cross the street only in the freshly painted pedestrian zones. But they seemed more set in practising their old ways than the cyclists. I watched an old woman attempt to cross the street in the midst of heavy automobile, bus, and truck traffic. A policeman ran up and stopped her. He pointed to the area where she could cross and told her to go there. Then he turned around and started walking away. No sooner had he done this than she continued walking across the street. Noticing this, he ran toward her again. He grabbed her arm and started pulling her toward the pedestrian zone. Then he saw another offender, dropped the old lady's arm, and pursued his new target. At that point the old woman turned abruptly and managed to get across the street without being caught. This stubbornness was typical of cyclists and pedestrians, who defied the new traffic rules as soon as a back was turned or the authorities had disappeared.

At bus stops on main streets, however, order reigned. Previously the queue had turned into a tidal wave when the bus arrived. Now monitors stood at the busiest stops and saw that people filed into the bus in an orderly way. But on side streets the squeeze-and-shove method was still the only means of entering the bus.

When I asked a Chinese friend about his reaction to the traffic campaign he said, 'We are used to campaigns. They last three or four months, and then there is a new one. You will see, as soon as this one is over, people will go back to their old ways.'

There was more discipline on the streets, but Mrs Shu enthusiastically told me about the new spirit in the classroom. Previously, *The People's Daily*—the party newspaper—had praised a primary school student who had criticised his teacher for being an authoritarian. In one article a teacher had been reprimanded for not accepting the written exam of a student who had copied from his neighbour. The student justified his action by explaining that everything must be done with the co-operation of the masses. When those articles were published I had tried to get a reaction from Mrs Shu, but she had stayed silent. Now she wanted to talk.

'Now the teachers will be respected and students must behave themselves and work hard in the classroom,' she said. The new educational reform pleased her also. 'My son has the possibility of going directly to the university from middle school, instead of to the countryside, if he passes the exams. Before, the children of intellectuals had a very difficult time. Many students who had the right political connections entered the university through the back door. Now students will be judged on their academic qualifications, and no one will be admitted to the university because of his contacts.'

Chinese had told me stories about leading musicians, artists, and professors who had been sent to the countryside during the last years to work as farmers because they did not support Chiang Ching's policies. But since the fall of the Gang of Four, many of these people had returned to their old positions. Although Mrs Shu did not mention it, I heard from other sources that her husband, a musician, had been a victim of the Gang. Only recently had he been permitted to resume his work. However, she was still unwilling to discuss her past.

She was willing to answer more abstract questions. 'What did the Tien An Men incident mean?' I asked. 'It demonstrated the strength of the people to resist the evil influence of the

Gang of Four. We Chinese understood the significance of the written posters. It was our way of showing our resistance to these people.' She added, 'I used to flip through the newspaper, not wanting to read any articles. They made me very angry. But now I read every article carefully.' I did not understand the meaning behind everything she told me and wanted more details, but I was afraid that if I interrupted she would clam up.

Toward the end of my stay, Mrs Shu and Mr Gu joined me for dinner. To my amazement, our interpreter monopolised the conversation. When he had worked for Gerd, he had been the model of a Chinese interpreter, never expressing an opinion, giving advice, or suggesting that one phrase in an article was more important than another. He was there to translate and he did that very well.

At this dinner he started to talk about how difficult the past years had been. Unwilling to elaborate with details, he said, 'So many times, I wanted to answer Mr Ruge's questions, but I could not. Indeed I felt very unhappy about what was happening in China, but I had to be silent.' Mrs Shu nodded and said, 'You had no idea how difficult life was for us.'

The highlight of my Peking stay was a reunion with old friends from the Information Department. Mr Ma and Mr Chee joined me for dinner in a journalist's flat. Their first words were, 'We did not want you to leave Peking without seeing us.' This warm greeting set the tone for the most relaxed and candid session I spent with Chinese in Peking.

I had liked Mr Ma and Mr Chee from the first time I had met them. They had been abroad and understood our humour and manners. Both spoke excellent English and often I joked with Mr Chee about his upper-class English accent, which he had learned in England.

Mr Ma and Mr Chee were very important to us during our years in China. They were the principle contacts Western journalists had with the Information Department, and therefore they were the targets for everyone's frustration.

Reporting in China was difficult because official information was limited to the text of newspaper articles and Chinese publications. Interviews and press conferences were rare because the Chinese maintained that everything they had to say was included in the press. Journalists, therefore, sought other sources for news. When delegations arrived in Peking, they would meet with government leaders, and information from these sessions would leak to the press. In addition, there was the press abroad and an active rumour mill in Peking that offered controversial information. Confirmation or denial of a report was necessary, and so the journalists turned to the Information Department for help.

When a journalist called the Information Department, the voice on the other end never identified himself, but Mr Chee's accent was recognisable and he was the man who usually received the inquiries. 'I will note your question and get back to you,' the voice would say. If a response came it was usually 'no comment', or, more often, the question went unanswered. On occasion, the voice would say, 'I would not print that story if I were you,' without giving an indication if it was true or false.

Angry and frustrated, some journalists turned against Mr Ma and Mr Chee and blamed them for all their difficulties. But I defended them. They were like a slice of ham between two pieces of bread. The journalists wanted the truth while the government demanded silence. The Information Department did not initiate policy. They were the instruments for passing on policy.

At the dinner that evening, Mr Ma confirmed my beliefs.

'Had I answered Gerd's question about Tien An Men, I would have risked my job for political reasons. I could better serve the journalists by not expressing my personal opinion. The Gang of Four tried to suppress all opposition by publishing rumours in the newspaper that could be attributed to many people. In this way they could point an accusing finger at anyone they chose. At that time I did not dare to express my opinion to anyone except my best friend,' Mr Ma said, as he glanced quickly at Mr Chee.

Knowing that they liked classical music, I had Mozart for background music. This brought us to the topic of Western music. 'I have been a party member for twenty years and believe in the great future of China. When I listen to classical music and appreciate it, it does not mean that I like Chinese music any less. I can enjoy them both,' Mr Ma remarked.

All of the Chinese I met were delighted with the change during the last year and hoped, as I did, it would continue. Their lives had improved and they saw a bright future for their country. They wanted nothing to interfere with the present development, but knew that the pendulum could swing in another direction just as quickly. The last twenty-seven years of frequent changes had made them cautious. 'The present situation might remain stable five years,' a friend said. After that no one could predict what would happen.

Mr Chee wanted to talk about an interview Gerd had had with a ballet group at the end of his stay in Peking. 'That was the only time we could arrange anything with the Ministry of Culture,' he said, chuckling. The meaning was clear. It was well known that culture had been Chiang Ching's main interest. Obviously, the relations between the Information Department and the Chiang Ching group had been strained, and this was Mr Chee's way of telling me.

Then I asked about positive results of the Cultural Revolution. Mr Ma thought carefully, and then replied.

'The main outcome was to give the masses the strength and ability to see through the Gang of Four. There had been a growing awareness of what they were doing. But the last straw was the attack on Chou En-lai and the subsequent removal of wreaths in April. After the death of Chairman Mao we were all frightened and did not expect things to happen so quickly. But as soon as Hua Kuo-feng was named chairman, it was clear that Teng Hsiao-ping would come back. The Western journalists were very impatient that it took so long for this to happen, and therefore started printing rumours. We are patient people and knew it was necessary for Hua to do things slowly in order to prepare the nation.'

After dinner we covered the world arena, discussing the American economy, terrorism, the political instability in Italy, the peace movement of the late sixties. They were interested in what was going on outside China because they realised it would have an impact on their country. At the same time China was sending many delegations abroad, and Mr Ma informed us that he would soon be leaving with one of these groups.

We were passing so quickly from one theme to the next that I felt both confused and elated. There were so many more questions to ask, but time was running out. After spending almost four years in Peking, I was slowly realising how little I knew about the Chinese, except as they appeared to my round Western eyes, and these were perhaps the main obstacle to my understanding. But Mrs Lee, our former cleaning woman, gave me hope that a more personal and human contact might be possible in the future. She told me, 'The next time you return to China you must meet my children.'